Poverty: the outcomes for children

Edited by: Jonathan Bradshaw, University of York

Occasional Paper 26

ECONOMIC AND SOCIAL RESEARCH COUNCIL
FAMILY POLICY STUDIES CENTRE
SOCIAL POLICY RESEARCH UNIT

Published by Family Policy Studies Centre
9 Tavistock Place, London WC1H 9SN

Tel: 020 7388 5900
Fax: 020 7388 5600

ISBN 1-901455-50-5

April 2001

The Family Policy Studies Centre is an independent
body which analyses family trends and the impact of
policy. It is a centre of research and information. The
Centre's Governing Council represents a wide spectrum
of political opinion, as well as professional, academic,
faith, local authority and other interests.
This Occasional Paper, like all those in the series,
represents the views of the authors and not necessarily
those of the Family Policy Studies Centre.

The Social Policy Research Unit (SPRU) is an
autonomous research unit at the University of York.
SPRU's work is concerned with the development of
policies and the delivery of services to support people
made vulnerable by poverty, ageing, disability or chronic
illness. Most of the Unit's work is within the related
fields of social security, social care and health care.

Cover photographs by Format Photographers: Jacky Chapman,
Maggie Murray, Ulrike Preuss & Brenda Prince
Design and print by Intertype

Contents

List of Tables

List of figures

Abbreviations

ACORN	A Classification of Residential Neighbourhoods
B&Bs	Bed and Breakfast Hotels
BCS	British Crime Survey
BHPS	British Household Panel Survey
BPVS	British Picture Vocabulary Scales
BSAG	Bristol Social and Behavioural Adjustment School Guides
Carstairs Index	Measure of deprivation based on a number of variables from the 1991 census
CIDI	Composite International Diagnostic Interview for Psychiatric Disorder
CSO	Central Statistical Office
DETR	Department of the Environment, Transport and the Regions
DfEE	Department for Education and Employment
DoH	Department of Health
DSM	Diagnostic and Statistical Manuals, fourth revision
DSS	Department of Social Security
ECHP	European Community Household Panel Survey
EHCS	English Housing Condition Survey
ESWNI	England, Scotland, Wales and Northern Ireland
FFT	Family Fund Trust
FSMs	free school meals
GAP	Government Accountability to the People
GHS	General Household Survey
GHQ12	General Health Questionnaire 12
HEA	Health Education Authority
ICD-10	International Classification of Diseases, tenth revision
IS	Income Support
KS1	Key Stage 1

LA	local authorities
LEA	local education authorities
LIS	Luxembourg Income Survey
NCDS	National Child Development Study
	a longitudinal survey of children born in 1958
NCAS	National Congenital Anomaly System
NSHD	National Survey of Health and Development
	longitudinal study of children born in 1946
NCIPA	National Commission of Inquiry into the Prevention of Child Abuse
NLSCY	National Longitudinal Survey of Children and Youth
NSPCC	National Society for the Prevention of Cruelty to Children
NSSAL	National Survey of Sexual Attitudes and Lifestyles
	random survey of nearly 19,000 men and women aged 16 to 59 completed in 1990 and 1991
NUT	National Union of Teachers
OFSTED	Office for Standards in Education
ONS	Office for National Statistics
ONS Longitudinal Survey	*a follow-up study of one per cent of the population enumerated at the 1971 census and followed up for 25 years*
OPAs	Output and Performance Analysis
OPCS	Office for Population Censuses and Surveys
PHLS	Public Health Laboratory Service
PSA	Public Service Agreements
PSI	Policy Studies Institute
RGCS	Registrar General's Occupational Classification System
SATs	Standardised Assessment Tests
SDQ	Strengths and Difficulties Questionnaire
SEH	Survey of English Housisng
SEN	Statement of Educational Need
SEU	Social Exclusion Unit
SMR	Standardised Mortality Ratios
YRBS	Youth Risk Behaviours Survey

Contributors

Helen Barnes is a Research Fellow at the Policy Studies Institute.

Jonathan Bradshaw is Professor of Social Policy and Associate Director of the Social Policy Research Unit at the University of York.

Paul Higate was a Research Fellow in the Centre for Housing Policy at the University of York and is now a Lecturer in Social Policy at the University of Bristol.

Francis McGlone is a Freelance Researcher.

Deborah Quilgars is a Research Fellow in the Centre for Housing Policy at the University of York.

Julia Johnson is a DPhil student in the Department of Social Policy and Social Work and attached to the Social Policy Research Unit at the University of York.

Acknowledgements

The authors acknowledge the Economic and Social Research Council's (ESRC) funding of the project 'Poverty: outcomes for children'. The project was part of the ESRC's £2.9 million research programme on 'Children 5–16 growing into the 21st century'.

The Family Policy Studies Centre and the authors thank the Economic and Social Research Council and the National Children's Bureau for their support of this publication.

Foreword

This book contains the results of parts of a project *Poverty: the outcomes for children* funded as part of the Economic and Social Research Council's programme of research on Children 5–16. This project involved:

i)   A programme of secondary analysis of large datasets exploring child poverty and using the child as the unit of analysis. This has included British data: the Family Resources Survey, the Breadline Britain Survey and the British Household Panel Survey; and comparative data: the Luxembourg Income Survey and the European Community Panel Survey. This element of the project has been completed and written up elsewhere (Whiteford, Kennedy and Bradshaw (1996), Adelman and Bradshaw (1998), Bradshaw and Barnes (1998), Bradshaw (1997), Bradshaw (1999), Clarke, Bradshaw and Williams (2000), Bradshaw (2000)).

ii) A comparative study to discover how other countries attempt to monitor the well-being of their children. Chapter 18 summarises the results of that study.

iii) A review of existing evidence on the impact of poverty on the outcomes for children. This is the work that is included in Chapters 1–17 of this book.

For the purposes of these reviews we have divided outcomes into four domains:

* **physical outcomes** including mortality, morbidity, accidents, child abuse, teenage pregnancy, environmental degradation and homelessness;
* **cognitive outcomes** including educational attainment;
* **behavioural outcomes** including school exclusions, youth crime, smoking, alcohol, drugs, suicide and child labour;
* **emotional outcomes** including self-image, happiness, subjective well-being.

The purpose of these reviews is:

* to assess whether there is evidence that poverty is associated with poor outcomes for children; and
* to assess whether there is evidence that increased poverty has led to worse outcomes for children – whether during the period that child poverty has increased child outcomes have got worse or have improved more slowly than they might have.

In answering both questions although we have had some regard to comparative data, the evidence drawn on in the reviews is deliberately concentrated on British data, and on British data in the last 20 years.

It builds on earlier (less detailed) reviews (Bradshaw 1990 and Kumar 1995) undertaken as part of the UNICEF efforts to monitor the well-being of children in industrialised countries (Cornia and Danziger, 1996; Micklewright and Stewart, 1999).

The work for this project was originally going to be undertaken with my wife, Carol Stimson, but when she was killed in a car crash on 9 May 1997 a number of colleagues and ex-colleagues from the University of York and the Family Policy Studies Centre stepped into the breach. For their generous support I am eternally grateful. I am also grateful for the patience of Professor Alan Prout, University of Stirling, who was the co-ordinator of the ESRC Children 5–16 Programme.

Jonathan Bradshaw
Venabu, Norway

1 Introduction

Jonathan Bradshaw

It is now clear that among Western industrial countries the United Kingdom is an outlier in terms of child poverty. We know from national data (DSS, 2000) that the proportion of children living in households with income below half national average increased more than threefold – from 10 per cent in 1979 to 35 per cent in 1998/99. We also know from administrative statistics that the proportion of children living in families receiving basic social assistance increased from 7 per cent in 1979 to 23 per cent in 1998.[1] A third of children are presently being born to mothers receiving Income Support.

The European Community Household Panel Survey found that the UK had the highest child poverty rate among the twelve EU countries included in 1994 (Ditch *et al.*, 1998). The Luxembourg Income Survey reveals that around 1995 the UK had the third highest child poverty rate of 25 countries included – only exceeded by Russia and the United States (Bradbury and Jantti 1999). The same analysis shows that while most countries have managed to maintain stable, or even reduce, their child poverty rates in the face of the economic and social changes of the last two decades or so, the UK has had one of the fastest-growing child poverty rates – an annual increase between 1974 and 1995 of twice the rate of the United States, for example (Bradbury and Jantti 1999).

The reasons for this record are also fairly clear. Our family demography does not help; a comparatively high fertility rate, low age of first marriage, high divorce rate, low mean age of child-bearing, high birth-rate outside marriage, high proportion of lone parents, high proportion of cohabiting couples, high proportion of families with three or more children (Ditch *et al.*, 1998). All these factors are likely to be associated with high rates of child poverty. However, purely demographic explanations for child poverty are unsatisfactory. There are countries with low or lower child poverty rates than the UK but with similar demographic characteristics. Take France – in its family demography it is remarkably similar to the UK, but has a much lower child poverty rate.

The comparative evidence indicates that it cannot be argued that increasing child poverty is the inevitable result of economic restructuring, globalisation, demographic transitions or whatever. In Britain it is the consequence of successive Conservative Governments pursuing *laissez faire* economic policies, aspiring to reduce public expenditure and taxation and relying on theories about the trickle-down of economic growth. The result is an unprecedented and remarkable increase in overall inequality, with children the group most seriously affected.

Among the factors associated with high levels of child poverty in Britain are the following:

- the percentage of children in Britain living in households without a full-time paid worker has been higher and diverging from the overall unemployment rate since the 1980s (Atkinson, 1998)

- worklessness (households without a worker) in Britain is second highest out of 15 countries for both lone parents and couples with children (OECD, 1998);
- the proportion of lone mothers in employment is fourth from lowest out of 20 countries (Bradshaw *et al.*, 1996a);
- the proportion of married mothers in employment is middling, but the proportion working full-time is third from lowest out of 20 countries (Bradshaw *et al.*, 1996);
- the level of the short-term unemployment compensation package was the lowest among the EU12 in 1992 (Papadopoulos, 2000); and Eardley *et al.*, (1996) found that, out of 26 OECD countries in 1994, social assistance for couples with children ranked fifteenth in purchasing power parity terms. Bradshaw *et al.* (1996) found the social assistance replacement rate for lone parents was comparatively low;
- the value of the in-work package for families with children is also comparatively low. Bradshaw *et al.*, (1993) found that Britain's package was below average out of 18 countries and the work of the EU Observatory (Ditch *et al.*, 1998) confirmed that the UK package was below average, and considerably lower than countries like Luxembourg, Belgium, France and Finland.

In short, our transfer package is relatively ineffective in the UK, both the out-of-work package and the package of tax allowances, cash benefits and services in kind which mitigate the costs to parents of raising children.

In, 1997, after 17 years of Conservative rule, a Labour Government came to power. Before the election Tony Blair had declared 'If the next Labour Government has not raised the living standards of the poorest by the end of its time in office it will have failed' (Interview in the *Independent on Sunday* by Tony Blair, 26 July 1996). However, during the election campaign the Labour leadership had promised not to increase public expenditure for two years and not to increase taxation in the lifetime of the Parliament (up to five years). Almost their first social policy act was to implement Conservative proposals to abolish One-Parent Benefit and the lone-parent premium in Income Support – thus further impoverishing more than two million of the poorest children in Britain.

However the state of child poverty in the UK, and the evidence of our comparative position, has begun to seep into the political consciousness. On 18 March 1999 Tony Blair announced:

'Our historic aim will be for ours to be the first generation to end child poverty, and it will take a generation. It is a 20-year mission but I believe it can be done'.

In the context of both Government rhetoric and action in their first two years this was a most unexpected declaration – and a brave and welcome one. The Government has claimed that policies already announced will lift 800,000 children out of poverty and the Chancellor has promised that measures announced will lift a further 200,000 out of poverty in 2001 and 2002. We have not yet been told what poverty standard is being employed in these estimates but an indication of the challenge facing the Government is that the latest Department of Social Security statistics (DSS, 2000) indicate that in 1998/9 there were 4.5 million children living in households with equivalent income below half the average.

The Government is pursuing four strategies:

- **redistribution** (a minimum wage from April 1998, Family Tax Credit, Childcare Tax Credit, Child Tax Credit, real increases in Child Benefit and the child scale rates of Income Support for children under 11, a starting rate of income tax of 10 per cent);
- **employment** (the New Deals);
- **prevention** (Sure Start, Social Exclusion Unit, a strategy to reduce teenage mothers);
- **investment in human capital** (schools, training, the NHS and the Childcare Strategy).

What this book contributes

The proposal for the work contained in this book was written and submitted to ESRC long before child poverty became a key political issue. It was submitted out of a concern that the impact of poverty on the well-being of children was being neglected because the United Kingdom does not produce a routine comprehensive analysis of the well-being of children. There is no Ministry for Children (or the Family) in the UK and no Children's Council or Ombudsman that might produce such a report. As one recent commentator noted:

> ... there is no annual report on the state of UK children, no systematic collection or publication of statistics, no requirement to assess or publish information on the impact of government policies on children and no analysis of overall or departmental budgets to assess the amount and proportion spent on children. (Hodgkin and Newell, 1996:13)

Of course there are official sources of data on children's well-being (for example Botting *et al.*, 1996; Woodroffe *et al.*, 1993) and the Central Statistical Office published a *Social Focus on Children* in 1994 (CSO, 1994), which collected together some of the relevant data – but not focused on the consequences of rising poverty. There are also a variety of sources of data on children's well-being generated by the research community, with *inter alia*, the support of government funding – including especially the birth cohorts of children born in one week in, 1949, 1958 and, 1970 (with another being planned for 2001) and the British Household Panel Survey (which includes a young person's questionnaire). However, although these sources are useful none of them is designed to monitor child well-being over time.

The new Government committed itself to producing an annual report on its progress in reducing poverty in the Green and White Papers on welfare reform (Cm 3805, 1998 and Cm 4101, 1998). The New Policy Institute published a model version of such a report which includes indicators of child poverty some of which are measures of outcome[2] (Howarth *et al.*, 1999(a)) and followed it up with a second report (Howarth *et al.*,

1999(b)). In September 1999 the Government published its own proposals (DSS, 1999) for monitoring its performance which included 13 indicators covering children and young people some of which were indicators of outcome.[3]

As we shall see it is easier to examine the relationship between poverty for some outcomes than for others. For many of the outcomes we examine there are no good time-series measures and/or there are no good cross-sectional measures that allow one to associate variations in outcomes to poverty. Very often the only indicators of poverty that are available are very indirect – such as social class, employment status or family composition. There are a number of problems in seeking to explore the relationship between poverty and the outcomes for children. First, child poverty has only been increasing since the late 1970s in Britain and then only relatively.[4] Effectively what we are attempting to observe is the impact of an increase in relative poverty on child outcomes. Nevertheless that increase has been very great, unprecedented, threefold and even if such a dramatic change in the lives of children has not been associated with a deterioration in their well-being it might have been expected to have slowed down the rate of improvement in their well-being.

However, there are also problems (as ever in social science) in understanding the nature of any associations observed. The finding that increasing poverty has or has not been associated with an outcome, or that an outcome varies at any one time for children from different backgrounds, does not prove that the association is direct and it does not identify the causal mechanisms involved. Interpreting the results of this analysis is a complex, and inevitably politicised, activity.

The outcomes of poverty may be short-term or long-term. Although concentrated in the poorest sections of society, they also have consequences for other social groups. The experience of poverty may be mediated (whether positively or negatively) by a number of other factors, and the form which poverty takes will vary from one person to the next. Equally, it is clear that some of the negative outcomes which are experienced by children are not a necessary consequence of poverty, although they may be strongly associated with poverty at an aggregate level.

The objective of this book is to present a review of evidence about the association between child poverty and indicators of well-being. It is in attempt to do some of the ground work that is necessary before a Government agency – perhaps most appropriately the Office for National Statistics takes on the important task of monitoring the impact of social and economic change on our children.

The brief of the contributors to this book was to review British evidence on the association between poverty (and proxies for poverty) and the outcome. They have interpreted that brief in different ways and that explains why the reviews are not the same length, are structured somewhat differently and presented in different styles. They were also written at different times and some of the most recent evidence on the subject may be missing from some of the chapters. This is not the last word on the subject; indeed, it is more or less the first.

Notes to Chapter 1

1   During this period the scales of benefit declined as a proportion of average earnings. For a couple with two children under 11 the scales of benefit were 42 per cent of average earnings in November 1979 and by April 1998 they were 32 per cent of average earnings.

2   They include the following indicators: children living in work-less households; children living in households with below average income; percentage of babies born with low birth-weight, number of accidental deaths, numbers gaining no GCSE above grade D, numbers permanently excluded from school, number of children whose parents divorce, births to girls conceiving under age 16, number in young offender institutions.

3   They are:

   1   An increase in the proportion of seven-year-old Sure Start children achieving level one or above in the Key Stage 1 English and maths tests.

   2   Health outcomes in Sure Start areas: a reduction in the proportion of low birth-weight babies in Sure Start areas; and a reduction in the rate of hospital admissions as a result of serious injury in Sure Start areas.

   3   An increase in the proportion of those aged 11 achieving level four or above in the Key Stage 2 tests for literacy and numeracy.

   4   A reduction in the proportion of truancies and exclusions from school.

   5   An increase in the proportion of 19-year-olds with at least a level two qualification or equivalent.

   6   A reduction in the proportion of children living in work-less households, for households of a given size, over the economic cycle.

   7   Low income indicators: a reduction in the proportion of children in households with relatively low incomes, with low incomes in an absolute sense, and with persistently low incomes.

   8   A reduction in the proportion of children living in poor housing.

   9   A reduction in the proportion of households with children experiencing fuel poverty.

   10 A reduction in the rate at which children are admitted to hospital as a result of an unintentional injury resulting in a hospital stay of longer than three days.

   11 A reduction in the proportion of 16 to- 18-year-olds not in education or training.

   12 An improvement in the educational attainment of children looked after by local authorities.

   13 Teenage pregnancy: a reduction in the rate of conceptions for those aged under 18 and an increase in the proportion of those who are teenage parents, in education, employment or training

4   In fact there was an increase in the numbers of children living below the 1979 real-terms poverty threshold by, 1995/96 of 300,000 (DSS, 1998) but that series has been suspended since that date.

Physical outcomes

Deborah Quilgars, Julia Johnson and Francis McGlone

2 Child mortality

Deborah Quilgars

Introduction

The link between poverty and infant and child mortality in Britain is well established, and has been highlighted by all the key health documents in the last 20 years, from the Black Report (Townsend and Davidson, 1982) to the recent *Inquiry into Inequalities in Health* (Acheson, 1998). Infant and child mortality rates are often cited as one of the major indicators of the level of development and health of a nation (Botting, 1997). Whilst mortality rates fell substantially during the twentieth century, including over the last 20 years, the evidence indicates that steep differentials between the rates of mortality for poor children compared with better-off children are still evident, and show little sign of improving. This evidence is reviewed in detail below, looking at inequalities in child mortality by occupational social class of both father and mother, area deprivation indicators as well as evidence on differences by ethnic origin.

Infant and child mortality: definitions and statistical sources

Mortality statistics are produced on an annual basis in all countries in Britain. In England and Wales annual reference volumes are produced by the Office for National Statistics (ONS), whilst an Annual Report of the Registrar General is produced in Scotland and Northern Ireland. The publications *Population Trends*, and from 1999, *Health Statistics Quarterly*, also present analysis of mortality statistics. Annual statistics routinely include information on infant mortality rates by father's occupational class (see below). Official publications refer to five types of infant mortality (ONS, 1998d):

Perinatal: still births plus early neonatal deaths;
Early neonatal deaths: deaths up to six completed days of life;
Late neonatal: 7–27 completed days of life;
Post-neonatal: more than 28 days but under one year;
Infant deaths: all deaths at ages under one year.

In practice, early and late neonatal deaths are usually presented together, and still births are often presented separately. In addition, data on child mortality is usually presented in three age groups: ages 1–4; 5–9 and 10–14.

Recording of parental occupation

At the birth of a child, there is a legal requirement for the occupation of the child's father to be recorded whenever the birth is a 'joint' registration (registered by both the mother and father). If the father is unemployed, the registrar records the last full-time occupation. Employment status (ie. whether economically active or not) is collected, as well as the type of industry or line of work that the father is in. In contrast, there is no legal requirement that the mother's occupation should be recorded. Since 1986 the registrar has been encouraged to ask the mother whether she was in gainful employment at any time before the birth, but the provision of this information is voluntary.

When a child dies, information used in ONS statistics may come from details supplied by the doctor certifying the death, by the informant to the registrar, and/or by a coroner if a post-mortem or inquest is carried out. Again, the father's occupation is recorded routinely, but registrars are only told to record the last full-time occupation of the mother of the child if she has been in employment for most of her adult life (this practice began in 1982). This means that unemployment or not being economically active is recorded differently for men and women (Botting and Cooper, 1993).

Since 1991, the information on occupational class collected on birth and death records is classified using the Standard Occupational Classification Codes for social class used in the Census. It should be noted, however, that this allocation is inevitably approximate as not all the questions used in the Census on occupation groups are collected on birth or death records. In addition, whilst parents' occupations, if given, are coded for all still births and infant deaths, for live births they are only coded for a ten per cent sample.

Recording of other factors

Birth registrations in England and Wales record a number of other details about the parents and child, including birth-weight, age of mother, country of birth of mother, marital status and whether the birth was a single or multiple birth. As much of this information is not collected at death, since 1975 ONS has linked the death records of infants (under the age of one) to births using NHS numbers to identify the birth registration. Linkage of birth and death records is achieved for nearly 100 per cent of cases. More recently, in 1994, ONS started linking records for childhood deaths at ages one, two and three, giving more scope for analysis of mortality trends by these other social and biological factors.

Trends in mortality during childhood

Mortality rates in children are highest around, and just after, birth. Rates then show a sharp drop during the first year of life, continuing to fall as the child increases in age. Child mortality rates are at their lowest between the ages of five and nine and then show a gradual increase through the teenage years (Dattani, 1999). Table 2.1 shows the rates for still birth, infant and child mortality for the period 1981–1997 for England and Wales (data for Scotland shows similar trends). As can be seen, rates for all types of

Table 2.1 **Still births, infant and child mortality rates, 1981–1997, England and Wales**

Year of death	*Still births	**Neonatal deaths	**Post-neonatal deaths	**Infant deaths	Ages 1–4	Ages 5–9	Ages 10–14
1981	6.6	6.6	4.3	11.0	50	23	24
1982	6.3	6.3	4.6	10.8	47	21	23
1983	5.7	5.9	4.3	10.1	44	23	22
1984	5.7	5.5	3.9	9.4	42	21	22
1985	5.5	5.4	4.0	9.4	45	20	23
1986	5.3	5.3	4.3	9.6	42	19	19
1987	5.0	5.1	4.1	9.2	42	18	20
1988	4.9	4.9	4.1	9.0	42	19	20
1989	4.7	4.8	3.7	8.4	40	19	19
1990	4.6	4.6	3.3	7.9	38	17	19
1991	4.6	4.4	3.0	7.4	36	18	19
1992	4.3	4.3	2.3	6.6	32	16	17
1993	4.4	4.2	2.2	6.3	32	14	18
1994	4.4	4.1	2.1	6.2	29	14	17
1995	4.2	4.2	2.0	6.1	26	14	17
1996	4.0	4.1	2.0	6.1	28	12	15
1997	3.9	3.9	2.0	5.9			

* Still birth rates per 1,000 total births; figures are based on still births which occurred after 28 or more weeks' gestation

** Neonatal, post-neonatal and infant mortality rates per 1,000 live births

Source: Schuman (1998).

child mortality decreased substantially over this 17-year period. Infant deaths overall have reduced from 11 per 1,000 total live births in 1981 to nearly half this rate, at 5.9 per 1,000 in 1997. Still births and neonatal deaths have both seen the same reduction, from 6.6 per 1,000 live births to 3.9 per 1,000 over the period, with post-neonatal deaths more than halving from 4.3 to 2 per 1,000 live births – much of this latter a result of a reduction in deaths due to sudden infant death syndrome (cot deaths). Child mortality rates at ages 1–4 remained at over twice the rate for child deaths at ages 5–9 and 10–14 during the period 1981–96, with all three rates also almost reducing by half during the period. Whilst not shown in Table 2.1, gender differences are pronounced, with boys experiencing higher rates of mortality at all ages: for example, rates for boys were 30 per cent higher than for girls aged between 1 and 14 during 1987–91 (Botting and Crawley, 1995). Causes of death are different at different ages. Low birth-weight accounted for nearly 60 per cent of neonatal deaths in 1991 (Botting and Crawley, 1995). Injury and poisoning are the most common causes of death for boys over one and girls over the age of four (see Chapter 4). Deaths from cancer accounted for 27 per cent of deaths in 1991 for 5- to 9-year-olds and 19 per cent of 10- to 14-year-olds.

Whilst this review is concerned solely with British evidence on infant and child mortality, it is important to note that, whilst Britain's infant mortality rates have decreased, they still remain higher than many other comparable Western European countries including France, Germany, the Netherlands, Finland and Sweden (WHO Eurostat/PC, 1992, in Woodroffe *et al.*, 1993). For example, a comparison with Sweden, a country often regarded as setting the standard in this area (although Japan and Finland have both shown lower infant mortality rates recently), showed that neonatal risk was 1.5 times higher in England and Wales than Sweden in the mid-1980s, whilst post-neonatal rates were nearly twice (1.9 times) as high (Leon *et al.*, 1992).

Mortality and father's social class

Infant mortality

The most up-to-date examination of ONS data on father's social class for linked birth–death records of infants and children aged 0–3 is for the years 1993–1996 (Dattani, 1999). This analysis includes all births registered by both parents (within and outside marriage) and accounts for 95 per cent of births. Table 2.2 shows a clear class gradient for mortality rates by social class of father, with mortality rates for social class V more than double those in social class I for infants in 1996 (815 compared with 370 deaths per 100,000 births), representing an increasing class differential compared with 1993 (664 compared with 458 deaths per 100,000 births – 1.4 times greater), 1994 (1.5 times greater) and 1995 (1.7 times greater). A difference of more than twofold was evidenced for children aged one between social classes I and V for all three years 1993–5, however the gradient through the classes was not as clear. For children aged two the gradient was 1.75 times higher between classes I and V (1993/4); but again the pattern was less than clear for other classes, whilst the smaller numbers of children aged three meant that no clear association could be found. This evidence appears compelling, but also reveals the difficulties of working with small numbers when analysing trends. A number of researchers have combined years to give more robustness to the data, and Dattani (1999) points out that data will improve as more linked data sets are available for ages 1–3.

Botting (1997) combined data for years 1993–5 to observe the mortality ratios for different categories of infant mortality (Table 2.3). This shows a ratio between social class I and V of 1.7 for infant deaths over 1993–5. Botting noted that the differential between classes increases with age – whereas the rate for still birth is 1.7, perinatal and neonatal 1.6, the differential for post-neonatal deaths is as high as 2.2. The author suggests that these differences may partly be explained by the fact that earlier deaths are more likely to be a result of factors relating to birth, like prematurity, rather than external influences which are likely to be more prominent when the child is living in its home environment.

Table 2.2 **Infant and childhood deaths, ages 1, 2 and 3, by father's social class for births inside or outside marriage, joint registration, England and Wales**

Social class	Year of birth	Rates per 100,000			
		Age under 1	Age 1	Age 2	Age 3
All classes	1993	598	42	28	18
	1994	581	43	26	–
	1995	596	42	–	–
	1996	582	–	–	–
Social Class I	1993	458	22	28	9
	1994	433	28	15	–
	1995	422	13	–	–
	1996	370	–	–	–
Social Class II	1993	480	25	22	18
	1994	451	27	16	–
	1995	476	31	–	–
	1996	440	–	–	–
Social Class IIIN	1993	544	45	13	13
	1994	520	40	27	–
	1995	528	53	–	–
	1996	516	–	–	–
Social Class IIIM	1993	562	34	24	13
	1994	541	31	27	–
	1995	536	42	–	–
	1996	552	–	–	–
Social Class IV	1993	553	48	26	20
	1994	611	50	37	–
	1995	659	35	–	–
	1996	605	–	–	–
Social Class V	1993	664	64	36	8
	1994	663	61	39	–
	1995	710	35	–	–
	1996	815	–	–	–

– Data not collected

Source: Dattani (1999).

Table 2.3 **Still birth, perinatal and infant mortality rates, by father's social class, 1993–95, England and Wales**

Father's social class	Still birth rate	Perinatal rate	Neonatal rate	Post-neonatal rate	Infant rate
I	4.5	7	3.1	1.3	4.5
II	4.5	7.3	3.5	1.3	4.8
IIIN	5.4	8.4	3.9	1.6	5.5
IIIM	5.4	8.5	4.1	1.8	5.9
IV	6.2	9.9	4.6	2	6.6
V	7.8	11.5	4.9	2.8	7.7
England and Wales	**5.5**	**8.7**	**4.1**	**1.8**	**5.9**

Source: Botting (1997), Tables 7.2 and 7.3.

A number of authors have looked at the trends in infant mortality rates over a longer period of time to observe whether differentials have reduced or increased. Botting and Crawley (1995), looking at data from 1981 and 1991, using standard mortality statistics, noted the continuation of social class gradients (Table 2.4). Unfortunately this data is limited by the fact that it was only able to compare rates for children of parents who were married. Nonetheless, for children of married parents, the data indicates that rates reduced proportionately more for manual social classes than non-manual classes, with, for instance, nearly a 50 per cent reduction for class V compared with only a third (34 per cent) for class I over 1981–91 – meaning that whilst rates were twice as high in 1981 between classes V and I, this had reduced to 1.6 times as high in 1991. However, it should be noted that a reduction of less than a quarter (23 per cent) was evidenced for the 'other' category which is likely to comprise high proportions of economically inactive households. Botting (1997), using similar analysis, confirms this trend in a second paper by stating that the ratio between infant mortality rates for class V and I (inside marriage) fell from 2.0 to 1.7 in the 1980s, and to 1.6 in 1995.

Most recently, Whitehead and Drever (1999) looked at trends in couple registrations by social class of father over the period 1975–1996 for joint registrations both within and outside marriage, using the linked birth–death record database (with the ten per cent sample of births coded to social class). Whitehead and Drever combined social classes I and II, and IV and V to make their calculations more robust, and for the same reason used three-year moving averages to observe changes over time. Table 2.5 shows that major reductions in infant mortality occurred through the period, particularly in the late-1970s and early-1990s. A slight reduction in excess mortality between those in classes IV–V compared with I–II was evidenced over the period, but only from 64 per cent to 52 per cent. Again, following Botting's analysis (1997), the differentials for infant deaths between classes were greatest in the post-neonatal period, with an excess of 118 per cent in 1989–9, compared with 47 per cent for perinatal and 40 per cent for neonatal

Table 2.4 **Infant mortality rates by social class (based on father's occupation), 1981 and 1991, England and Wales**

Social Class		Rate (per 1,000 live births)	
		1981	1991
All		10.9	7.2
Within marriage	All	10.2	6.3
	I-IV	10.0	6.0
	I	7.7	5.1
	II	7.9	5.3
	IIIN	8.5	6.1
	IIIM	10.3	6.2
	IV	12.6	7.1
	V	15.8	8.2
	Other	15.0	11.5
Outside marriage		15.2	9.4

Source: Mortality Statistics – perinatal and infant: social and biological factors 1981, 1991, in Botting and Crawley (1995), Table 6.4.

deaths in the same period. Differentials appeared to have reduced for all types of infant mortality, although the data for post-neonatal mortality showed excess mortality to be highest in both 1975–77 and 1989–91, with a dip in 1982–84 and later in 1994–96.

Child mortality

The OPCS occupational mortality childhood supplement (OPCS, 1988) produced figures for child mortality rates for the period 1979/80 and 1982/3 (around the 1981 Census) by the social class of the head of household which was subsequently analysed by Botting and Crawley (1995). Table 2.6 shows mortality of children aged 1–15 by standardised mortality ratios (SMR) for this period for both girls and boys. Class differentials were most marked at ages 1–4 with social classes I and II having a SMR of 65 for boys and 73 for girls compared with 145 and 139, for boys and girls, in social classes IV and V. Differentials were least amongst those aged 10–15.

Botting went on to compare childhood mortality rates for the period 1979/80 and 1982/83 with those from 1991–93 (1997). Unfortunately analysis by social class is only possible around the times of the Census as population denominators by social class are not available each year, and therefore analysis relates to the periods of 1981 and 1991 Censuses. Table 2.7 shows mortality rates per 100,000 (rather than SMRs) for all age groups and both sexes.

Looking at class differentials for ages 1–15, it can be seen that differentials persisted over time and in fact widened slightly, with class V having twice the death rate of those in class I in 1979/80–1982/3 but this being 2.3 times greater in 1991–3. However, it is important to note that most of the observed difference, in both periods, was be-

Table 2.5 **Trends in infant mortality (95 per cent confidence interval) for couple registrations by father's social class, 1975–1996, England and Wales**

Year	Class I–II	Class IV–V	Excess mortality classes IV–V over I–II (%)
Perinatal mortality per 1,000 total births			
1975–77	13.8	20.6	50
1982–84	8.2	12.4	51
1989–91	6.5	9.5	47
1994–96	7.2	10.2	41
Neonatal mortality per 1,000 live births			
1975–77	7.6	11.3	48
1982–84	4.7	7.0	50
1989–91	3.7	5.2	40
1994–96	3.4	4.8	42
Post-neonatal mortality per 1,000 live births			
1975–77	3.0	6.1	105
1982–84	2.9	5.2	78
1989–91	2.0	4.3	118
1994–96	1.3	2.2	78
Overall infant mortality per 1,000 live births			
1975–77	10.6	17.5	64
1982–84	7.6	12.2	61
1989–91	5.7	9.6	67
1994–96	4.6	7.0	52

Source: Whitehead and Drever (1999), Table 4.

Table 2.6 **Mortality of children aged 1–15, Standard Mortality Ratios (all causes) – by age, sex and social class, 1979/1980 and 1982/1983, England and Wales**

Social class	1–4 years		5–9 years		1–15 years	
	Boys	Girls	Boys	Girls	Boys	Girls
I & II	65	73	72	80	71	77
IIIN	79	82	83	92	77	81
IIIM	101	96	93	96	95	95
IV & V	145	139	130	128	126	121

Source: OPCS (1988) reproduced in Botting and Crawley (1995), Table 6.3.

Table 2.7 **Childhood mortality rates per 100,000, by age, England and Wales**

	Children		Boys		Girls	
	1979–80, 1982–83	*1991–93*	*1979–80 1982–83*	*1991–93*	*1979–80, 1982–83*	*1991–93*
Age 1–4						
I	34	27	34	34	34	21
II	34	23	35	24	32	22
IIIN	41	23	44	24	37	22
IIIM	47	37	53	40	42	33
IV	57	30	63	33	51	28
V	98	71	111	75	84	67
England & Wales	**48**	**34**	**53**	**37**	**44**	**30**
Age 5–9						
I	21	14	25	16	18	12
II	19	12	21	13	16	11
IIIN	22	11	25	13	19	7
IIIM	23	19	26	21	19	16
IV	28	14	32	16	23	13
V	42	30	51	34	31	26
England & Wales	**25**	**16**	**29**	**18**	**20**	**14**
Age 10–14						
I	19	14	21	15	16	13
II	19	13	23	14	16	12
IIIN	18	15	21	17	14	12
IIIM	23	22	26	25	19	18
IV	24	20	30	26	17	15
	30	29	36	41	24	17
England & Wales	**23**	**18**	**28**	**22**	**19**	**15**
Age 1–15						
I	24	18	26	21	21	15
II	22	16	25	17	19	15
IIIN	25	16	28	19	21	14
IIIM	28	25	32	29	24	22
IV	33	22	38	26	27	19
V	49	42	57	49	40	35
England & Wales	**30**	**23**	**35**	**26**	**25**	**19**

Source: Botting (1997), Table 7.6.

tween classes I–IV and V, with class V having 1.5 the rate of class IV in the earlier period and 1.9 times the rate in the early 1990s. The slight increase was mainly due to increasing differentials at ages 10–14 (1.6–2), and a minor increase at ages 5–9 (2.0–2.1). Whilst ages 1–4 show the greatest differentials in each period of time, here differentials between classes I and V decreased from 2.9 to 2.6 over the period.

There were also some differences by gender. For example, differentials between classes I and V actually increased more for girls over the time period, from 1.9 to 2.3, compared with only 2.2 to 2.3 for boys. A reduction in class differentials at ages 1–4 was achieved only for boys during the period, rates for girls showed an increase. Conversely, whilst differentials increased for boys aged 10–14 between the two time periods, girls showed a slight reduction.

Another important source of data on trends in child mortality is the ONS Longitudinal Study (Botting, 1997). This study uses a representative sample of one per cent of the population of England and Wales, where everyone born on one of four days since the early 1970s has been selected for interview. Whilst the numbers in this study are obviously smaller than routine mortality statistics, the study is linked to the Census and so benefits from access to full information on the occupational details of the head of household. Table 2.8 demonstrates that, whilst absolute numbers differed substantially from Table 2.7 (due to the inclusion of infants aged under one in the calculation), social class gradients are once again evidenced in all periods. Similarly, slightly widening differentials are observed with social class V having 2.8 times the chance of childhood mortality (aged 0–14) in 1982–86 and 3.3 times the chance in 1987–91. Once again, differentials are most marked between classes I–IV and class V, particularly in 1982–86, whilst there was an absence of a stepped increase between classes II and IV (for example, in all periods class IIIN had higher mortality rates per 100,000 than class IIIM).

Table 2.8 **Mortality rates (ages 0–14, 0–4) per 100,000 population, England and Wales**

Social class	1982–1986	1987–1991	1982–1986	1987–1991
	Ages 0–14		Ages 0–4	
I	57	37	162	88
II	74	68	169	164
IIIN	86	122	240	291
IIIM	75	67	216	162
IV	86	88	208	205
V	161	122	399	268
England and Wales	**87**	**81**	**219**	**188**

Source: Botting (1997), Table 7.7.

Causes of death

Most causes of mortality within childhood show class gradients, although some more than others. Sudden infant death syndrome has a particularly strong relationship with class – three times as many babies died from cot death in social class V compared with social class I over the period 1990–95 (Botting, 1997). In childhood, accidental deaths shows the clearest class gradients across all ages (OPCS, 1988 and see also Chapter 4). The only major cause of death which does not show clear class gradients and, if anything seems to be inversely related to class, is cancer (OPCS, 1988; Fear *et al.*, 1999). Whilst there is some evidence that some forms of cancer are associated with 'exposure' to potentially harmful substances within fathers' occupations, for example, childhood kidney cancer with occupational exposure to either agrochemicals, agriculture or animals, recent data also suggests that cancer may be more likely, for example, amongst the children of clerks, teachers, sales-staff and managers than labourers and construction workers (Fear *et al.*, 1999). These patterns, however, have not been fully analysed, nor adequately explained.

Mortality and mother's social class

As outlined earlier, mother's social class has only been collected on a voluntary basis for births since 1986 and on child death records since 1982 only for women who have been in full-time employment for most of their adult life. It is generally agreed that there are, therefore, potentially a number of sources of unreliability associated with using mother's occupation in analysis (Cooper and Botting, 1992). These include a high proportion of missing information, and a possible under-representation of those in lower grade jobs where mothers may have recently changed jobs and choose not to volunteer this information. There is also a broader question about how appropriate social class, as measured by occupation, is as a measure of what women do. For example, the manual / non-manual divide is not as appropriate, and certain jobs in some classes may reflect different positions in the labour market to men (for example, shopwork and car sales are both class IIIN but the latter usually offers higher wages and better promotion prospects). The effects of childbearing on occupation may be significant; for example, 61 per cent of first births in marriage record mother's occupation compared with only 26 per cent of third births, and it is likely that a proportion of women may have changed social class from birth to the death of a child. Finally, it is suggested that 'infant mortality rates for manual social classes will be artificially reduced by the higher non-statement of the women's occupation at death registration' (as the recording of mother's occupation is more likely for those in higher classes with careers) and that 'this will account, at least in part, for the reduced social class differentials … for the mother's social class as defined by her occupation compared with those of the father' (Botting and Cooper, 1993).

Botting (1997) updated previous analysis by Botting and Cooper (1993) of infant mortality rates by mother's social class for the period 1991–5 (Table 2.9). Here, similar, but smaller, differentials in infant mortality are seen as compared to father's social class. No clear pattern is evident between classes I and IIIM, although figures increase significantly for class V. Between 1986–90 and 1991–95, the largest fall in infant mortality was for class I (fall of 29 per cent), whilst the rates for others fell between 17 and 20 per cent, with the overall gap between social classes increasing from 1.5 in 1986–90 to 1.7 in 1991–95. It is likely that the latter figures are the more robust due to the lower proportion of missing data: therefore it is possible that some of this effect over time is due to bias in the statistics rather than real differences.

Table 2.9 **Infant mortality rates, by mother's social class, England and Wales**

Mother's social class	1986–1990	1991–1995
I	6.6	4.7
II	5.9	4.9
IIIN	5.7	4.7
IIIM	6.5	5.2
IV	7.1	5.9
V	9.7	7.8
England and Wales	**8.8**	**6.5**

Source: Botting (1997), Table 7.5.

Whilst a number of commentators have drawn attention to the worrying lack of detail and analysis of parents classified in the 'unoccupied' social class category (for example, Dennehy et al., 1996; Judge and Benzeval, 1993), few detailed research studies have looked at mortality rates in this area. For example, only one significant paper has been prepared on the position of lone mothers – that by Whitehead and Drever (1999) looking at trends in infant mortality, for sole registrations at birth compared with couple registrations. The authors point out that the traditional way of looking at social class differentials in infant mortality, using father's social class, has become increasingly problematic, excluding a growing proportion of children, particularly lone-mother registrations (which increased from 5 per cent of births in 1975 to 8 per cent in 1996). Sole registrations were chosen to examine the position of lone mothers on the assumption that most sole registrations will be made by lone mothers. One limitation of the study, however, is that it excludes registrations made by both parents but who are resident at separate addresses (a quarter of joint registrations outside marriage), some of which may represent lone-mother households.

Perhaps surprisingly the authors found that the gap between infant mortality of lone mothers and couples had reduced: whereas the excess mortality was 79 per cent in 1975, it was only 33 per cent in 1996 (Table 2.10). The paper, however, pointed out that most of the improvement was within the neonatal period (now very little difference – only two per cent) as well as perinatal (improved from 100 per cent to 24 per cent difference), leading the authors to suggest that improvements may be chiefly a product of improved healthcare around, and following, the birth, rather than any change in lone

Table 2.10 **Trends in infant mortality (95 per cent confidence interval) for sole and couple registrations, 1975–1996, England and Wales**

Year	Sole registrations	Couple registrations	Excess mortality/ sole/couple (%)
Perinatal mortality per 1,000 total births			
1975–77	34.2	17.2	100
1982–84	17.8	10.1	77
1989–91	11.5	7.8	47
1994–96	10.6	8.6	24
Neonatal mortality per 1,000 live births			
1975–77	17.1	9.5	81
1982–84	8.2	5.7	43
1989–91	5.3	4.4	19
1994–96	4.2	4.1	2
Post-neonatal mortality per 1,000 live births			
1975–77	7.6	4.4	74
1982–84	7.5	3.9	91
1989–91	6.6	3.0	123
1994–96	3.7	1.8	103
Overall infant mortality per 1,000 live births			
1975–77	24.7	13.9	79
1982–84	15.7	9.6	63
1989–91	11.9	7.4	61
1994–96	7.8	5.9	33

Source: Whitehead and Drever (1999), Table 3.

mothers' social and economic situation. In contrast, over the period, the excess mortality for lone mothers compared with couples for the post-neonatal period rose from 74 per cent in 1975–77 to 103 per cent in 1994–96 – the period of time more likely to be associated with the child's environment. It should be noted that in 1975–77 the rate of infant mortality for lone mothers was 24.7 per 1,000 live births, which was much higher than 17.5 for classes IV–V. Whilst differentials reduced between 1975 and 1996, lone mother registrations still had higher infant mortality (7.8 per 1,000 live births) compared with classes IV–V (7.0) and I–II (4.6).

Mortality and area and other deprivation indicators

Mortality, within all age groups, is known to differ widely by geographical area, and infant and child mortality rates are no exception, with higher mortality rates being prevalent in economically depressed, often inner-city and northern areas of the UK (Woodroofe *et al.*, 1993). A number of studies have examined the relationship between area and childhood mortality in more detail by looking at smaller geographical areas using a variety of measures of deprivation indicators. Few studies, however, are very up-to-date.

Carstairs and Morris (1991), using a classification of areas of deprivation using measures of overcrowding, male unemployment, not having a car and low social class found gradients between the most deprived areas and the more affluent areas for deaths in childhood at all ages. In the lower age group (0–4 years old) boys in the most deprived area in 1980–82 had a SMR of 138, and girls of 124, compared with SMRs of 63 and 79 for boys and girls, respectively, in the most affluent area. Another study, by Williams and Lloyd (1990), looked at the period 1979–83 for still births, perinatal, neo-natal, post-neonatal and infant mortality in Scottish communities using four socio-economic variables (social class, overcrowding, lone-parent density, housing tenure). Using bivariate analysis a relationship was found for perinatal mortality and social class, overcrowding and housing tenure; neonatal and post-neonatal mortality were correlated with housing tenure and overcrowding; although no correlation with infant mortality was found. The authors concluded that socio-economic characteristics ex-plained between 10–32 per cent of the variation in mortality.

Robinson and Pinch (1987) examined the relationship between early childhood mortality and socio-economic conditions (rather than social class) by looking at the records of 254 deaths of children aged 0–5 in Southampton between 1977 and 1982. Using addresses of families' residences, the records were grouped into different areas by combining census enumeration districts with similar socio-economic circumstances, which were then allocated to one of 15 cluster types. Cluster types typified by high levels of unemployment, lone-parent density and poor housing were found to have significantly higher levels of early child mortality. Finally, Elbourne *et al.,* (1986) looked at perinatal outcomes in Aberdeen and Cardiff during the period 1976–1981 and also found area differences for a range of outcomes including low birth-weight and perina-tal death.

Mortality and parents' ethnic origin

In a consideration of the links between childhood mortality and poverty, social class indicators, and to a much lesser extent, indicators of social deprivation, tend to domi-nate discussions. Nonetheless, another important cross-cutting issue is that of ethnic origin and child mortality. There is an established close association between poverty and ethnic origin in the UK, although this relationship is a complex one. Unsurprising-ly, the literature also shows an association between ethnic origin and childhood mortality.

Unfortunately data on ethnic origin is not readily available on childhood births and deaths. In the last 20 years, country of birth has been used as a proxy for ethnic origin, being collected at birth registration for the mother of the child. Soni Raleigh and Balarajan (1995) have pointed out that this proxy is becoming increasingly inad-equate as the UK-born population includes an increasing proportion of minority ethnic populations resident in Britain. In addition, a proportion of births to mothers born in other countries have always included white expatriates. Notwithstanding these problems, routinely collected mortality data (linked to birth) shows some clear patterns by mother's country of birth. Firstly, perinatal deaths are generally higher for infants born to mothers born in the New Commonwealth – a relationship which holds in all social classes. For example, in the late-1980s and early-1990s, the rate of perinatal deaths of children from mothers born in Pakistan was almost double that for UK-born children (Soni Raleigh and Balarajan, 1995; Parsons et al., 1990). Low birth-weight is cited as one reason for this as much higher proportions of low birth-weight babies are born to mothers themselves born outside the UK, which is partly related to ethnic predisposition. Deaths from congenital anomalies are also much higher for infants of Asian-born mothers, especially for Pakistani mothers (although lower for Caribbean and African [other than East] compared with the UK) (Soni Raleigh and Balarajan, 1995; Gillies et al., 1984). Other reasons may include diet, uptake of screenings and abortion, different immunities to viruses, a greater proportion of consanguineous marriages in some communities and childbearing at older ages (Soni Raleigh and Balarajan, 1995). Trends for perinatal deaths appeared to narrow between 1975–85 but this trend did not continue thereafter. Neonatal rates also show generally higher rates, similar to perinatal deaths.

However, in contrast, post-neonatal rates are *lower* for infants born to mothers born in India, Bangladesh and East Africa, although they remain higher for Pakistani, Caribbean and mothers born in the rest of Africa. One partial explanation for this may be the fact that lower rates of cot death occur in Asian and African-born mothers, possibly because such babies are more likely to sleep face upwards rather than prone (Balarajan et al., 1989), as well as fewer births being outside marriage and to smoking parents (both factors are known to be associated with cot deaths, although cot deaths are also associated with lower social class and lower birth-weight infants).

Rates of childhood mortality also seem to be higher amongst children born in non-UK countries, that is recent immigrants (Soni Raleigh and Balarajan, 1995). Using standardised mortality ratios, at ages 1–4, children born in the African Commonwealth have a SMR of 192 and those born in the Indian subcontinent a SMR of 152. SMRs are also higher in the 5–14 age group but differences are not as pronounced.

Mortality rates and other factors

In addition to social class, area deprivation and ethnic origin, a number of other factors are associated with higher infant mortality. Firstly, there is an association between maternal age and mortality, with rates being highest for mothers under 20, lowest for those between 25–29 and 30–34, with another rise for mothers aged 40 or over (Dattani, 1999). It is possible that there is some relationship between maternal age and social class as younger mothers tend to be disproportionately represented in the manual social classes. Higher mortality for those aged 40 or over is likely to be, at least in part, accounted for by medical reasons associated with late births.

Mortality rates have been consistently higher for babies born outside marriage, even when registered by two parents living at the same address. At first glance, this relationship seems difficult to understand; however it is known that there is a relationship between social class and higher rates of births outside marriage (90 per cent of births during 1993–5 of social class I were inside marriage compared with only 53 per cent of class V (Botting, 1997)). It is therefore important to include births outside marriage to gain a more accurate assessment of social class gradients (Botting, 1997). Data on births both inside and outside marriage, however, has only been published routinely since 1993.

A strong association has always been evidenced between low birth-weight and infant mortality. For example, over 1993–96, the infant mortality rate for babies born under 1,500 grams (the definition of low or very low birth-weight) was over five times the rate for those weighing 2,500 grams or more (Dattani, 1999). Again, it is known that low-income households have higher rates of children born with low birth-weight (Dattani, 1999), with the average baby being 115 grams lighter in class V than I (for inside marriage) and 130 grams lighter for outside marriage (3.3kg) (Botting, 1997). In addition, babies of the same birth-weight (1.5–2.5kg) are more likely to die from manual classes than non-manual classes, although most classes, except social class V, experience similar mortality outcomes for babies under 1.5kg.

A number of commentators have noted how a range of social and biological factors are likely to be interrelated but that these relationships have not been explored (Schuman, 1998; Dattani, 1999). It is clear that a more sophisticated analysis, using multiple regression techniques, is urgently required to more fully understand the associations between the different factors and to discover which best explain observed differences in mortality rates in childhood.

Conclusion

Evidence on the links between poverty and infant and child mortality is mainly derived from analyses of parental social class, usually that of the father, from birth and death records routinely collected by ONS. Clear evidence exists to demonstrate a strong association between father's social class and heightened risk of mortality for children at all ages.

For infant mortality, differentials between father's social class I and V were twice as high in 1996 (Dattani, 1999) and 1.7 times as high over the period 1993–5 (Botting, 1997). Differentials were greater in the post-neonatal period than for the peri- and neonatal periods. There is some evidence of slight reductions in differentials between classes, measured by father's social class, over time for infant mortality (Botting and Crawley, 1995; Whitehead and Drever, 1999). However, in contrast, evidence on child mortality indicates a slight widening of differentials between classes, accounted for by increases between classes within the older age groups (5–14). Class differentials have always been the widest for the age group 1–4, but some slight improvements have been evidenced over time for this younger age.

There are a number of acknowledged problems with using the mother's occupational social class in analyses, and it is possible that relative under-statement of mothers' occupation in the manual classes artificially reduces actual differentials (Botting and Cooper, 1993). Despite this, similar, although smaller, differentials are observed between social classes when measured by mother's occupation. In addition, one study shows a slight increase in differentials over time from 1986–90 and 1991–95. As with child (though not infant) mortality measured by father's social class, rates within social class V are particularly high when compared to the other classes.

Little research has been undertaken looking at differentials including the 'other' category in social class classifications, which represents a gap in the evidence base. One paper, however, did compare infant mortality between lone registrations with that of couple registrations to investigate child mortality in lone mothers. Much higher rates of infant mortality were observed for lone mothers, although excess mortality had reduced over time from 79 per cent in 1975 to 33 per cent in 1996. It is important to note, however, that improvements were confined to earlier infant deaths and differentials actually increased for the post-neonatal period. This period is more likely to be related to socio-economic conditions and poverty and requires closer investigation.

Links between infant and child mortality and a range of other factors have also been observed. Whilst there are few up-to-date studies, there is a clear relationship between area deprivation and childhood mortality. Again, whilst there are problems with data on ethnic origin, this also shows a relationship, although a complex one, with child mortality. Maternal age, births outside marriage and low birth-weight are also known to be associated with higher mortality rates. All of these additional factors are also associated with social class; however, to date no analysis has been undertaken which attempts to understand the inter-relationships between these factors.

Overall, the data on the links between poverty, particularly as measured by social class, and childhood mortality is comprehensive, robust and allows trends to be observed over time. Nonetheless, improvements are still required, particularly in the registration of mother's social class at birth and death of the child. Analysis also needs to be undertaken carefully, as small numbers or single years can sometimes be misleading, and it is therefore advisable to combine years and datasets when looking at trends. Most research has tended to concentrate on England and Wales rather than Scotland, possibly because of the smaller datasets involved. Finally, a greater understanding is still required of the reasons for the observed differences, particularly between age groups, and of how a range of factors inter-relate to produce such clear and enduring patterns of inequalities in the deaths of children in Britain.

3 Child morbidity

Julia Johnson

Introduction

Traditionally, infant and child mortality rates have been used as the indicators for gauging the health status of populations and the inequalities that exist between groups of the population (Spencer, 1996). However, the use of childhood mortality data as a proxy measure of health status fails to reflect the full range of child morbidity. Death in childhood is rare and open to random fluctuation. It may give an inaccurate and misleading picture of the patterns of child morbidity, therefore mortality rates are an inadequate indicator of the health status of children (Blane *et al.*, 1994). There are varied major factors influencing health. These include: biological, socio-economic, environmental and lifestyle factors. It is difficult, if not impossible, to isolate the effects that these influences have on the incidence of childhood morbidity. A number of authors have argued that there is a strong positive relationship between poverty and child morbidity (Spencer, 1996; Reading, 1997; Dennehy *et al.*, 1996). Evidence of the link between child morbidity and poverty is not immediately accessible. Much of the literature that has been generated has concentrated on the biological, rather than the social determinants of ill health. It is often the case that social factors are seen as 'incidental confounding factors' (Reading, 1997:463).

Definitions and measurement

Recently, studies have begun to redefine the health status of populations in terms of morbidity. It should be noted that the measurement of morbidity can be problematic (Spencer, 1996). There are two main methods of measuring morbidity, both of which can be criticised. Firstly, there are measures of medically-defined morbidity. Much of the medically-defined morbidity data is generated using health service contact data. This can be obtained from GP contact data or hospital admission rates. However, there are a number of factors which can create bias in data of this nature. Service contact may be influenced by a range of variables including access, availability and social and cultural differences in perceptions of ill health (OPCS, 1995; Spencer, 1996).

The second method used to generate morbidity data is self-reported morbidity. It is argued that self-reported morbidity overcomes some of the problems associated with the use of service contact as a measurement of morbidity (Spencer, 1996). However, the use of self-reported morbidity data is also not without its critics. As Staples and Pharoah (1994) note, self-reported measures are 'based on people's subjective assessment of their health, and may show temporal change as expectations vary' (Staples and Pharoah, 1994). It has also been suggested that self-reported morbidity data for young children is open to further bias, as the questions are addressed to the adult responsible for the child's care. This introduces an additional source of bias in so far as adult carers may either under-estimate or over-estimate the extent to which their children experience symptoms of ill health (Office for National Statistics, 1985). The studies that have been reviewed in this chapter, use data collected from surveys which may use either self-reported or medically-reported symptoms of illness, or a combination of both these methods, to measure child morbidity.

The literature uses a variety of methods to indicate poverty and / or socio-economic deprivation, some of which are, arguably, more reliable as indicators of the likelihood of poverty than others. These include demographic characteristics, area census characteristics, social class, housing tenure, income and parental educational levels. As Woodroffe (1993) notes 'Probably the most useful measure for such comparison would be income, but suitable data are not generally available' (Woodroffe, 1993:81). One of the most frequently used methods to indicate socio-economic position has been the Registrar General's Occupational Classification System (RGCS). The RGCS is historically based on men's full-time employment status. This has been increasingly criticised for the inadequacy of the measurement of the social position of women, children, households headed by a lone mother and the unemployed (Reading, 1997; Spencer, 1996). One recent study found that family structure, employment status and receipt of benefit were more closely associated with differentials in child morbidity than social class (Cooper *et al.*, 1998).

In spite of the difficulties involved in the measurement of poverty the general consensus is that there are strong links between socio-economic disadvantage and poor child health. In discussing the variety of measures used to measure social characteristics Reading (1997) notes that using all of the methods available similar health variations are found '… The one and only variable they all have in common is material and economic factors. As a general rule, methods of classification which specifically measure material factors result in wider and more distinct health variations' (Reading, 1997:464).

Morbidity Indicators

The term morbidity is used to describe all forms of ill health. The issue of mental health is dealt with in Chapter 17. The material reviewed concentrates on differing aspects of physical morbidity, focusing on particular morbidity indicators and examining some of the existing literature on them. The morbidity indicators to be included are:

- Low birth-weight
- Congenital anomalies
- Chronic illness
- Infectious diseases
- Dental caries
- Obesity
- Rates of physical exercise.

Low birth-weight

According to Reading (1997), the bulk of research into child health inequalities has focused upon growth and birth outcomes. Although low birth-weight is not strictly a measure of morbidity, it can act as a useful proxy measure (Osmond, 1993). A number of studies have revealed that low birth-weight babies are at greater risk of mortality and morbidity during childhood (McCormick, 1985; James, 1997). The optimum birth-weight for survival in developed countries is between 3,000–4,500g. Currently low birth-weight is defined as less than 2,500g and very low birth-weight is defined as being less than 1,500g. Recent data (1997) for England and Wales suggests that during the last twenty years the proportion of all births weighing over 3,500g has increased. Accompanying this increase, however, there has also been an increase in the number of low birth-weight and very low birth-weight babies being born (ONS, 1997). Table 3.1 indicates trends in birth-weights for various years since 1986. These are expressed as actual numbers and as percentages of total live births. It should be noted that this data is incomplete. For each year cited there are a varying number of births where information regarding birth-weight has not been available.

Table 3.1 **Live births, by total numbers and birth-weight, England and Wales, various years**

Numbers of live births	1986	1989	1992	1995	1996	1997
Total live births	661,018	687,725	689,656	648,001	649,489	642,093
>3,500g	242,821	257,191	265,894	254,272	257,401	253,401
<2,500g	45,728	44,978	44,831	47,324	47,187	47,742
<1,500g	6,081	6,547	6,642	7,538	7,920	7,873
Birth-weight not stated	624	21,113	25,937	2,217	1,538	1,101
Percentage of total live births where weight is stated						
>3,500g	36.70	37.30	38.50	39.20	39.60	39.40
<2,500g	6.91	6.54	6.50	7.30	6.34	7.43
<1,500g	0.91	0.95	0.96	1.10	1.20	1.20

Source: Data collated from ONS Mortality Statistics: Series DH3 Nos 20, 23, 26, 28, 29, 30.

The OPCS report 'The Health of Our Children' found that babies born in 1989 to mothers in social class V were, on average, 100g lighter than babies born to parents in social class I (Botting, 1997) More recent data suggests the average birth-weight differential between the two social classes has increased, with babies born to mothers in social class V being 115g lighter than that of their counterparts in social class I (ONS, 1997). In their study, Spencer *et al.*, (1991) examined the trends in birth-weight and their association with socio-economic status in a ten year birth cohort in Sheffield (1985–1994). Using the Townsend Deprivation Index to measure poverty, the authors concluded that 'The proportion of births <3,500g statistically "attributable" to social inequality for the ten year period was 9.6 per cent (range 4.3–15.5)' (Spencer *et al.*, 1991:138). A number of other studies, using a variety of indicators to measure socio-economic status, have found evidence that inequalities in birth-weight are strongly correlated to parental socio-economic status (Reading, 1990; Carstairs and Morris, 1992).

A variety of socio-demographic characteristics have been cited as risk factors of low birth-weight. As Table 3.2 indicates, these include: maternal age, marital status, parity within marriage, social class within marriage, and country of birth of mother. A number of these characteristics can also be said to be indicators of the risk of poverty. Children are more likely to be poor if they live in large families, have lone parents, are from ethnic minorities, or are the children of teenage parents (Fleming, 1998; Adelman and Bradshaw, 1998; Smith, 1999; Botting *et al.*, 1998). Analysis of 1991 mortality data by Soni Raleigh and Balajaran (1995) found that there was a higher incidence of low birth-weight babies born to mothers born outside the UK than among their indigenous counterparts. In 1991, low birth-weight babies constituted 7 per cent of all deliveries in England and Wales. The proportion of low birth-weight babies born to minority ethnic women ranged from 9 per cent in Caribbean-born women to 12 and 13 per cent respectively for mothers born in India and East Africa. The authors recognise that some difference in birth-weight may be attributable to genetic predisposition but also note that high proportions of the minority ethnic population face social and economic disadvantage (Soni Raleigh and Balajaran, 1995).

Congenital anomalies

Data on the prevalence of congenital anomalies appears contradictory and subject to inconsistencies in definition and errors in measurement. The National Congenital Anomaly System, (NCAS) was established in England and Wales in 1964, following the thalidomide epidemic. The main purpose of the NCAS is surveillance, but the system provides the best available national data on congenital anomalies. Registration is voluntary and only congenital anomalies identified in the first ten days after birth are included. This may lead to the under-reporting of congenital anomalies which are not identified within the first ten days after birth, such as congenital heart defects and muscular dystrophy (Wills, 1995; Woodroffe, 1993).

Data from the Annual Update for Congenital Anomaly Statistics (ONS, 1999) reveals that in 1998 there were 5,393 notifications of live births with some type of congenital anomaly. The notification rate was approximately 85 per 10,000 live births. During the 1990s notification rates have fluctuated; however, figures for 1998 (ONS, 1999) confirm that the number of babies with some form of congenital anomaly, per thousand live births, is at its highest rate since 1992 (ONS, 1999). Trends for individual types of congenital anomaly reveal a mixed picture, with the rates of some types of anomaly increasing whilst others appear to be decreasing. The notification of heart

Table 3.2 **Mean birth-weight by socio-demographic factors: live births, 1989, England and Wales**

	Mean birth-weight (g)	Number of live births	Birth-weight less than 2,500g %	Birth-weight less than 2,500g Number
All Groups	3,319	687,725	6.5	44,978
Maternal Age				
Under 18	3,205	15,869	8.5	1,360
18–19	3,223	39,674	8.1	3,231
20–24	3,283	185,239	6.8	12,670
25–29	3,343	242,822	5.9	14,348
30–34	3,357	145,320	6.3	9,089
35–39	3,336	49,465	7.1	3,533
35 and over	3,333	58,801	7.3	4,280
Marital status				
Within marriage	3,347	501,921	5.9	29,824
Outside marriage	3,242	185,804	8.2	15,154
Parity within marriage				
0	3,273	199,766	7.3	14,667
1	3,403	182,111	4.7	8,630
2	3,402	78,056	5.0	3,923
3 and over	3,354	41,988	6.2	2,604
Social class within marriage				
I	3,385	42,650	4.8	2,060
II	3,377	129,480	5.1	6,600
IIIN	3,369	49,850	5.9	2,950
IIIM	3,338	169,720	6.4	10,860
IV	3,306	65,230	6.8	4,430
V	3,285	22,560	7.7	1,730
Country of birth of mother				
UK	3,331	607,228	6.4	38,660
Irish Republic	3,362	6,561	6.1	397
Remainder of Europe	3,348	9,488	5.6	528
Australia, Canada and NZ	3,388	2,772	5.4	150
New Commonwealth and Pakistan	3,152	49,532	9.3	4,604
Bangladesh	3,095	5,085	9.4	480
India	3,066	8,830	11.1	980
Pakistan	3,164	12,249	8.9	1,094
Remainder New Commonwealth	3,247	5,362	6.1	327
East African Commonwealth	3,061	6,742	11.7	787
Rest of Africa	3,259	4,721	8.3	392
Caribbean Commonwealth	3,180	4,032	10.6	427
Mediterranean Commonwealth	3,319	2,551	4.7	117

Source: Mortality statistics – perinatal and infant: social and biological factors, 1989, OPCS unpublished data. *Cited in Botting, 1997:1.*

Table 3.3 **Trends in the numbers of reported live births with congenital anomaly. Total numbers and selected anomalies, 1992–1998, England and Wales**

Condition	Year of Notification						
	1992	1993	1994	1995	1996	1997	1998
Central nervous system	264	210	203	203	186	163	199
Eye	69	69	99	53	76	67	73
Cleft lip and palate	479[a]	431[a]	423[a]	565	542	563	567
Other face, ear and neck	241	241	190	194	183	208	232
Heart and circulatory	535	487	462	444	454	495	601
Respiratory	56	60	63	64	54	64	51
Alimentary	135[b]	122[b]	123[b]	321	273	289	316
Genital organs	699	697	672	575	614	598	608
Urinary system	354	369	336	381	370	456	451
Musculoskeletal	1,008[c]	886[c]	886[c]	2,108	1,944	1,971	1,899
Skin and integument	457	413	438	192	206	224	215
Chromosomal/	495	400	397	393	417	365	475
Down's Syndrome	383	299	303	303	316	273	356
Congenital infections	-	-	-	1	-	2	3
Other[d]	222	239	249	438	425	469	490
Total Notifications	5,909	5,656	5,536	5,365	5,280	5,319	5,393
Notifications per 10,000 live births	86	84	80	83	80	83	85

a Data refers to notification of cleft lip only
b Data refers to 'other anomalies of upper alimentary tract'
c Data refers to 'certain congenital musculoskeletal anomalies' (ICD Chapter 754)
d Data refers to other congenital anomalies not elsewhere classified.

Sources: ONS, Health Statistics Quarterly 04, Winter 1999.
ONS Series MB3 Nos 8, 9, 10, 11, 12, 13.

and circulatory system anomalies have risen, as has the rate per thousand of babies born with cleft lip and palate.

Evidence from a study by Bax and Lawton (1998) also suggests that some types of congenital anomaly are in decline whilst others are increasing. These authors do, however, argue that there has been an increase in the prevalence of children with severe disabilities. In their study Bax and Lawton (1998), using Family Fund Trust (FFT)[1] data, estimate that 1.5–1.7 per cent of children in the UK have a severe disability. Analysing data from 1968 to 1992, the authors found that there had been an overall increase in the numbers reporting specific congenital anomaly and severe disability. Within this overall increase particular types of congenital anomalies and disabilities appear to be declining whilst others are increasing. Table 3.4 summarises trends for the period 1968–1992 using the data held by the Family Fund Trust (1998).

Table 3.4 **Trends in the prevalence of reported congenital anomalies and severe disabilities, 1968–1992, United Kingdom**

Decline (significant trend)	Static (no significant trend)	Increase (significant trend)
Spina Bifida	Deafness	Prada Willi
Congenital Rubella	Learning difficulties	Fragile X
	Muscular dystrophy	Cerebral Palsy
	Down's Syndrome	Heart disease
		Autism
		Asthma

Source: Bax and Lawton (1998).

A report by the Chief Medical Officer (1997) cites contradictory evidence, suggesting that the notification rate for live births with congenital anomalies is falling. 'In 1997, the notification rate for live births with congenital abnormalities fell to 79.2 per 10,000, 5 per cent lower than in 1996 and 8 per cent lower than in 1992. Approximately 5 per cent of all babies in England and Wales are born with a congenital malformation or other developmental defects such as Down's Syndrome and spina bifida' (Chief Medical Officer, 1997 cited in BMA, 1999:21–22).

Examining the data from the Family Fund Trust it is apparent that the biggest rates of increase, during the period 1968–1992 have been observed for cerebral palsy, autism and asthma (Bax and Lawton, 1998). A study conducted in the Republic of Ireland between 1976 and 1981 demonstrated a clear social class gradient in the overall prevalence of cerebral palsy (Dowding, 1990). It has been suggested that there is a possible relationship between very low birth-weight and the prevalence of cerebral palsy (Woodroffe, 1993). Evidence from data generated in 1994 suggests that there is a social class gradient for the majority of reported congenital anomalies, with those from manual social classes reporting a higher incidence of congenital anomaly than non-manual social classes (Drever, 1997). The only type of congenital anomaly to show a reverse social class gradient is Down's Syndrome. It is possible that that this is due to the tendency for mothers from non-manual classes to delay childbearing until beyond age thirty-five, thereby putting them at greater risk of having a child with Down's Syndrome (Drever, 1997).

Chronic sickness: long-standing illness and long-standing limiting illness

The General Household Survey (GHS) has collected data on childhood chronic sickness since 1972. Child health data, (aged 0–15), is supplied by the adult living in the household who is responsible for their care. The questions asked provide a two-stage measure of chronic sickness. Informants are asked if they have any long-standing ill-ness and if this limits their activities in any way (ONS, 1985). GHS data for the period 1972–1994 reveals an upward trend in the numbers of children reported to have both long-standing and long-standing limiting illness (Table 3.5). Data for the subsequent years, 1995 and 1996, indicate a slight decrease or stability in the percentage of males aged 0–15 reporting long-standing and limiting long-standing illness. There was how-ever, no decrease in the numbers of females in this age group reporting either long standing or limiting long-standing illness. For females aged 0–4 there was a slight in-crease in the numbers reporting long-standing illness.

The data regarding social gradients in the prevalence of self-reported morbidity reveals relatively slight differentials when measured by social class. It is possible to suggest that this is a consequence of the inadequacy of the RGCS as an indicator of poverty. This is supported by the findings of Prescott-Clarke and Primatesta (1998), who found no strongly-marked differences in the prevalence of self-reported long-stand-ing limiting illness by social class. However, there were differences found when using

Table 3.5 **Trends in self-reported sickness by boys and girls, 1975–1996, England and Wales**

	1975	1985	1991	1993	1994	1995	1996
Percentage who reported long-standing illness							
Boys aged							
0–4	8	11	13	15	15	14	14
5–15	11	18	17	21	21	20	19
Girls aged							
0–4	6	9	10	12	11	11	13
5–15	9	13	15	16	18	17	16
All							
0–14	7	10	12	13	13	13	13
5–15	10	16	16	19	20	19	18
Percentage who reported limiting long-standing illness							
Boys aged							
0–4	3	4	4	5	5	5	4
5–15	6	8	7	9	10	8	8
Girls aged							
0–14	2	3	3	3	4	3	4
5–15	4	6	5	8	8	8	8
All							
0–4	2	3	4	5	4	4	4
5–15	5	7	6	9	9	8	8

Sources: OPCS/ONS, General Household Survey 1985, 1995 and 1996.

equivalised income as a variable. Children aged between 2 and 15 in the lowest income quintile were more likely to report long-standing limiting illness than those in the highest income quintile. (Prescott-Clarke and Primatesta, 1998).

Table 3.6 **Prevalence of reported long-standing illness and long-standing limiting illness, by age and sex, 1985–1996, Great Britain**

Year	Boys (aged 0–15) %		Girls (aged 0–15) %	
	Non-manual	Manual	Non-manual	Manual
Reported long-standing illness			**Reported long-standing illness**	
1985	14	18	11	12
1995	17	20	15	16
1996	17*	18*	15*	16*
Reported limiting long-standing			**Reported limiting long-standing**	
1985	6	8	4	5
1995	7	9	5	7
1996	7*	6*	6*	8*

* General Household Survey, OPCS 1996.

Sources: Drever and Whitehead, 1997

There is some evidence to suggest that social inequalities in childhood morbidity vary by age. Macintyre and West (1991), in their study of 15-year-olds in the West of Scotland found little evidence of socio-economic differentials during the period of adolescence. The authors note that this is in contrast to the socio-economic differentials present in earlier childhood and which re-emerge during early adulthood.

There are also gender differentials found in childhood morbidity. Across most categories of illness and disease there appears to be a greater prevalence of morbidity amongst boys in early childhood; in mid-adolescence, however, reported morbidity becomes more prevalent in girls.

The literature reviewed so far regarding general health has mainly concentrated upon self-reported data. What follows is an examination of the data relating to health service use. Medically-defined child morbidity, measured by service contact, also identifies an upward trend of morbidity in children during the period 1981–1992 (OPCS, 1995). Morbidity data generated by the recording of service contact has been criticised as leading to the possible under-estimation of socio-economic differences in morbidity. It is argued that there are social gradients in the uptake of health services, most especially preventive services and child immunisation programmes (Marsh and Channing,

1987). There is evidence to suggest that those in the higher non-manual social classes are more likely to make disproportionate use of health services. Relative to need, professional and managerial groups receive over 40 per cent more NHS expenditure per capita than those in semi-skilled or unskilled occupations (Le Grand, 1978).

Table 3.7 **All diseases and conditions, category of severity: prevalence rates per 10,000 person years at risk, 1991/1992, England and Wales**

		Persons		
		Ages 0–4	Ages 5–14	Ages 15–24
All diseases and conditions	1981/82	9,846	6,686	7,054
	1991/92	10,221	7,243	7,536
	Change	+4%	+8%	+7%
Serious	1981/82	649	538	653
	1991/92	1,200	995	940
	Change	+85%	+85%	+44%
Intermediate	1981/82	6,200	4,004	3,682
	1991/92	6,843	4,446	4,390
	Change	+10%	+11%	+14%
Trivial	1981/82	8,843	5,187	5,922
	1991/92	9,376	5,603	6,396
	Change	+6%	+8%	+8%

Source: Data extracted from Table 3A. OPCS, (1995) Morbidity Statistics from General Practice 1991/1992.

Table 3.7 shows that prevalence rates for children and young people rose significantly during the decade 1982–1992. Self-reported data from the GHS (1996) supports this upward trend in the prevalence rates for children. Morbidity data, which classifies patient consultation ratios by a range of socio-economic variables, found significant social gradients across a range of diseases. Social gradients were also found on analysis of illness/disease severity in a number of cases. In their national study of morbidity statistics from General Practice, McCormick et al., (1995), found that children from council housing were significantly more likely to consult a doctor than their counterparts in owner-occupied accommodation. Other studies examining other socio-economic and demographic variables have reached similar conclusions. Fleming and Charlton (1998) conducted a study of morbidity and the health care utilisation of children in households with one adult. The authors argue that children from lone-parent households are likely to consult more often and have higher rates of illness compared with children living in households with more than one adult. The authors go on to suggest that this supports the argument that single-parent households are an appropriate indicator of deprivation (Fleming and Charlton, 1998). Research by Saxena (1999) also found social gradients in child morbidity in the frequency of consultation and severity of illness. 'Childhood consultation rates for episodes of illness increase from social classes I-II through to classes IV-V. The findings on the severity of underlying illness suggest that the health of children from lower social classes is worse than that from higher social classes' (Saxena, 1999:643).

Respiratory disease is a major cause of morbidity amongst children (Prescott-Clarke and Primatesta, 1998; GHS, 1996). The prevalence of asthma has increased dramatically since the 1960s. It would appear that the prevalence of severe asthma is also increasing. During the period 1962 to 1985 there has been a 1,300 per cent increase in hospital admission rates for asthma in the age group 0–4 years (OPCS, 1995). Bax and Lawton (1998) notes that children with asthma have to be severely affected before they come within the remit of the FFT. According to their data, during the period 1968–1990 the numbers registered on the FFT database had increased 'by an order of magnitude of 14–15 fold' (Bax and Lawton, 1998:10). There is also evidence that the prevalence of asthma is higher amongst children from certain minority ethnic groups. The incidence of asthma amongst Afro–Caribbean children born in England is more prevalent than amongst Caucasian children or Asian children born in England and higher than Afro–Caribbean children born abroad (Morrison-Smith and Cooper, 1981). Children of minority ethnic groups are also disproportionately affected by the increasing incidence of tuberculosis.

> 'A report from the Medical Research Council based on a national survey of notifications in 1978/1979 reported high levels of tuberculosis in children of Asian origin, including those born in Britain. The rates for British-born children (per 10,000 children under 15) were 72 in Indians and 95 in Pakistanis and Bangladeshis, compared with 3.6 in Caucasians. The environment of inner cities, with overcrowded poor quality housing, is reported to have contributed to the spread of the disease in populations of Asian origin' (Soni Raleigh and Balarajan: cited in Botting (ed.) 1995:82).

The evidence for a social gradient in childhood respiratory illness/disease is extensive (see, for instance, Saxena *et al.*, 1999; Woodroffe *et al.*, 1993; Reading, 1997).

Infectious diseases

The trends in childhood infectious diseases reveal a decline in some infections alongside a rise in others. According to data last updated in June 1999, by the Public Health Laboratory Service (PHLS), the number of notifications of measles continues to decline. In 1991 there were 9,680 notified cases; by 1996 the number of notified cases had fallen to 5,614. Data regarding the notification of whooping cough reveals a similar pattern. In 1980 there were 20,301 notified cases of whooping cough in children aged 14 years and under, by 1998 notifications in the same age group had fallen to 1,425 (PHLS, 1999). The declining incidence of measles and whooping cough can be attributed to increases in the uptake of childhood vaccinations. In 1980 approximately 53 per cent of children were vaccinated against whooping cough and 58 per cent of children were vaccinated against measles. In 1997/1998 these figures had risen to 96 per cent and 91 per cent respectively (PHLS, 1999).

Whilst some infectious diseases are declining others have emerged and are of increasing importance. Notification rates of meningitis in children aged under 14 have been increasing since 1984. Meningococcal meningitis (accounting for approximately 40 per cent of all cases) has risen particularly sharply amongst young children (PHLS, 1999). There have also been recent regional increases in the notification of childhood dysentery, with the West Midlands reporting a 50 per cent increase in notifications between June 1998 and June 1999. The greatest age-specific increases were amongst boys aged five to nine years. HIV and AIDS pose new threats to child health and survival through sexual abuse, infection *in utero* and, among adolescents, through intravenous drug use.

According to Reading (1997), infectious diseases are probably the major cause of acute morbidity among children and a significant contributory factor to the health inequalities that exist between children. Following a comprehensive review of a number of medical studies, Reading (1997) found that with very few exceptions children from deprived backgrounds are more likely to be at risk of infection than their more affluent counterparts. 'In the context of steadily increasing proportions of children growing up in conditions of poverty and a resurgence of infectious disease it is important to re-examine the contribution of infectious disease and its consequence to the burden of social inequalities in health in children' (Reading, 1997:409). Table 3.8 summarises a number of recent studies, which have identified strong evidence of a social gradient in the incidence of infectious disease.

Dental caries

The incidence of dental caries is a useful predictor of childhood morbidity and, historically, the incidence of dental caries has revealed persistent social gradients. Data from the National Dietary and Nutrition Survey (1996) suggests that the incidence of dental caries has been increasing in recent years. A number of risk factors associated with dental caries were identified. The authors note 'Dental decay is strongly related to social background. The factors most strongly associated to caries prevalence are: receipt of income benefits in 1.5 to 2.5-year-olds; low educational status of the mother in 2.5 to 3.5-year-olds; low social class of the head of the household in 3.5 to 4.5-year-olds' (Moynihan and Holt, 1996 cited in BMA, 1999:54). As Table 3.9 shows, data from the Children's Dental Health Survey 1993 found that children from manual social classes are more likely to have tooth decay, more likely to have teeth missing due to tooth decay, and are also likely to have more teeth affected than children in the non-manual social classes (O'Brien, 1994).

Table 3.8 **Social differences in childhood infection: conditions with strong evidence of a social gradient**

Type of infection	Details of the evidence	Odds ratio[1]	Source
	Occupational mortality data	3.0	OPCS, 1988
Infant respiratory infections / bronchiolitis	NSHG[2] longitudinal cohort study	N/A	Taylor et al., 1982 Butler and Golding, 1986
	Longitudinal cohort, Tayside, UK	1.4	Ogston et al., 1987
	Occupational mortality data	2.6	OPCS, 1988
Childhood respiratory infection	NSHG[2] longitudinal cohort study	1.6 Bronchitis 2.5 Lower resp	Taylor et al., 1982 Butler and Golding, 1986
	NSHG[2] longitudinal cohort study	2.0	Taylor et al., 1982
Gastroenteritis	Hospital-based control study	3.2	MacLure and Stewart, 1984
	Longitudinal cohort, Tayside, UK	2.0	Ogston et al., 1987
	Ecological study, Liverpool, UK	N/A	Spence et al., 1993
Tuberculosis	Ecological study, New York, USA	5.6	Drucker et al., 1994
	Ecological study, London, UK	N/A	Mangtani et al., 1995
HIV	Ecological case control study of pregnant women with HIV	17	Johnstone et al., 1992

1   Disadvantaged:Advantaged calculated from original data where possible.
2   National Survey for Health and Growth (1970 birth cohort).

Source: data for table cited by Reading, 1997:404.

Obesity

There is a paucity of data relating to the prevalence of obesity amongst young children. It is argued that obesity in children is an indicator of obesity in adulthood. There is some uncertainty over the precise aetiology of obesity but it is likely that socio-economic inequalities in nutritional status have a role to play in determining the risk of obesity (BMA, 1999). There are marked differences in the quality of foods eaten by children from different socio-economic groups. Children's eating habits appear to be related to

Table 3.9 **Incidence of dental caries by age and social class, 1993, England and Wales**

Condition	Social class			Social class		
	I, II, IIIN	IIIM	IV, V	I, II, IIIN	IIIM	IV, V
	% of children with condition			mean number of teeth affected		
Age 12						
Any known decay	45	51	68	1.1	1.4	2.0
Actively decayed	17	27	32	0.3	0.5	0.6
Filled	35	38	50	0.7	0.7	1.1
Missing due to decay	3	6	15	0.1	0.1	0.3
Age 15						
Any known decay	58	68	72	2.0	2.7	3.4
Actively decayed	25	25	36	0.5	0.6	0.9
Filled	48	59	59	1.4	2.0	2.2
Missing due to decay	4	6	19	0.1	0.1	0.3

Source: Moynihan and Holt (1996).

social class and equivalised income. Children in the social classes IV and V and those in the lowest income quintile were more likely to consume larger amounts of sweet foods, sugary drinks, crisps and chips, and less fresh fruit and vegetables than their counterparts in social classes I and II and those in the highest income quintile (Prescott-Clarke and Primatesta, 1998). A study of the food intake of British infants also found similar results (BMA, 1999).

The consumption of high energy 'unhealthy' foods such as processed-meat products, biscuits, sweets and white bread is thought to be related to low income rather than ignorance of what constitutes a 'healthy' diet. A survey by the National Children's Home (1991) found 'Poor diet was correlated with food expenditure. The survey showed that there was no evidence to suggest that parents are ignorant about what constitutes a healthy diet. They were unable to provide themselves or their families with an adequate diet because of income' (NCH, 1991 cited in BMA, 1999:58).

It has been argued that benefit levels in Britain are inadequate to allow claimants to afford a 'Low Cost but Acceptable' standard of living. During their study Parker *et al.*, (1998) made a detailed list of the goods and services, and their prices, needed for two differing family types to maintain a low cost but acceptable standard of living. When compared with Income Support (IS) levels the authors found that for two parents and two children there was an IS shortfall of £32.00 per week. For a single mother with two children the shortfall was £24.00. Other studies have identified 'gross inadequacies' in the diets of families on welfare benefits and resultant deficiencies in a number of essential vitamins and minerals (Lobstein, 1988; Bradshaw and Morgan, 1987; Bradshaw and Holmes, 1989).

A recent study by Prynne *et al.*, (1999) analysed the nutrient intake of members of a birth cohort study of young children in 1950, to investigate differences from present-day children's diets. They concluded that 'The relative austerity of post-war food supplies resulted in food and nutrient intakes in 1950 which in many respects may well have been beneficial to the health of young children, despite fat intake being higher than present day recommendations' (Prynne *et al.*, 1999). It should be noted that the modern food economy provides a perverse incentive to eat 'unhealthy' foods. According to the BMA (1999) it is much cheaper to provide the necessary calories by filling up on a diet of meat products, biscuits, sweets, white bread and margarine than on a healthier diet of fresh fruit and vegetables. It has also been suggested that it costs more to purchase 'healthy' foods in deprived areas than it does in more affluent areas. Table 3.10 details the results of part of a study undertaken by the Food Commission (1995).

Table 3.10 **The cost of a basket of healthier food items (wholegrain rice, wholemeal bread, low fat mince, etc.) compared with a basket of similar, less healthy, foods**

	More healthy basket	Less healthy basket	Extra cost of more healthy basket
Deprived areas	£15.25	£10.84	41%
More affluent areas	£14.87	£11.38	31%

Source: The Food Commission, 1995:31 cited by BMA, 1999:56.

Physical Activity

The contribution of physical exercise to good health is recognised in the Government White Paper *'Our Healthier Nation'* (1999). Research by Prescott-Clarke and Primatesta (1998) found evidence of socio-economic gradients in the prevalence rates of some forms of physical exercise amongst children aged 2–10 (Table 3.11). This pattern was not evident in all forms of physical activity included in the survey. When questions were asked regarding active play, walking and housework/gardening the data suggests that children from the manual social classes are, in general, more likely to participate. It could be suggested that these forms of activity are the least likely to involve financial expenditure and are therefore more accessible to children living in poverty.

A number of studies have found that significant gender differences exist in the rates of participation in physical exercise/activities. Gender differences in exercise become more pronounced between the ages of 11 and 16 years (Woodroffe *et al.*, 1993; Haselden *et al.*, 1999; Prescott-Clarke and Primatesta, 1998). In his study of young people in Wales (Nutbeam, 1989) found that boys aged 11–16 were almost twice as likely to be involved in physical exercise than girls of the same age.

Table 3.11 **Percentage of children who had participated in sports and exercise (for at least five minutes) in the last week, England and Wales**

	Social class of head of household			
	I and II	IIIN	IIIM	IV and V
	%	%	%	%
Boys aged 2–10	60	57	44	45
Boys aged 11–15	73	78	75	71
Girls aged 2–10	63	53	46	35
Girls aged 11–15	63	59	53	47

Source: Prescott-Clarke and Primatesta, 1998:258.

Conclusion

In spite of the definitional problems relating to morbidity and the large number of indicators used to illustrate socio-economic variance, the majority of the literature reviewed in this chapter supports the argument that children living in poor socio-economic circumstances are likely to have poorer health than their more affluent counterparts. There are a range of factors which can influence the prevalence of childhood morbidity. These include those which are biologically or genetically determined, factors relating to the environment and lifestyle factors. It is not possible to isolate poverty as a single causal factor or prove that poverty causes ill health. As Reading (1997) notes 'Definitive proof that poverty causes poor health is unlikely ever to be available because the experimental design (that is, to randomly assign one group of families to poverty and one to affluence) is unethical. However the evidence points strongly to economic and material factors being at the root of the causes of social differences in child health' (Reading, 1997:36). One of the most striking features noted during this literature review has been the definitional obstacles and statistical vagaries that have been encountered. Neverthless the consistency of the findings are sufficient to confirm that little has changed since the early 1940s when, following the publication of *Birth Poverty and Wealth* by Richard Titmuss, newspapers reported 'Poor folks babies stand less chance' (cited by Roberts, 1997:1,113).

Note to Chapter 3

1   The Family Fund Trust (FTT) – formerly the Family Fund – was established in 1973 by the British Government and provides financial support in the form of grants to families with severely disabled children with incomes of less than £18,801 (April 1998). The Trust holds a database containing information on approximately 200,000 severely disabled children and their families whom it has assisted since its inception. Although the Trust's database only holds information on 'severely disabled' children it is the largest database of its type in the UK and provides a valuable source of information on the nature of severe childhood disability. It should be noted that the reporting of congenital anomaly to the Trust is self selecting; therefore prevalence may be subject to under-reporting. There will also be omission of many cases whose disability is not considered to be severe enough to be eligible for financial assistance from the Trust.

4 Childhood accidents

Deborah Quilgars

Introduction

Two decades ago in 1980, when relative child poverty rates were less pronounced than today, the Black Report on Inequalities in Health (Townsend and Davidson, 1982), hot on the heels of the 1976 Court Report, drew attention to the fact that the widest inequality in childhood mortality rates was for accidents. In the 1970s, the risk of death of a child pedestrian by a motor vehicle was five to seven times greater for those in class IV than for those in social class I, with deaths by fires, falls and drowning showing even sharper class gradients. As the authors pointed out: 'While the death of an individual child may appear as a random misfortune, the overall distribution clearly indicates the 'social' nature of the phenomena' (Townsend and Davidson, 1982).

This chapter examines the accident rates for children over the last 20 years, looking at whether the class gradient has changed. The Black Report found that there had been little improvement in class differentials between 1959–63 and 1970–72. The 1992 Department of Health strategy, Health of the Nation, identified the reduction in childhood accidents as a governmental target, and more recently the publication of *Variations in Health* (DoH, 1995b) reasserted the importance of tackling inequalities in health. But have any improvements in class differentials of childhood accidents been evidenced over the last 20 years? The general trends in childhood accidents are set out, before a detailed consideration of social class gradients, and finally a discussion of the possible causes of differences in childhood accident rates.

Incidence of child accidents

Child accident mortality rates

A useful review of the data on childhood accidents is provided by Roberts (1996) and Jarvis *et al.* (1995). Jackson and Towner (1997) have written a report, for the Child Accident Prevention Trust, on socio-economic influences on unintentional injury in childhood. There are a number of reviews of the international literature on the effectiveness of ways of preventing unintentional injuries to children, including the NHS Centre for Reviews and Dissemination (1996) and Towner and Ward (1998).

Accidents remain the single largest cause of death for all children over the age of one in the UK 'and there is strong evidence that childhood injuries are closely linked with social deprivation and that socio-economic mortality differentials for childhood injury are increasing. Social gradients also exist for morbidity data. Data on morbidity is generally of poor quality and evidence related to causal mechanisms is patchy and unbalanced.' (Jackson and Towner, 1997:3). In 1990, 24 per cent of deaths of those aged 1–4 were due to injury/poisoning. This rose to 37 per cent of deaths of children aged 5–9 and 39 per cent, nearly two-fifths of all deaths, in the age range 10–14 (Roberts, 1996 using OPCS/ONS data). The majority of accidents to children under five occur in the home, whilst the majority of accidents in older age groups occur outside the home. Accident rates for boys are higher than for girls at all ages, with boys accounting for 60–65 per cent of all accident deaths (Jarvis *et al.*, 1995). In 1994 in England and Wales, 952 children and young people under the age of 19 died as a result of unintentional injury. Ten per cent of children who died were under five, 12 per cent aged 5–9, 16 per cent 10–14 years and 52 per cent aged between 15 and 19. Over half (62 per cent, of the young people died as a result of motor vehicle traffic accidents. Other important causes of death were poisonings (7 per cent), drownings (5 per cent), fire and flames (5 per cent), inhalation and ingestion (4 per cent), falls (4 per cent) and mechanical suffocation (3 per cent). However, a different profile of accidents occurs for different age groups (Jackson and Towner, 1997).

The data relating to child accidental deaths are mainly derived from reports from the Registrar General for England and Wales, Scotland and Northern Ireland in the form of mortality statistics (in England and Wales OPCS/ONS DH1 (surveillance), DH2 (cause) and DH6 (childhood)), as well as from information collected by the Department of Environment, Transport and the Regions (DETR) on road accidents and from the Home Office on residential fires. Information on the number of deaths, place of death, age and gender tend to be reliably recorded (Roberts, 1996). However, ONS information on social class (of the head of household, usually the father) appears to be collected only in certain years. Local coroners' reports represent a rich but relatively unexplored data source on child deaths (Roberts, 1996); Jarvis *et al.* (1995) also outline a number of other problems with the data, for instance definitions of categories of injury being subject to change.

Despite these problems, mortality data do allow time trends in child accidents to be observed. The number of accidents to children have decreased, with mortality rates for children aged 1–9 halving over the period 1970–90, although the decline has been less pronounced for older age groups (OPCS data in Jarvis *et al.*, 1996). However, because the decline in accident rates has not been as steep as for other causes of death, such as whooping cough, measles and TB, accidents account for an increasing proportion of child deaths as a whole (Jarvis *et al.*, 1995).

Child accident morbidity rates

Accidents are a major cause of morbidity in childhood. Whilst there are a number of data sources on non-fatal accidents, including the General Household Survey, the Home Accident/Leisure Accident Surveillance Scheme, as well as school and GP records and hospital admission rates (Roberts, 1996; Jarvis *et al.*, 1995), no source provides comprehensive evidence on child morbidity rates from accidents. For example, it is not known how many minor accidents occur which do not result in a GP or hospital visit, although local studies have attempted to go some way towards understanding such patterns

(Roberts *et al.*, 1995). In contrast to falling child mortality rates, hospital admissions for unintentional injuries have shown a slight rise (except for a decline in the late 1970s) although it is not known whether this represents an increase in accidents or in hospital use (Jarvis *et al.*, 1995).

A new source of information on non-fatal childhood injury is now available in the recently-commissioned Health Survey for England. Since 1985, the survey has included data on children aged 2–15, collected using a self-report questionnaire filled out by young people and parents of children (Prescott-Clarke and Primatesta, 1998). Major non-fatal accident rates were 31 and 42 per 100 persons for boys and young men respectively, and 22 for girls and young women, for the period 1995–7. Minor accident rates were estimated at 216 and 385 per 100 persons for boys and young men, and 144 and 184 for girls and young women respectively.

In addition, the Family Fund Trust (previously the Family Fund) provides a database on severely disabled children which includes children disabled following accidents. The database contains information on approximately 200,000 children who have been helped by the Fund since 1973. Between 1980 and 1997, 1,173 children were recorded as disabled as a result of an accident, including head injuries (782), burns (245), paralysis (83), brain damage (47) and eye injuries (16). The Trust only supports children who are 'very severely disabled' and families where the gross household income is less than £18,801 (April 1998). The database is therefore not representative of all children with disabilities but nonetheless provides a rich source of data on the nature of severe disablement in childhood, and highlights how accidents, for some children, mean long-term or permanent disability.

Relationship with social class

Child accident mortality rates

Jarvis *et al.* (1995) provide details of the standardised mortality ratios for accidents to children as recorded by OPCS (for England and Wales) in the decennial supplement for 1970–72. This shows steep class gradients for all fatal injuries with particularly high differences between social classes I and IV for certain deaths, most notably deaths by fire and flames (ratio of 1:9). Data on social class collected for the subsequent decennial supplement using 1979/80 and 1982/3 data by Jarvis *et al.* (1995) confirm that differentials in injury mortality rates persisted from 1970/71 to 1982/3. For the four years 1979/80 to 1982/83, the accident death rate (for all accidents) for children in social class V was 3.5 times greater than for those in social class I.

Since the early 1980s, few studies have investigated the class gradient of child injury mortality, with most reviews of the area relying on old data. Only two studies have considered the relationship between poverty and all types of childhood accident mortality over time: a comparison of class-specific mortality in England and Wales over the period 1981–1991 by Roberts and Powers (1996) and a similar study for 1981–95 by Morrison and colleagues (1999) examining evidence for Scotland.

The Roberts and Powers research (1996) compared the data for 1979/80 to 1982/83 with anonymised records provided by OPCS for all child injury deaths for the period

1989–92 for children aged 0–15, supplemented by denominator data[1] from the 1991 census. The research showed that the class gradient for child deaths by injury had increased over the period, with children from social class V being five times (an increase from 3.5 times) more likely to die from an accident than children in class I. They demonstrated that whilst child injury rates had fallen for all classes, the decline in death rates for those in social classes IV and V was less than for those in classes I and II. For social classes I and II the decline was about a third but for social class IV the decline was a fifth and only two per cent for social class V (Table 4.1). Furthermore, whilst deaths on the road (accounting for 44 per cent of all deaths in 1989–92, 51 per cent in 1979–83) had decreased for all classes (although again the gain was more for social classes I and II), deaths by fire actually increased for social classes IV and V, by 18 per cent and 39 per cent respectively (representing ten per cent of all deaths, up from eight per cent in 1979–83). Although different classification systems were used by OPCS in 1981 and 1991 for social class, the authors concluded that this could not account for the increase in class differentials. However, it is important to note that a seemingly inconsistent finding from the study was that the largest decline in child injury mortality rates actually occurred in the 'other' group, mainly consisting of economically 'unoccupied' households. Roberts and Powers explain this by the changing composition of such households, from mainly lone parents in 1981 to a more heterogenous population in 1991. The 'other' category, however, is very important as 17 per cent of all children lived in such households in 1991 compared with only six per cent in 1981 (Roberts and Powers, 1996).

The Morrison *et al.* (1999) research took a slightly different approach to investigating socio-economic differentials in child injury rates. Accident rates for children aged 0–14 were provided by the Registrar General for Scotland, whilst socio-economic status was based on the Carstairs' Area Deprivation Index. As with the Roberts and Powers study, a decline in the child accident death rate for all classes was observed over 1981–95. However, the study did not find any evidence of either widening or narrowing inequalities between areas of deprivation; very similar rates of inequality were maintained. Children living in areas of greatest deprivation were 2.29 times more likely to experience accidents than those in the least deprived areas. The authors point out that their and Roberts and Powers' studies are not directly comparable as one used occupational status and the other an area-based deprivation measure, particularly as there is evidence that the characteristics of communities may exert a different impact on health to that of individuals.

A more specific study, looking at area variations in fatal childhood accidents involving head injuries, was undertaken by Sharples and colleagues (1990) for the period 1979–86. Looking at all child fatalities from head injuries for ages 0–15 in the Northern Regional Health Authority, the authors found that children living in the local authorities which ranked the lowest on the Townsend deprivation index were fifteen times more likely to experience fatal head injuries than children living in the least deprived areas. A majority of fatalities were road traffic accidents (73 per cent of sample of 255 children) occurring, two-thirds of the time, within 2 km of the child's home.

Table 4.1 **Mortality from injury and poisoning per 100,000 children aged 0–15 years by social class, 1979–83* and 1989–92**

| | Rate per 100,000 (No.) | | | | % Decline (95% confidence interval)** | |
	1979–83*		1989–92			
Social Class						
I	24.2	-144	16.5	-94	32	(12 to 47)
II	25.0	-580	15.8	-388	37	(28 to 45)
IIIN	24.2	-248	19.1	-171	21	(4 to 35)
IIIM	35.7	-1,267	34.3	-828	4	(-5 to 12)
IV	47.5	-710	37.8	-417	21	(10 to 30)
V	84.7	-423	82.9	-297	2	(-13 to 16)
P value for trend						P<0.001
Other	93.4	-1,169	51.2	-966	45	(40 to 50)
Non-manual v manual						
Non-manual	24.7	-972	16.6	-653	33	(26 to 39)
Manual	52.5	-3,569	43.5	-2,508	17	(13 to 21)

* Excludes 1981
** Based on rates before rounding

Child accident morbidity rates

Whilst there is a large body of work on child accident morbidity generally, few studies have been completed on the social class differentials for non-fatal child injury. The studies that do exist have not demonstrated a particularly consistent relationship between poverty and morbidity arising from accidents, and, due to the problems with data sources, the findings must be treated with some caution.

The most up-to-date information allowing social class and income to be examined for child accident morbidity rates comes from the Health Survey of Young People (Prescott-Clarke and Primatesta, 1998). Here, as the authors note, somewhat surprisingly in the light of Roberts and Powers' study (1996), no strong relationship was found between reported (major and minor) accident rates and social class for children and young people aged 2–24. If anything, there appeared to be some suggestion that accident rates were higher for males, in both social classes I and V (although accident rates were lower for females in social class I). The authors suggest that the equality of experience of non-fatal accidents across social classes would seem to indicate that a higher proportion of accidents in social classes IIIM, IV and V prove fatal. Interestingly, the survey results showed a slightly stronger relationship between equivalised income and accident rates, although here again it appeared that those young people (both males and females) living in households with either a particularly high or low income were at greatest risk of accidents.

Williams *et al.* (1997) also used a self-completed questionnaire, administered through schools, to collect data on non-fatal injuries and socio-economic status for 4,710 Scottish adolescents aged 11, 13 and 15 years. They used two measures of socio-economic status in the study: a description of the adolescent's father's job and a four point measure of material wealth using the number of cars in household and whether or not the child had their own bedroom. The study found that there was no relationship between overall incidence of medically-attended injuries and father's job or material wealth of the family. However, Williams *et al.,* did observe marked differences between socio-economic groups in both the circumstances in which injuries occurred and in the different types of risk and protective behaviour. For example, relative material deprivation was predictive of injuries occurring on the roads, in public parks and in the home, whereas increased material wealth was associated with injuries at school. High-status father's job was associated with sports injuries, whilst a lower-status father's job was predictive of bicycle injuries. High material wealth was associated with being injured as a passenger in a car whilst lower family affluence was predictive of being knocked down by a car.

Other studies, however, particularly those looking at hospital use, have found differences for child accidents by socio-economic group and / or type of area. A recent study by Reading and colleagues (1999), looking at pre-school accident and emergency rates over two years in Norwich, found higher rates of attendances for accidents in the most deprived parts of the city (using the Townsend material deprivation index) dominated by large local authority housing estates. The risk of a pre-school child attending for a severe accident was 1.49 times greater in these most deprived areas, with a weaker but still significant relationship for more minor injuries. Variation in rates of severe injuries was also accounted for by individual factors, including male sex, young maternal age, number of elder siblings and being a lone parent, with all these factors, except lone parenthood, being important for more minor injuries. Analysis of the Family Fund Trust database has also indicated a relationship between lone parenthood and accidents, particularly for severe burns. Bradshaw and Lawton (1995) found that over a third of children with burns were from lone-parent families, whilst only 14 per cent of Family Fund recipients were lone parents.

It is known that child morbidity rates vary by both age and gender with older male young people being at the greatest risk of both major and minor accidents (Prescott-Clarke and Primatesta, 1998). More recently, it has also been suggested that the relationship between socio-economic group and accident morbidity varies according to the age group of young people. West (1997) reviewed UK and international studies in this area and, whilst noting the lack of consensus about whether a relationship with class existed, and the problems of comparing different types of injuries, concluded that 'there does appear to be suggestive evidence for a change in class patterning between childhood and youth'. This would explain why studies of accidents amongst pre-school children might reveal a greater class gradient than studies of adolescents; however the Health of Young People survey data provides little evidence to confirm this assertion. Williams *et al.,* (1997) have asserted that adolescents might be 'comparatively resilient to the effects of parental socio-economic status because of greater personal autonomy and common environments'.

Reasons for childhood accident rates

The precise causes of childhood accident rates and of the high class gradient remain, to a large degree, unknown (Jarvis *et al.,* 1995). A number of possible causes have been discussed but the complexity and inter-relationship of the different risk factors make interpretations difficult. Most studies on the subject provide evidence of 'associations' between risk factors rather than causes of accidents. Spencer (1996) has identified four main type of explanations for the varying social class gradient in health: artefact, social selection, behavioural and cultural, and structural or life circumstances.

Artefact explanations, relating to the lack of uniformity within and between data sources, and problems with recording methods, have been discussed above. Whilst some of the variations between studies may be explained by artefact, for example between the Roberts and Powers and the Morrison *et al.* studies, the social class gradient for childhood accidents overall is too strong to be explained away by artefactual considerations. Social selection explanations, arguing that health leads to social class rather than vice versa, have been shown to explain poorly any differences between classes (Spencer, 1996). This is particularly likely to be the case with childhood accidents.

The behavioural or cultural explanation for variations in child accident rates has been advanced by many commentators. Child behaviour has been implicated in higher accident rates, and this to some extent may explain some of the differences between accident rates for boys and girls. However the parental role has come under the most questioning with it being suggested that higher injury rates to the children of younger parents, and lone parents (Wadsworth *et al.,* 1983), can be largely accounted for by the lack of parental supervision of the children. One study looking at residential fires concluded that child fatalities were largely a result of lack of responsibility, and also alcohol-related behaviour, of adults in the household (Squires and Busuttil, 1995).

However, the weight of evidence argues most strongly for an explanation on the basis of structural factors and life chances. Roberts and Powers (1996) assert that: 'the most likely explanation for the steepening social class gradient in child injury death rates is a deepening of the differential exposure to health damaging or health promoting physical and social environments resulting from greater inequalities in income'.

A recent review of fatalities amongst children of lone parents concluded that increased rates could be explained by poor housing conditions, lack of income and social isolation of lone parents (Roberts and Pless, 1995). The absence of day care was also mentioned as one of the failings of social policy in attempts to make an impact on accident rates. The effect of living in a deprived area has also been shown to be associated with poorer health and higher accident rates, independently of individual family poverty (Macintyre *et al.,* 1993; Reading *et al.,* 1999).

Environmental factors, and rates of exposure to the risk of accidents, clearly play an important role in accounting for childhood rates of injury mortality. Children in families without a car, who are more likely to be in a lower socio-economic group, are more likely to walk and are therefore exposed to higher risks of accidents (Towner *et al.*, 1994; Roberts *et al.*, 1996). Poorer children are more likely to live in built-up areas with high traffic volume which put them at greater risk (Roberts, 1995); studies have shown how reductions in traffic speed can result in fewer road accidents, for example, introducing a 20 mph zone leads on average to a 67 per cent drop in child pedestrian and cyclist casualties (DETR, 1997).

It is important to restate that there has been a decline in child accident mortality rates over the last twenty years. However, studies have repeatedly demonstrated that this has primarily been as a result of parents and children changing the patterns of childhood travel in response to the rise in traffic (DoT, 1995; Hillman *et al.*, 1990). Children are now much less likely to walk or cycle to school than in past decades, with much-discussed consequences for the extent of childhood mobility and the long-term health impact of the lack of exercise and independence of children (Hillman *et al.*, 1990; Dixey, 1998). However children from lower socio-economic groups are still less likely to travel by car, and to be accompanied by an adult, than middle-class children (Towner *et al.*, 1994).

Conclusions

A strong relationship between social class and/or levels of area deprivation and childhood accident fatality rates has been demonstrated in the UK. In contrast, studies investigating the links between poverty and child accident morbidity are less than consistent in their findings. A number of studies have found that children in poverty, particularly young children, and children of lone parents are at greater risk of non-fatal accidents. However, other studies have found no correlation between social class and accident rates. No studies, however, have found poverty to be associated with fewer accidents; the balance of the evidence suggests that a relationship does exist, at least for some poor children, but further research is clearly required to demonstrate the precise nature of this relationship.

The steep social class gradients for fatal accident rates amongst children highlighted in 1980 by the Black Report have been maintained over the last twenty years, despite an overall reduction in the numbers of child fatal accidents in all classes. There is some evidence to suggest that the class gradient might have actually increased over the period 1981–1991 in England and Wales (Roberts and Powers, 1996), although research in Scotland shows that accident rates by levels of area deprivation have continued to exhibit the same levels of inequality (Morrison *et al.*, 1999). There are no reliable studies on rates of childhood accident morbidity over time, although the new Health Survey of Young People will begin to provide such data.

An overall reduction in childhood fatal accidents appears to have been largely achieved through changing patterns of childhood travel, whereby children are now less mobile than they were in past decades. Exposure to the risk of accidents, which is closely associated with levels of family poverty and area deprivation, appears to explain much of the variations in childhood accidents. However, better sources of information are required to understand the links between childhood accidents and poverty. Whilst the data available for fatal accidents are fairly robust, information sets on childhood accident morbidity rates are beset by problems of definition and measurement and are unable to capture data reliably over time.

Note to Chapter 4

1   The number of children in this age group from which the mortality rate can be calculated

$$\frac{\text{number of deaths}}{\text{number of children of a particular age}} = \text{death rate}$$

5 Child abuse

Deborah Quilgars

Introduction

The chapter begins by outlining the problems surrounding both the definition and measurement of child abuse, presenting the limited information available on the incidence and prevalence of abuse in Britain. The evidence for a link between child abuse and poverty (including socio-economic status, unemployment, numbers of families receiving benefit, and neighbourhood deprivation), is then reviewed, as well as links with other characteristics such as family composition which may also be associated with poverty. The important link between domestic violence and child abuse is also discussed. The limited information on time trends is briefly presented. Finally, the evidence is assessed through a consideration of existing explanatory models of the aetiology of child abuse.

Defining child abuse

There are no absolute definitions of child abuse. Whilst in any one society at any one time what constitutes child abuse, particularly severe abuse, may be broadly agreed and understood, child abuse is inevitably defined within cultural understandings and standards. Even within the British context understandings have changed over time, with child abuse being synonymous with physical abuse until the 'discovery' of child sexual abuse in the 1970s. In addition, different sections of the population (for example, professionals, researchers and members of the public) may understand child abuse differently at any one time (National Commission of Inquiry into the Prevention of Child Abuse (NCIPCA), 1996).

The most commonly cited definitions of child abuse in the UK are derived from child protection legislation and practice. Here, four main types of abuse are defined: physical, sexual, emotional and neglect (see Table 5.1). However, child abuse can be defined more broadly than these main child protection categories. For example, the recent National Commission of Inquiry adopted the following definition: 'Child abuse consists of anything which individuals, institutions, or processes do or fail to do which directly or indirectly harms children or damages their prospects of safe and healthy development into adulthood', (NCIPCA, 1996:2)

This much broader type of definition includes what has been termed 'institutional' or 'system' abuse, as well as abuse by individuals. Within this definition, it may be argued that institutional (children's homes) practices such as 'Pin-down',[1] as well as more general poor standards of care, may result in the abuse of children. Arguably, poverty itself, if understood as being a result of state policies, could be interpreted as a type of 'system' abuse of children. Higher rates of mortality and morbidity of children, as well as other outcomes of poverty, could be cited as evidence that the State 'system' is damaging the safe and healthy development of children (NCIPCA, 1996).

Table 5.1 **Definitions of child abuse**

Neglect	The persistent or severe neglect of a child or the failure to protect a child from exposure to any kind of danger, including cold or starvation, or extreme failure to carry out important aspects of care, resulting in the significant impairment of the child's health or development, including non-organic failure to thrive
Physical Injury	Actual or likely physical injury to a child, or failure to prevent physical injury (or suffering to a child), including deliberate poisoning, suffocation and Munchausen's syndrome by proxy
Sexual Abuse	Actual or likely sexual exploitation of a child or adolescent; the child may be dependent and/or developmentally immature
Emotional Abuse	Actual or likely severe adverse effect on the emotional and behavioural development of a child caused by persistent or severe emotional ill-treatment or rejection. All abuse involves some emotional ill-treatment

Source: Working Together, Department of Health, 1991 reproduced in National Commission of Inquiry into the Prevention of Child Abuse (1996) *Childhood Matters, Volume 1: The Report*, London: The Stationery Office, p.4.

The extent of child abuse

It is impossible to be precise about the extent of child abuse in the UK. It will obviously be determined largely by the definition which one adopts. However, over and above this, any attempt to arrive at a figure for abuse is confounded by almost insurmountable problems of measurement. The very nature of child abuse means that much abuse is hidden. Table 5.2 presents an estimate, using a wide range of statistics, of children at risk of harm in the UK. The available information sources on the incidence and prevalence of child abuse are outlined below.

Incidence of child abuse

The child protection system offers the best information on the incidence of abuse in Britain. Other information is available on criminal convictions for child abuse-related crimes and from OPCS statistics on child deaths from abuse; however these are very specific and no less reliable than the child protection statistics.

The Department of Health collects regular statistics from local authorities on the number of children placed on the child protection register. Table 5.3 shows the number of children registered as being abused, by the different types of abuse, for 1995. It should be noted that this represents a count at one point in time: most children are on the register for less than a year, so more children in the course of a year will be registered

Table 5.2 **Estimates of total numbers of children at risk of harm annually**

In the legal system	
Convictions/Cautions (England)	4,500
In child protection system	
On register at risk of abuse or neglect	70,000
Not on register but in process family visit/conference (England)	100,000
Referred to social services, no visit (England)	40,000
Harmful experiences similar to registration categories	
Severe physical punishment	150,000
Witness violence between parents/carers	250,000
Sexual	100,000
Living in homes which are low in warmth/high in criticism	350,000
Other 'in need' categories	
Poverty	4.3 million
Disability in private homes	171,000
Record of offending	130,000
Parents' marital problems/divorce	250,000
Homeless	250,000
Other harm/risk	
School:	
bullied	600,000
permanent exclusions	11,181
Institutions/care (LA)	62,000
Child carers	40,000

Note: The figures cannot be added across groups as one child may appear under several headings

UK figures unless otherwise stated

Source: National Commission of Inquiry into the Prevention of Child Abuse (1996):17.

than the figures indicate (NCIPCA, 1996). In addition, many more families are subject to child protection inquiries than these figures show: it is estimated that only about one-fifth of referrals for child abuse are finally registered by local authorities (Creighton, 1995). It is also generally acknowledged that some types of child abuse are more likely to result in registration: cases of neglect, in particular, are thought to be under-represented. Stevenson (1996), examining the 'neglect of neglect' has demonstrated how social workers are often unwilling to register such cases until an actual 'incident' of abuse occurs.

Another problem with the Department of Health statistics is the wide variation in rates of registration of children in different areas of the country, even between areas with similar social compositions. Many commentators (Little and Gibbons, 1993; Miller *et al.*, 1993) have asserted that local authority discretion accounts for much of this variation. Gordon and Gibbons (1998) examined this assumption through primary research

Table 5.3 **UK Child Protection Registers:
reasons for registration at 31 March 1995**

	England	Scotland[a]	Wales	N. Ireland
Total Children on register	34,954	2,601 (1,532)	1,668	1,523
Physical abuse	–	–	44%	10%
Physical injury	37%	48%	–	–
Physical neglect	–	22%	–	–
Neglect	32%	–	30%	25%
Failure to thrive	–	1%	–	–
Sexual abuse	26%	21%	19%	12%
Emotional abuse	13%	9%	15%	10%
Grave concern	–	–	–	41%
Categories not recommended	*	–	–	–
Other	*	–	–	4%
More than one category	9%	0%	7%	2%

– indicates category not specified in statistics.

* = very low

a The percentages shown for categories for abuse for Scotland are based on those registered during the year to 31 March 1995 in all regions except Grampian (1,532 cases: there were 162 registrations in Grampian). Only the main category is recorded.

Source: National Commission of Inquiry into the Prevention of Child Abuse (1996):12.

in eight local authorities, comparing the vulnerability 'risk' factors (including socio-economic status, parental characteristics, and other factors thought to be associated with abuse) of children registered across areas. The study concluded that similar children are actually registered in different parts of the UK (although the research itself rests on the assumption that such indicators are associated with abuse).

The concern over differences in local child protection practices highlights the fact that child protection is not a science. For this study, the main problem with the Department of Health statistics is that they only represent cases which have been identified and judged serious enough to warrant investigation or registration by social workers. The child protection process does not operate in a cultural vacuum: it is widely accepted that the abuse of children within poor families is more visible and that cases amongst middle-class families are less likely to come to the attention of agencies (Frost, 1993), and that abuse, once suspected, is more likely to be labelled as such within poor families (Creighton, 1995). Creighton (1992) cites an interesting American study (O'Toole *et al.*, 1983) which supports this view. Doctors were presented with a hypothetical case study of child abuse. Where the parents of the child were described as 'low social status', 70 per cent of the doctors judged it to be child abuse: but where the parents were said to be of 'high socio-economic status', only 51 per cent judged it as abuse (although nurses and more experienced professionals were less likely to be influenced in this way). The potential bias towards identifying poor families in the child protection process presents a huge problem for research examining the link between child abuse and poverty: even the best data available on incidence is likely to be fundamentally flawed. This should be borne in mind when examining the evidence below. It is necessary to question the extent to which observed relationships reflect a true association and how far they represent an artefact of the statistics.

Prevalence studies

Surveys of the general population offer a better chance of establishing the prevalence of abuse amongst the population (NCIPCA, 1996). Nonetheless, such studies are also beset by their own problems: surveys are necessarily retrospective, asking adults about childhood abuse, and even sensitive interviewing skills will not overcome the understandable reluctance of some people to disclose episodes of abuse to an interviewer.

Despite these difficulties a number of surveys have been carried out focusing on the prevalence of child sexual abuse. Baker and Duncan (1985) reported on the first national study of the prevalence of child sexual abuse, which consisted of a MORI representative sample of 2,019 men and women, aged 15 or over. Using a definition of sexual abuse which included both contact and non-contact types of abuse, ten per cent of respondents reported that they had been sexually abused before the age of 16 (12 per cent women, 8 per cent men). On the basis of these figures, the authors estimated that over 4.5 million adults were likely to have been sexually abused as a child. A similar study, the BBC Childwatch, with a sample of 2,041 adults (cited in Creighton, 1995) found a prevalence rate of 3 per cent when confining abuse to contact forms of abuse. Finally, Kelly et al.'s (1991) study of child sexual abuse amongst a sample of young people attending a further education college found the highest prevalence: by the broadest definition of sexual abuse (an unwanted sexual event or interaction) 1 in 2 women and 1 in 4 men reported an incident before the age of 18, whilst 1 in 50 men and 1 in 25 women reported being subject to forced sex, rape or coerced masturbation before the age of 16. The varying prevalence rates across these studies demonstrate the difficulties of undertaking such a survey. Recently, Ghate and Spencer (1995) carried out a study on the feasibility of conducting prevalence studies on child sexual abuse in an attempt to overcome some of these problems. Prevalence studies have the advantage of reducing the bias found in incidence studies as respondents can be selected from all social classes.

The links between child abuse and poverty: presenting the evidence

Most research into the links between child abuse and poverty has been carried out in the USA; very little research has been carried out in the UK. The UK research that does exist is almost entirely reliant on information collected as part of child protection enquiries, usually conducted in special surveys, as the Department of Health statistics of children registered for abuse provide no information on poverty indicators. As noted above, it is known that, probably to a large extent, the information is biased towards selecting poorer families. As a result, as pointed out by the Department of Health (1995a) 'little is known about middle-class parents who mistreat their offspring'. This significant gap in knowledge must be borne in mind when reviewing the studies below.

The link with unemployment, social class and means-tested benefits

The richest data source on cases of child abuse is the (now defunct) NSPCC register research (Creighton, 1992) which ran for 18 years, up until 1990, and represented the largest continuous study of child abuse in the UK (with a total of 26,300 children registered by all professionals in between 12 and 20 local authorities over the course of the research). Amongst many other variables, the register collected information on the social class and employment status of the parents, whether the family was receiving Income Support and a professional assessment of 'stress factors' thought to be experienced by the family. The last report for the register covered the period 1988–90, involving 9,628 registered children (Creighton, 1992).

In the NSPCC research, parents of the registered children had much higher unemployment rates than average rates in the regions included in the study. Table 5.4 shows that only 14 per cent of mothers and 36 per cent of fathers were employed.[2] Parents of children registered for non-organic failure to thrive, neglect, and neglect and physical abuse were the most likely to be unemployed. In contrast, the parents most likely to be

Table 5.4 Employment of parents by reason for registration (1988–1990 combined)

Reason for registration	Mothers				Fathers			
	Employed		Unemployed		Employed		Unemployed	
	No	(%)*	No	(%)	No	(%)*	No	(%)
Physical injury	470	19	1,506	59	887	43	771	37
Sexual abuse	297	19	906	57	489	37	450	34
Neglect	40	6	506	78	147	32	216	47
Emotional abuse	24	11	167	75	66	39	86	51
Failure to thrive	6	6	93	85	15	17	54	63
Neglect and physical abuse	7	7	72	72	16	20	39	48
Physical and sexual abuse	4	7	40	71	15	37	16	39
Grave concern	372	10	2,340	65	903	33	1,164	42
All registrations	1,222	14	5,640	64	2,541	36	2,807	40
No information	1,945	22			1,634	23		

* Percentages relate to the different numbers of mothers and fathers in the sample when parental situation adjusted for

Source: Creighton (1992), Table 14, p.29.

in employment were parents of children sexually abused and those physically abused. Data on occupation was recorded for ten per cent of mothers and 27 per cent of fathers. Only 4 per cent of mothers and 5 per cent of fathers were in non-manual occupations, with parents of physically injured and sexually-abused children most likely to be in non-manual occupations, and the parents of children registered for failure to thrive and neglect being the least likely. One per cent of mothers and 11 per cent of fathers were in skilled manual jobs and 5 per cent of mothers and 11 per cent of fathers in unskilled or semi-skilled occupations. In addition, Table 5.5 shows that over half (56 per cent) of the registered children's families were receiving Income Support, rising to nearly three-quarters of the families of neglected children. The families of sexually abused children were the least likely (46 per cent) to be on Income Support.

Professionals also recorded for the research register the factors in the families they assessed that were placing stress on the household. Here debts (23 per cent of cases) and unemployment (22 per cent) were both among the five most frequently mentioned stress factors. The highest stress-related factor, though, was marital problems, (assessed to be present in 35 per cent of families), followed by an inability to respond to the 'maturational needs' of the children (24 per cent), whilst marital violence was causing stress in over a fifth of cases (22 per cent). Marital problems were highest in cases of physical abuse, sexual abuse, emotional abuse and grave concern, whilst debt and inability to respond to maturational needs were highest in neglect and failure to thrive cases.

Gordon and Gibbons (1998), in their study of local authority rates of registration, collected information on poverty indicators of children referred and registered in eight

Table 5.5 Families on Income Support by reason for registration (1988–1990 combined)

Reason for registration	Percentage of families on Income Support	
	Total	Form 37*
Physical injury	36	51
Sexual abuse	34	46
Neglect	52	74
Emotional abuse	51	71
Failure to thrive	50	69
Neglect and physical abuse	48	65
Physical and sexual abuse	48	63
Grave concern	43	59
All registrations	40	56

* Income Support is recorded on Form 37. Some 28 per cent of the Form 37s were not completed. The second column of percentages is derived from the 72 per cent of the total sample who completed a Form 37.

Source: Creighton (1992), Table 27, p.42.

local authority areas in England. Table 5.6 shows six indicators of poverty: whether the family was claiming Income Support, was homeless, had a wage earner in the family, four or more children, any debts, and other financial problems. Consistent with other research, sexual abuse referrals had fewer poverty indicators, then physical abuse, with neglect cases showing the strongest relationship. For example, 44 per cent of sexual abuse families were in receipt of social security payments, compared with 58 per cent of physical abuse cases and 69 per cent of neglect cases. Interestingly, when comparing referrals with registered cases, Gordon and Gibbons found that neglected children and lone parents were the most likely to be filtered out. They explained that the poverty association appeared to be highest at referral, that is, at the point of the identification of risk in the first place, which would lend support to the idea that such factors might increase the visibility of families.

One of the only studies to examine explicitly the link between poverty and child abuse has been the study by Gillham *et al.* (1998) of 5,551 child abuse referrals and 1,450 registered cases of abuse in Glasgow, Scotland over the period 1991–3. The research looked not only at child poverty, but also at the links between abuse and adult unemployment and single-parent density. However, it is important to note that the study was examining the *characteristics of the local area* in which the families lived, rather than the individual characteristics of families. Measures used included receipt of means-tested clothing grants and free school meals as indices of child poverty (using unpublished data from the Education Department), rates of male and female unemployment (obtained from the Chief Executive's office), and unpublished 1991 census data on single-parent density for each social work area. All measures were found to be correlated with at least some forms of abuse. However male unemployment was found to account for two-

Table 5.6 **Poverty indicators in families referred for suspected child abuse or neglect**

Indicator Test	Neglect		Physical abuse		Sexual abuse		All	
	%	No	%	No	%	No	%	No
Social Security	69	258	58	535	44	285	57	1,078
Homeless/temporary accommodation	18	310	12	669	6	376	12	1,355
No wage earner	69	268	57	561	42	293	56	1,122
Four or more children	19	391	22	835	23	521	21	1,747
Debts	37	367	31	803	22	475	30	1,645
Other Financial	33	368	33	802	18	476	29	1,646

Note: All findings are statistically significant at 0.19 level

Source: adapted from Gordon and Gibbons (1998), Table 2, p.427.

thirds of the variance of total abuse rates, and to be particularly good at predicting physical abuse rates, although much less so for sexual abuse and neglect. Child poverty and female unemployment also correlated with abuse measures, but they did not significantly improve the prediction. Single-parent density increased the prediction marginally. The authors concluded that localised high male unemployment rates were likely to put vulnerable families at greater risk of child physical abuse and neglect. They argued however, that it is likely to be the associated poverty, rather than unemployment *per se*, which bears the causal responsibility.

A number of other studies have also focused on links between the neighbourhood or locality and child abuse, asserting that child abuse may be associated directly with environmental or neighbourhood factors, rather than simply the likelihood of an individual family being in poverty. 'Clustering' of children on child protection registers has certainly been observed in deprived areas of cities (Cotterill, 1988). In an Australian study, examining two adjoining economically-depressed localities with contrasting rates of child abuse, Vinson *et al.*, (1996) found significant differences within the structures of networks. They found that a higher rate of abuse was associated with lower levels of interaction between family and friends, acquaintances and neighbours, whilst the equally deprived neighbourhood with better networks exhibited lower rates of abuse. Drake and Pandey's (1996) American study found that child neglect, out of all types of abuse, was most powerfully associated with neighbourhood poverty rates.

Summing up: different links for different types of abuse

The evidence presented above indicates clearly that any link between poverty and child abuse varies by the type of abuse.

There appears to be some evidence for arguing for a link between physical abuse and poverty, however the strongest link is for cases of neglect and failure to thrive. It is here that families tend to be characterised by extremely high levels of poverty, debt and unemployment. Baldwin and Spencer (1993) reviewed the evidence for an association between material deprivation and child abuse and concluded that: 'The strength and consistency across studies of the deprivation / abuse correlation would seem to be greater than could be explained by reporting bias, or the more ready identification of abuse among the poor'. (Baldwin and Spencer, 1993:363)

However, this analysis does not hold for sexual abuse. All the child abuse studies using child protection registers have noted that child sexual abuse appears to be the least correlated with poverty indicators. The few prevalence studies specifically on child sexual abuse have strongly suggested that there is no link between sexual abuse of children and poverty. Baker and Duncan's survey (1985) of the prevalence of child sexual abuse found no significant difference by social class (using market research categories which approximated to the Register General's Classification). Accounts of adult survivors suggest that sexual abuse is common to all social groups (La Fontaine, 1990). The Gillham *et al.*, (1998) study commented on the much weaker correlation between child sexual abuse and poverty indicators: 'It seems reasonable to infer that sexual abuse does have a different ecology, less related to poverty and social disadvantage, even amongst the selected clientele of the Social Work Department. The fact that this difference is apparent, even in the 'biased', in other words, non-representative sample would demonstrate a markedly different ecology'. (Gillham *et al.*, 1998)

Child abuse and other family characteristics

The evidence above mentioned the link with other family or household characteristics as well as with poverty indicators, including single-parent density and marital stress. Here, the possible link with other family characteristics, which it is argued are often highly associated with poverty, is examined.

The NSPCC research register (Creighton, 1992) was also able to provide detailed information on other family characteristics, including family composition and parental characteristics, of the abused children. The registered children's families were characterised by a much greater degree of instability in parental relationships than national demographic data would predict, even for similar social classes. Registered children were considerably less likely to be living with both natural parents (only 36 per cent of children) and eight times more likely to be living with a natural mother and father substitute compared with the national distribution from similar social classes. Just over a quarter (26 per cent) of the families were lone mothers (although 39 per cent of neglect cases), and only 3 per cent lone fathers. Mothers were over five times as likely to have been a teenager at birth of child than mothers from similar social classes nationally. Nearly twice as many families included four or more children than nationally. A previous criminal record was recorded for 12 per cent of mothers and 40 per cent of fathers of registered children (less than one-third of fathers, and only half of mothers were recorded as having no criminal record).[3] Seven per cent of mothers and 5 per cent of fathers had attended special schools compared with one per cent nationally in 1971. Fathers (and particularly stepfathers) were more likely to be suspected in physical abuse and sexual abuse cases than mothers (taking into account who lives with the children), whilst mothers were more likely to be implicated in cases of emotional abuse or neglect.

The Gordon and Gibbons' (1998) study also examined a range of 'vulnerability' indicators, as well as poverty indicators, including the criminal record of parents, mental illness or drug use by parents, domestic violence, lone parent, reconstituted family, child under five, perpetrator living in the home, previous recorded incident, and serious incident. Interestingly, it was the child's vulnerability factors, rather than poverty, which were more strongly associated with decisions to put the child on register, univariate analysis showing registration to be most highly associated with parental criminal activity, marital violence, abuse (previous and abuse not neglect) and mental illness. Taitz *et al.* (1987), in a Sheffield children's hospital study, found that the criminal record of the male partner was the strongest predictive factor of child abuse.

Sheppard (1997) investigated the specific link between child abuse and maternal depression in two district teams focusing on all mothers in care-managed families on child and family care social work caseloads. In this study, the self-completed Beck Depression Inventory was used to assess depression in the last week, and the Depression Social Assessment Schedule was filled out by a social worker to look at social and demographic factors, including deprivation. The study found that 36 per cent of the 116 women were depressed and that child abuse was significantly more likely to be present in families with depressed mothers (62 per cent) than families where mothers were not depressed (41 per cent). In addition, mothers who were depressed and where child abuse was suspected, were also found to suffer the greatest deprivation; for example there was no wage earner in 77 per cent of this group compared with 60 per cent of non-depressed mothers. The second schedule also looked at 'social problem domains' (social, health, relationship, parenting and child) and found that the depressed–abuse group had much higher frequencies of problems compared with other groups (who were similar). They also reported much higher levels of domestic violence: 54 per cent of depressed – abuse group compared with 30 per cent of non-depressed/abuse and only 10 per cent of non-depressed/non-abuse group. They were also more likely to be isolated from family and friends, and to experience marital problems. The authors stated that the women 'lived their lives in the context of extensive relationship problems with other adults … living in families pervaded by abuse and violence' (p.99), and concluded that 'maternal depression, on the evidence of this research, constitutes a central element of the context for child abuse'.

Baldwin and Spencer (1993) have pointed out how: 'material deprivation, though often treated as such, is not a one-dimensional variable but a complex web of circumstances acting and reacting upon each other'.

It may be asserted that variables such as criminality and education are also implicated in the link between poverty and child abuse, in so far as they are strongly correlated with deprivation. They also serve to demonstrate the complexity of the interrelationships between deprivation and abuse.

Child abuse and domestic violence

A number of the studies looking at poverty and deprivation cited above have identified a problem with marital conflict, and in particular the high incidence of domestic violence associated with child abuse cases. In the last five years in Britain, this factor has received increasing attention both by researchers and at a policy level. The witnessing of domestic violence by a child has been asserted to represent a form of emotional abuse in itself (Stark and Flitcraft, 1988; Kelly, 1994; Hester and Pearson, 1998). In 90 per cent of cases of domestic violence with children in families, children are in the same or next room (Hughes, 1992 in Kelly, 1994). The effects on the children are thought to include depression, suicidal behaviour, bed-wetting, insomnia, tics, fears and phobias, and aggression (Morley and Mullender, 1994). There are also concerns about the effect on the children of the stress placed on the mother (Wolfe *et al.*, 1985, cited in Morley and Mullender, 1994). Kelly (1994) has also pointed out that some acts of family violence 'defy categorisation as either child abuse or domestic violence' for example, the humiliation of a mother in front of her children.

The link between child abuse and domestic violence has been recognised for some years in the USA. The seminal study by Stark and Flitcraft (1988), which looked at the medical records (for 1977/1978) of mothers of all children referred to Yale–New Haven hospital on suspicion of abuse (physical and neglect), found that 45 per cent of the women had a recorded trauma history of battering. In the UK small-scale studies have found consistently that in about one-third of child abuse cases, the mothers were also experiencing domestic violence (for example, a study into child abuse conducted by the London Borough of Hackney, 1993, cited in Morley and Mullender, 1994). More recently, Hester and Pearson (1998) examined the impact of introducing a systematic means of identifying domestic violence in cases of child abuse within an NSPCC team. Using a monitoring form which gave families a number of opportunities to disclose violence, they found evidence of domestic violence at the start in one-third of cases taken on by the team, increasing to two-thirds of cases at the end.

Studies clearly predict that men who abuse women are more likely to abuse children in the household as well, and vice versa. Increasingly, guidance to local authorities advises professionals to be aware of the possible link between child abuse and domestic violence and to look into the possibility of the existence of the other when one is present (for example, LGA, 1998; DoH, 1999). In addition, there is some evidence that abused women are more likely to abuse children. The link between domestic violence and physical child abuse is fairly well established, but much less research is available on any links with sexual abuse. It has been observed that although men are heavily under-represented in child care, they are responsible for about half of the incidents of abuse reported (Creighton, 1992) and the majority of reported sexual abuse (La Fontaine, 1990). Stark and Flitcraft (1988) argued that child abuse could be best explained as a component of female subordination. In their analysis, poverty was not seen as a primary reason for explaining men's behaviour. However, if as they argue, female empowerment is the best means of preventing child abuse, women's economic independence is crucial in determining whether women and children can escape the violence and abuse.

Trends over time

Very little data exists on the nature of child abuse over time. The Department of Health statistics allow broad trends to be observed of the numbers and proportion of children registered for different types of child abuse, as did the NSPCC research register from 1972–1990. However, even here, comparisons are made difficult by changes in the categorisation of abuse over time. The main change occurred in 1991, when registrations for abuse changed to include both those abused as well as those *thought likely to be* abused, replacing the previous category of 'grave concern'. The NSPCC study showed that the registration rate trebled between 1984 and 1990, but this largely reflected the change from child abuse registers to child protection registers and the increase in registrations of 'grave concern' at that time. Looking at the period up until the early 1990s, the number of sexual abuse cases was highest in 1987, at the time of the Cleveland enquiry. Physical abuse cases increased gradually from 1979 to 1984, with a marked increase in 1985, but then fluctuated year on year (Creighton, 1992, 1995).

However, the only time–trend data which allows a comparison of poverty indicators over time remains the NSPCC research register. The main trend observed over the period 1972–74 to 1990 was the decrease in the number of children living with both natural parents compared with those living with a father substitute: this change was greater than that for the population as a whole. In contrast, the proportion of lone parents saw only a small increase and became less over-represented over time. When looking at unemployment, the national rate increased over the latter period but not to the same extent as for fathers of those registered. In 1975, 30 per cent of fathers were unemployed; in 1985, 54 per cent were unemployed, although reducing to 40 per cent in 1990. Large families and early parenthood remained over-represented over the period. Marital problems, debts and unemployment were the stress factors most consistently found over time, with marital problems representing the single most significant factor over the period. In short, most factors remained prominent, but the parental situation become more atypical, with more unemployed fathers or father substitutes.

Understanding the evidence: explanatory models of child abuse

A review of studies on child abuse and poverty appears to indicate that a link exists between a range of poverty indicators and some (but not all) types of abuse. Other family characteristics, such as family composition, parental depression and criminality, also seem to be significant. However, whilst associations can be made with a range of factors, including poverty, the extent to which these associations reflect causal mechanisms is uncertain. Perhaps, partly, because of the methodological challenges involved, no major study has been undertaken in the UK which has attempted to establish the causes of abuse (for example, the Department of Health recently commissioned 20 studies on child protection, but not one of these was designed to understand the origins of abuse (DoH, 1995a)).

It is useful to consider the present review within a more conceptual framework by looking at the main explanatory theories of child abuse. Corby (1993) has provided a useful typology of explanatory models, identifying three main types:

(i) *Psychological theories:* Theories which seek to understand child abuse primarily through the psychology of the abuser, including biological explanations (natural selection etc), attachment theory (separation of mother-child), psycho-dynamic perspectives (similar to attachment theory but stressing mental processes) and learning theory and cognitive approaches (learning poor parenting skills).

(ii) *Social psychological theories*: Theories focus on both the role of the individual and social factors, including the 'individual interactionist' perspective (stresses current personal interactions), the 'family dysfunction' model (stressing family dynamics), and 'social ecological' (role of social environment) theories.

(iii) *Sociological perspectives:* Corby includes four main perspectives which in varying ways emphasise the role of social, economic and/or cultural factors: the 'social cultural' theory (argues that violence is the cultural norm and abuse is part of a continuum); the 'social structural' perspective (emphasises the contribution of stress caused by poverty, deprivation, and, to a lesser extent, the State); the 'feminist perspective' (sexual and physical violence is a result of male socialisation and patriarchal attitudes to power and control); and the 'children's rights perspective' (emphasises that childhood is fundamentally an oppressed state).

The role of poverty is seen as central within the social structural perspective of child abuse. The main proponent of this theory in the UK has been Parton (1985 and 1993, Parton *et al.*, 1997).

The starting point for Parton's argument of his 'politics of child abuse' was a critique of the 'disease' or 'medical' model of child abuse which he identified as the dominant explanatory theory on child abuse. The 'disease' model can be characterised as being concerned primarily with the psychology or 'pathology' of abusers, usually family members (the theory could be seen as an umbrella category for psychological/ social-psychological theories). Psychological or interpersonal family factors were seen as of prime importance in the aetiology, although it was acknowledged that stress (which could be caused by poverty) may be a secondary factor. Parton's theory was heavily influenced by Pelton's (1978) seminal American article on 'the myth of classlessness' which argued that commentators offered disclaimers to account for any link between poverty and child abuse (for example explaining away any observed effect by arguing that poor people are more subject to scrutiny etc.) to support a view of child abuse as basically a 'psychodynamic' problem requiring 'treatment'. Accepting the 'disease' model meant that solutions would need to be tailored to the individual case. Parton, in the UK context, argued that a social–structural account of child abuse meant that an anti-poverty strategy would be one of the main measures required to address child abuse. He argued that the 'disease' model: 'Fails to recognise the importance of inequality and the sense of frustration, repression and aggression that results: by concentrating on dangerous people it ignores dangerous conditions. And it blinds us to the abusive but non-individualistic practices of industrial, corporate and government agencies' (Parton, 1985:152).

Parton (1993) has, however, reflected more recently on his own important contribution to the social–structural account of child abuse by outlining a number of inadequacies in the theory. Firstly, he admitted that the theory had ignored the different aetiology of child sexual abuse. Related to this, he acknowledged that the theory failed to take account of broader considerations of gender politics. In short, Parton admitted that his original model did not explain why abuse occurs in middle-class families, why only some poor families, but not others, experience abuse and why men commit more child abuse yet have fewer child care responsibilities. The importance of the development of feminist theories in explaining child abuse, alongside social–cultural accounts, is clear. Some studies (for example, Gelles, 1989) have found that lone fathers are more violent than lone mothers: here, poverty, but also gender, are important factors. Parton has since emphasised the importance of developing a 'socialist–feminist' approach. Whilst not arguing for a unifying theory of child abuse, he notes that 'power' is a crucial factor in explaining child abuse, at both an individual and structural level.

It may be concluded that poverty and structural accounts of child abuse are of primary, but not sole, importance in explaining child abuse. There is no doubt that stresses associated with poverty have an impact on the likelihood of some types of child abuse occurring within families. However, other factors may also need to be present. For example, one American study on physical abuse (Straus, 1980) demonstrated how child-abuse rates increased as the number of stressors during the year increased (using modified Holmes and Rahe stressful life events). Fathers' rates of abuse increased more under stress, highlighting the gender dynamic. Stress was related to increased child abuse when other variables were also present – including beliefs about the efficacy of using violence, experience of violence in family of origin, male dominance in marriage, isolation from networks, with parents in low quartiles (measuring occupational level, education and income) having a child abuse rate double that of those in the highest quartile. Gillham *et al.*, (1998) have asserted that: 'It is probable that deprivation factors have both direct and indirect effects and that families, vulnerable in this and other re-spects, are brought to the critical edge of abuse by an interaction of individual/familial characteristics and the characteristics of their immediate social environment' (Gillham *et al.*, 1998:81).

It is now broadly accepted that child abuse can only begin to be explained ade-quately by an integrated model which acknowledges the roles of all factors including psychological, social, economic and environmental (Corby, 1993; DoH, 1995a). Belsky (1980, cited in Corby, 1993) has proposed a four level approach to child abuse (using an ecological framework): ontologic development (individual psychology); the microsys-tem (interaction of individuals); exo/ecosystem (social environment); macro-system (broader structural factors such as cultural attitudes to violence). This, however, makes explanations much more complex (Corby, 1993) and the precise role (both nature and relative importance) of each factor remains unknown. There is, however, no doubt that poverty represents one important factor in explaining child abuse.

Conclusions

The link between poverty and child abuse is a complex one. The causes of child abuse are multi-dimensional. Poverty is unlikely ever to be the only factor leading to, or asso-ciated with, child abuse. The inherent bias within child protection statistics, and the lack of prevalence studies in this area, mean that there is very little hard evidence to prove the link. However, notwithstanding these caveats, the available evidence does predict a relationship between poverty, as measured by factors such as unemployment, dependence on benefits and living in deprived localities, and child abuse. This relation-ship is different for different types of abuse. The strongest relationship appears to be between poverty and cases of neglect and failure to thrive. In addition, a link may be asserted between poverty and physical abuse. There is, however, very little evidence to suggest that child sexual abuse and poverty are related. It should also, perhaps, be remembered that, given the likely bias in child abuse register data, the observed rela-tionships for the links between physical abuse and neglect, as is predicted in the case of sexual abuse, may be weaker than observed. It is clear that there are many other factors at work, including issues of gender and cultural attitudes to violence. Over and above this, poverty itself could be said to represent a form of child abuse in so far as poor

children have much reduced opportunities in many aspects of life and have significantly worse health.

There is clearly a need for the collection of more robust measurements of child
abuse, including the collection of poverty indicators. The National Commission of Inquiry into the Prevention of Child Abuse has recommended that data on abuse, including
not only statutorily-defined categories of abuse but also information on poverty, health
and estimates on the number of children 'in need', should be collected systematically
and published annually. A better understanding of the underlying causes of child abuse
may ultimately help design more effective interventions and programmes of assistance. Abused children not only suffer abuse at the time it occurs; robust evidence exists
to indicate that sustained abuse can have major long-term effects on children's development, physical health and mental health and well being, often extending into
adulthood (DoH, 1999). The draft guidance for child protection (DoH, 1999), in a depar-
ture to previous guidance, identifies a number of sources of stress which they understand
to have a link with child abuse, including social exclusion, domestic violence, parental
mental illness and drug/alcohol abuse. The challenge remains, however, as to how
these problems – as seen to be related to child abuse – can be addressed.

Notes to Chapter 5

1   A form of inappropriate and potentially injurious physical restraint.

2   These figures are calculated using a base figure including missing cases – excluding the missing
    information would increase the figures to 18 per cent and 48 per cent, as well as increasing the
    proportion unemployed to 82 per cent and 52 per cent for mothers and fathers respectively).

3   Figures included missing data

6 Teenage pregnancy

Francis McGlone

Introduction

This chapter examines existing data sources for a link between poverty, social deprivation and young motherhood. Before examining this research, the chapter looks at trends in teenage conception rates, their outcomes, the changing marital status of teenage mothers, geographical variations, and comparisons with other countries.

Teenage conceptions

The Office for National Statistics (ONS) – the only national source of information on conceptions, abortions and maternities – defines conceptions as pregnancies that result in live births, still births or legal terminations. Based on this definition, ONS figures show that there were 95,500 conceptions to women under 20 in England and Wales in 1997. The figures also show that teenage conception rates (per 1,000 girls aged 15–19) fell sharply in the 1970s, although they have remained relatively unchanged since the early 1980s (Table 6.1).

For girls under 16 there has been very little change in conception rates since the early 1970s, with approximately eight girls in every 1,000 becoming pregnant before their 16th birthday. However, the number of girls under 16 becoming pregnant rose slightly for the third year running in 1996, before falling back again in 1997 to 8,300.

One possible reason for the rise in teenage conception rates in 1996 was the media attention given to the Committee on Safety of Medicine's warning in 1995 that seven brands of contraceptive pill carried a higher risk of thrombosis than other pills. ONS has investigated this hypothesis and shown that conception rates rose in the December 1995, March and June 1996 quarters compared with earlier years. Concern over the pill is more likely to have affected younger women than older women as its usage is much more common among younger women (Ruddock *et al.*, 1998).

Proportion ending in abortion

The proportion of teenage conceptions terminated by abortion has increased since the introduction of the 1967 Abortion Act in April 1968, but since the mid-1970s there have been only small fluctuations in this proportion. In 1997, 37 per cent of all teenage conceptions ended in abortion compared with 52 per cent of conceptions to girls under 16 (Table 6.2).

Table 6.1 **Teenage conceptions and numbers. 1971–1997, England and Wales**

Year	Rates (conceptions) (thousands in age group)		Numbers per thousand	
	Under 16	Under 20	Under 16[1]	Under 20[2]
1971	8.8	132.7	8.7	81.3
1981	8.6	115.2	7.2	57.1
1991	7.8	103.3	9.3	65.1
1997	8.3	95.5	8.9	62.3

1 Rates per 1.000 women aged 13–15
2 Rates per 1,000 women aged 15–19

Source: ONS Birth Statistics series FM1 and *Population Trends,* Spring 1999.

Table 6.2 **Proportion of conceptions to teenagers terminated by abortion. 1971–1997, England and Wales**

Year	Under 16	16	17	18	19	Under 20
	%	%	%	%	%	%
1971	36	26	22	24	26	26
1975	52	40	33	33	37	38
1980	54	45	38	37	37	40
1985	56	44	35	30	26	34
1990	51	42	37	34	32	37
1995	50	39	36	33	30	35
1996	52	41	37	34	32	37
1997	52	42	38	34	33	37

Source: ONS Birth statistics series FMI and *Population Trends,* Spring 1999.

Live births and marital status

In England and Wales in 1997, there were 46,316 live births to women under 20, including 1,600 to girls under 16. Nearly nine out of ten (89 per cent) of these births were outside marriage (Table 6.3).

The marital status of teenage mothers has changed dramatically since the early 1980s. In 1981, 55 per cent of live births to teenagers took place inside marriage, com-

Table 6.3 **Live births to women under 20. 1997, England and Wales**

Age	Total	Births within marriage	Births outside marriage
11	1	-	1
12	3	-	3
13	26	1	25
14	258	1	257
15	1,312	7	1,305
Under 16	*1,600*	*9*	*1,591*
16	4,493	121	4,372
17	9,782	581	9,201
18	14,004	1,532	12,472
19	16,437	2,984	13,453
Under 20	*46,316*	*5,227*	*41,089*

Source: ONS Birth statistics series FM1 .

pared with 12 per cent in 1996. Over the same period there has been a corresponding rise in the number of live births outside marriage registered by both parents, possibly reflecting the increasing popularity of cohabitation since the 1980s (Botting *et al.*, 1998).

Conceptions to teenagers are unlikely to lead to marriage in the 1990s. In 1971, 45 per cent of conceptions to teenagers led to so-called 'shot-gun' marriages but by 1996 this had fallen to just 4 per cent (Burghes and Brown, 1995).

The number of births outside marriage to teenage mothers who registered the birth alone also remained fairly constant through the 1980s and actually fell between 1990 and 1995, before rising again slightly in 1996 (Botting *et al.*, 1998).

Geographical differences

Teenage conception rates and live birth rates vary considerably across England and Wales, with rates tending to be higher in the north of England and lower in the south. The same pattern is seen for girls under 16. The lowest conception rates for girls under 16 in 1994–96 were in East Anglia, the Oxford area and the South West. The highest rates were in the north and Yorkshire region. The geographical variation is due, in part, to different socio-economic characteristics of different parts of the country. Analysis by ONS shows that local authority areas described as 'ports and authorities', 'mixed economies', 'manufacturing', 'coal fields' and 'inner London' have above-average teenage birth-rates (Botting *et al.*, 1998). The National Survey of Sexual Attitudes and Lifestyles (NSSAL) similarly found the prevalence of teenage births to be higher in mining and industrial areas and lower in areas classified as growing and prosperous (Wellings *et al.*, 1996).

A number of studies have also demonstrated that teenage birth-rates are higher in deprived areas than in affluent areas. Using the Carstair index (a measure of deprivation based on a number of variables from the 1991 census), ONS has calculated that in the most deprived local authorities 12 per cent of all live births in 1994–96 were to teenagers, compared with 2 per cent in the least deprived. Similarly, Smith (1993) found pregnancy rates in girls under the age of 16 to be three times as high, and those under the age of 20 to be six times as high, in the most deprived areas, compared with the most affluent areas. Research by Garlick et al., (1993) found that district health authorities with high underprivileged areas scores were more likely to have high rates of teenage conceptions than those districts with low scores.

It is, of course, possible that higher teenage pregnancy rates in deprived areas are no more than a reflection of poorer access to health care services. However, there is no evidence that more affluent areas are better served by birth control and young people's services. Analysis of NSSAL by Wellings and her colleagues found that, although area and social class were clearly linked, the area effect was stronger and independent of social class. Women in manual jobs in the sample were no more likely to have had a teenage birth than those in non-manual ones, after controlling for area of residence (Wellings et al., 1996).

A number of studies have suggested that there is a causal link between the growth in lone parenthood and the growth of unemployment in certain areas. Knowsley on Merseyside was estimated to have a 'real' male unemployment rate of 36.4 per cent in 1997, and 39 per cent of its families were headed by lone parents in 1991, while the figures for Glasgow were 35.3 per cent and 36.4 per cent, respectively. At the other extreme in Kincardine and Deeside (a prosperous part of Aberdeen) the figures were only 6.0 per cent and 8.5 per cent (Webster, 1999). However, other research suggests that the association is due more to coincidence than any causal effect (Rowlingson and McKay, 1998). Also, the effect seems to be less among teenage parents than lone parents in general.[1]

International comparisons

As Table 6.4 shows, the UK has the highest rate of teenage births in Western Europe – twice that in Germany, three times that in France and six times that in the Netherlands – and is exceeded only by Canada, New Zealand and the United States (SEU, 1999). Teenage birth-rate levels in the UK are more similar to Eastern European countries than Western European countries (Table 6.5). During the last 20 years, unlike the UK, most other countries of Northern and Southern Europe have seen a significant fall in teenage birth-rates, particularly in Holland and Scandinavia (Clarke, 1999).

Reasons for the UK's high teenage fertility rates

ONS researchers have argued that the UK's higher teenage pregnancy rates cannot be explained by differences in sexual activity or greater recourse to abortion, but instead may be due to the effectiveness with which teenagers use contraception (Botting et al., 1998). However, others have suggested that poorer educational and job prospects may

Table 6.4 **International comparison of teenage fertility**

Country (ranked by 1990, or latest year)	Live birth rate per 1,000 women aged 15–19			
	1970	1980	*1990	**1995
USA	68.2	53.0	53.6	60
England and Wales	49.6	30.4	33.3	(1997) 30
Scotland	47.6	32.0	31.9	(1997) 31
Northern Ireland	42.9***	29.2	29.3	(1997) 29
Portugal	29.8	41.0	24.1	21
Greece	36.9	52.6	21.8	14
Austria	58.2	34.5	21.3	18
Norway	43.7	25.2	17.1	14
Republic of Ireland	16.3	23.0	16.2	15
Sweden	34.0	15.8	14.1	9
Spain	13.8	25.3	13.4	(1994) 9
Finland	32.2	18.9	12.4	10
West Germany	35.8	15.2	11.6	(1994) 10
Italy	27.1	20.6	9.8	(1993) 8
Belgium	23.2	14.9	9.3	(1991) 12
Denmark	32.4	16.8	9.1	(1994) 9
France	27.0	17.8	8.8	(1993) 8
Netherlands	17.0	6.8	6.4	4
Switzerland	16.0	7.2	4.6	4

*   1990 or nearest available year
**   Figures rounded
*** 1971

Source: Clarke, 1999.

Table 6.5 **International comparison of teenage fertility: selected Eastern European countries**

Country ranked by 1995	Live birth rate per 1,000 women aged 15–19			
	1970	1980	1988	*1995
Bulgaria	71.5	81	73.9	52
Romania	66.0	73	60.0	42
Hungary	50.5	69	41.2	31
Poland	30.0	46	31.6	22

* Figures rounded

Source: Clarke, 1999.

explain the difference. For example, Plotnick (1993, cited in Selman, 1996) contends that: 'policies that improve teenagers' education and earnings appear to contribute indirectly to reducing teenage pregnancy and childbearing … because better economic prospects lead teenagers to believe that they have something to lose by becoming parents'.

Similarly, Campbell (1993, also cited in Selman, 1996) argues that teenage motherhood is a rational economic choice propelled by economic crisis and that teenage pregnancy is most likely to be reduced by creating employment. Certainly, UK and US studies suggest that material disadvantage is associated with both early sexual activity and pregnancy (Wellings *et al.*, 1996). It has also been suggested that, for the most disadvantaged young women, motherhood may offer both a sense of purpose to life and a route to adulthood (FPSC, 1999).

Another possible reason may be the level of income inequality in a country. A study carried out in the 1980s found inequitable income distribution to be positively related to higher rates of teenage pregnancy in the US, New Zealand and Canada. In the 1990s, the United States and New Zealand had both the highest rates of teenage pregnancy and the largest gaps between rich and poor as measured by the proportions of national gross income received by the poorest and richest 20 per cent of households (HEA, 1999).

The Social Exclusion Unit's report on teenage pregnancy (SEU, 1999) identifies three reasons for Britain's higher teenage birth-rates:

* **low expectations** – more young people in the UK have no prospect of getting a job
* **ignorance** – young people lack knowledge about contraception
* **mixed messages** – young people are bombarded by the adult world with sexually-explicit messages and an implicit message that sexual activity is the norm, but another part of the adult world, including many parents and most public institutions, is at best embarrassed and at worst silent about sex.

The Unit's report also points out that there is some association between countries with low levels of teenage parenthood and benefit systems that require lone parents to be available for work before their children have reached their teens. For example, the Netherlands requires the mother to be available when her youngest child is five; in the UK it is 16.

Nevertheless, there is no evidence that teenage mothers deliberately get pregnant to get housing or additional social security benefits. A recent study by the Policy Studies Institute (PSI) found that teenage mothers knew little or nothing about housing policy, and most of what they knew was usually wrong. Moreover, the majority of the young mothers had not planned to get pregnant (Allen and Dowling, 1998).

Social factors associated with becoming a teenage mother

Longitudinal research has identified certain social factors associated with becoming a teenage mother. For example, the National Survey of Health and Development (a longitudinal study of children born in 1946) showed that teenage mothers were more likely to come from a lower socio-economic background, to have more siblings than their peers, and to have parents who showed little interest in their education (Kiernan, 1980).

Hobcraft (1998), using data from the National Child Development Study (NCDS) – a longitudinal survey of children born in 1958 – found that women who were in care or fostered were nearly two and a half times more likely than those brought up by both their natural parents to become teenage mothers.

However, the most detailed and comprehensive study of factors associated with becoming a young parent is by Kiernan (1995). She used data from the NCDS to investigate the social, economic and educational backgrounds of the women and men who became parents at an early age – women who had a child before their 20th birthday and men who became fathers before their 22nd birthday. Her analysis showed that, compared to other young people, young parents were:

- **More likely to have had mothers who were teenagers themselves when they first gave birth.** One in four young mothers and one in five young fathers had teenage mothers, compared with one in eight women and men who became parents at a later stage.
- **More likely to have parents whose socio-economic status was low.** Over seven out of ten of the young parents had parents from the lowest socio-economic status as compared with around one in two of their contemporaries who became parents at a later age.
- **More likely to come from families who had experienced financial hardship.** Teenage mothers were nearly five times more likely, and young fathers nearly three times more likely, to come from families that reported financial problems when they were aged 7 and 16, than children whose parents reported no such problems.
- **Less likely to have performed well in school.** Young parents were twice as likely to have registered lower scores in reading and mathematical tests when they were 7 and 16. Six out of ten teenage mothers also had no qualifications by their early twenties, compared with one in four women who became mothers after their teenage years.
- **More likely to have experienced emotional difficulties while growing up.** Thirty-eight per cent of girls and 19 per cent of boys who were assessed as having serious behaviour problems at both 7 and 16 went on to become parents, compared with 7 per cent of girls and 6 per cent of boys who had few observable behaviour problems on both occasions.

Because many of these factors were inter-related, Kiernan included a logistical regression analysis to assess their relative importance. This showed that amongst the women all the background factors, with the exception of social class, continued to have a significant influence on the probability of becoming a young parent. However, this was not the case for young men.

Net of the other factors, teenage mothers were more likely to have had a mother who had been a teenage mother herself. Living in a family that had experienced financial difficulties when the child was age 7 or 16 increased the odds relative to those who had not experienced financial difficulties at those ages. The odds were similar for these two groups, but were even higher if financial problems were experienced at both ages. Forty-three per cent of this group become young mothers, compared with 25 per cent of those who had experienced financial problems on one or other occasion, and only 9 per cent of those who reported no financial difficulties on either occasion.

Similarly for fathers: 25 per cent of the group with financial problems on both occasions become young fathers, compared with 13–15 per cent of those who had the problem at one age, and 8 per cent who had no reported financial problems.

Women with a high score on the emotional index[2] at age 16, and more so with high scores at both ages 7 and 16, similarly had greater odds of becoming a teenage mother, whilst the odds for those with high scores at age seven only were not significantly different from those with low scores at both ages.

Young fathers were not significantly more likely to have had a mother who herself was a teenage mother but, unlike women, social class in childhood was associated with a greater propensity among men to become young fathers. Financial adversity in early childhood increased the chances of becoming a young father whilst financial adversity in adolescence did not. After the introduction of controls, emotional factors were not significantly related to becoming a father at an early age.

Both men and women who had at the age of 16 expressed a preference for starting a family at a young age also had increased odds of becoming a young parent. But the most powerful single influence over the probability of becoming a parent at a young age for both sexes was educational attainment, with the connection with poor school performance stronger at age 16 than at age 7.

From a simplified logistic analysis, Kiernan further estimated the relative probabilities of becoming a teenage mother for girls with differing backgrounds. At one extreme were women whose educational scores were low at age 16, whose families had experienced financial adversity when they were aged 7 or 16, who had emotional and behavioural problems at either age, whose mothers had become a teenage mother, and who had expressed a preference for having a child at a relatively young age. Of this group, 56 per cent became teenage mothers. This compared with a 3 per cent chance for those with none of them.

New analysis of the NCDS by Hobcraft and Kiernan (1999) has found that women who experienced poverty during childhood are much more likely to become a teenage mother than those who did not. For example, 31 per cent of women who were assessed in the NCDS as 'clearly poor' became teenage mothers, compared with 8 per cent who were assessed as 'not poor'.

Confirmatory evidence

A problem with findings from the NCDS is that they are for a group who were in their late teens in the 1970s and the demography of the country is very different two and three decades later (Botting et al., 1998). Thus, it may not be possible to draw any firm conclusions about the present generation of teenagers from the 1958 cohort analysis.

Nevertheless, the longitudinal research findings have been confirmed by more recent research. The ONS Longitudinal Survey (a follow-up study of one per cent of the population enumerated at the 1971 census and followed up for 25 years) found that girls living in local authority rented accommodation were more than three times more likely to become teenage mothers than those living in owner-occupied accommodation, and almost ten times more likely to become teenage mothers if their family was in social class V compared with social class I. The girls were also at greater risk of becoming teenage mothers if their fathers were absent from the household, or if they had three or more siblings (Botting *et al.*, 1998).

Further confirmatory evidence comes from NSSAL – a random survey of nearly 19,000 men and women aged 16 to 59 completed in 1990 and 1991. This showed that teenage births were more common among men and women who had lived with neither or only one of their natural parents, and among those who grew up in families where discussion of sex was difficult or did not take place. Women with no educational qualifications were almost twice as likely to report having a child in their teens as those who achieved O level or CSE examinations, four times as likely as those who achieved A level or other higher educational qualifications, and more than twenty times as likely to do so as female university graduates. The effect was less marked for men but graduate men were more than eight times as likely to remain childless until after the age of twenty compared with those with no qualifications.

Similarly with abortion, though here the educational effect was less strong and was reversed – the higher the educational level the more likely that a young women will terminate a pregnancy. However, as with other cross-sectional data, it was not possible to establish the direction of influence, ie. whether those with poor educational qualifications seek in early motherhood a means of fulfilment or whether teenage motherhood impedes achievement through its disruptive effect on education or both. Nevertheless, research carried out for the Social Exclusion Unit has shown a strong link between teenage parenthood and not being in education, training or work, for 16- and 17-year-old women (SEU, 1999).

Other key factors in understanding the relationship between early sexual activity, contraceptive use and teenage fertility picked up by the NSSAL researchers were adequacy of information about sexual matters and the degree to which first intercourse was planned. Women whose first intercourse was unplanned were more than twice as likely to have a child in their teens, after controlling for current age, educational level and age at first intercourse. The researchers believe that they have picked up here a distinction between self-determination and a more fatalistic and passive approach to life, ie. what they describe as: 'a tendency to plan things in life versus simply letting them happen'. (Wellings *et al.*, 1996) Both of these perspectives, they argue, are generally linked with both class position and personality type.

Recent research has also affirmed that girls who have been in care or fostered are at higher risk of teenage pregnancy. In one study, one in four young women in care was either pregnant or already a mother by the time she left to set up home on her own (Corlyon and McGuire, 1999). A project for young parents run by the charity Barnardos in Skelmersdale, reported that 40 per cent had been in care, 70 per cent had experienced family breakdown, and 40 per cent were the children of teenage mothers. However, all had grown up in poverty, had done badly at school, and had a history of not attending school (SEU, 1999)

Conclusion

Despite government and public concern about teenage pregnancies, the rate of conception to girls under ten has remained fairly steady since the early 1980s. Also, the number of girls under 16 becoming pregnant each year is relatively small – approximately eight girls in every 1,000. Nevertheless, the UK has the worst record on teenage pregnancies in Western Europe.

The evidence from a wide range of studies suggests that there is a clear association between teenage pregnancy and social and economic disadvantage. Young mothers and fathers are more likely to come from financially disadvantaged families and to have lower educational attainment. Young mothers are also more likely to live in deprived areas, have a mother who was a teenage mother herself, and to have exhibited higher level of emotional problems, particularly in adolescence. Other identified risk factors for young women are: living in local authority accommodation, coming from a low socio-economic class, living with only one or neither natural parent, growing up in a home where discussion about sex is difficult, and, living in a deprived area. But, according to a number of studies, the most important factor is poor performance at school.

Clearly, many of these factors are linked and are transmitted across the generations, and across the life-course. However, they are only associations, if in some cases very strong associations, and cannot show causality, despite the plausibility of the links. Moreover – and the question needs explanation – why, compared with the 1970s, have teenage birth-rates fallen or at least remained stable, yet on a number of indices poverty and social deprivation in the UK have increased? Unfortunately, no research has, to date, attempted to answer this question.

Notes to Chapter 6

1   Personal communication with David Webster.

2   Emotional indicators on the NCDS include independent ratings of behavioural problems by parents and by teachers at the ages of 7 and 16, and interviews and information from health visitors at age seven (Kiernan, 1995).

7 The environment

Deborah Quilgars

Introduction

This chapter explores the relationship between poor or bad environments and the poverty of children through a critical review of the research evidence. There is an argument to be had about whether poor housing conditions and environmental squalor are outcomes of child poverty – in the sense that death or ill health are. Housing is, of course, an input, a social policy, a service. However, housing and the environment are arguably an outcome of child poverty, and one which has a major influence on children's daily experience.

A number of related areas of 'environment' are considered in this chapter. Firstly, poor housing, arguably the most direct form of poor environment, is examined. The most extreme form of bad housing, homelessness, is considered in Chapter 8; here the extent to which poor physical housing conditions and overcrowding are related to childhood poverty is evaluated. The focus is then broadened to consider the 'problem' of disadvantaged neighbourhoods or areas, encompassing issues of poor housing alongside other aspects of the socio-economic environment. Research evidence shows a complex relationship between housing tenure, particularly social housing, and poor environment, and this is briefly examined. Finally, the effects of poor physical environment, over and above housing conditions, particularly air pollution, are considered. Environmental factors which are linked to high child accident rates are looked at separately in Chapter 4.

This chapter seeks to answer four questions:
- How closely are poverty and environment related: are poor children more likely to live in bad environments?
- Has the likelihood of children living in poor environments changed over time?
- What are the effects on children of living in poor environments?
- How robust and reliable is the research and statistical evidence on the links between child poverty and poor environment?

Poor housing conditions

Housing conditions in the 1990s in the UK

National surveys of housing conditions are conducted on a regular basis, typically every five years, in England, Scotland, Wales and Northern Ireland providing information on the level of disrepair and unfitness of properties in all tenures.

Whilst surveys are undertaken in each UK country, unfortunately, different survey methods and measures of housing condition are used and it is therefore not possible to compare the survey findings across countries easily: 'The measurement of poor housing conditions is a difficult and complex task but the variety of definitions used in national surveys, differences in the way surveyors are briefed, and variations in the way in which repair costs are estimated make comparisons between countries in the UK impossible' (Leather and Morrison, 1997).

For this reason, the Joseph Rowntree Foundation recently funded a comprehensive review of the *State of UK Housing* (Leather and Morrison, 1997), using the 1991 English, Scottish and Northern Ireland House Condition Surveys and the 1993 Welsh House Conditions Survey.

In 1991, about 1 in 14 dwellings in the UK were either unfit for human habitation or below the Scottish tolerable housing standard, rising to 1 in 8 dwellings in Wales. Housing in disrepair was more widespread, with 1 in 5 dwellings in England and Wales needing urgent repairs of over £1,000 and £1,500 respectively, 1 in 10 Scottish houses requiring £3,000 of repairs, and 1 in 4 dwellings in Northern Ireland needing repairs of over £5,000. The private-rented sector had the highest level of disrepair and unfit dwellings in all countries. There were fewer differences between the other tenures, for example 6.9 per cent of local authority stock was unfit in England in 1991 compared with 5.5 per cent of owner-occupied dwellings (and 15.1 per cent of local authority properties required urgent repairs of over £1,000 compared with 17.3 per cent of owner-occupied dwellings). These comparisons however mask great variations within the owner-occupied sector.

The Leather and Morrison (1997) study also provided data on the extent of disrepair and unfit dwellings by household income and household type. Unsurprisingly, households on low incomes were much more likely to live in poor housing, with three quarters or more of households living in housing in serious disrepair or unfit housing having incomes of less than £12,000 per annum in 1991. The available data on household composition presented in the study was difficult to analyse and inconsistent: there were indications that lone parents in Scotland and Wales, although not in England and Northern Ireland, and large families in England and Wales, were more likely to be living in unfit dwellings. The data on serious repair showed no discernable trends. Households from minority ethnic backgrounds in Scotland and England were over twice as likely to live in unfit dwellings (no data collected for Wales and Northern Ireland) and one and a half times more likely to be living in dwellings with urgent repair costs.

Information in the English House Condition Survey 1996 (DETR, 1998) showed a clearer pattern for households living in houses in poor condition. Here, 11 per cent of lone parents (compared with 6.7 per cent of all households) were living in unfit dwellings, and 10 per cent of lone parents, compared with 6.1 per cent of all households, were living in dwellings in need of substantial repair. The English House Condition Survey 1996 also provided a useful measure of 'poor housing', using a composite measure of 'poor housing' for houses which were either unfit, in substantial disrepair or requiring essential modernisation. Using this measure, 14.2 per cent of households were living in 'poor housing'. Lone parents were clearly more likely to be living in poor housing (18 per cent) whereas a lower proportion (10.7 per cent) of couples with children were living in poor housing. Whilst households with infants (less than five years old) were no more likely to be living in poor housing (13 per cent), strikingly, about one-fifth of households where the head of household was unemployed, in part-time employment or inactive lived in poor housing, with a quarter of unemployed lone parents with infants living in poor housing, compared with only 10 per cent of lone parents employed full-time. Younger households (29.1 per cent), and ethnic minorities (26.3 per cent) were also more likely to be in poor housing. A third (31.3 per cent) of private sector tenants were living in poor housing compared with 16.6 per cent of local authority tenants, 11.7 per cent of owner occupiers and only 7.6 per cent of Registered Social Landlord tenants.

A study of housing deprivation (Dale *et al.*, 1996) using the Office for National Statistics (ONS) Longitudinal Study found, perhaps unsurprisingly, that in 1991 households with children were more likely to be overcrowded than households without children. Whilst 6 per cent of couples with children were overcrowded (compared with 4 per cent of all households), 8 per cent of lone parents, 12 per cent of couples with children with other family members, and 35 per cent of households with two or more families, were overcrowded. An extremely high incidence of overcrowding was recorded for people from ethnic minorities: 57 per cent of Bangladeshi and 46 per cent of Pakistani households were overcrowded. A strong social class relationship was also found, with households in social class V being four times as likely to be overcrowded as those in class I. Households in social housing were over three times as likely to be overcrowded as owner occupiers.

Lone parents seemed to fare consistently badly on all elements of housing deprivation in the ONS study (Dale *et al.*, 1996). For example, whilst only 12 per cent of couples with children, and 17 per cent of all households did not have central heating in 1991, the figure for lone parents was 22 per cent. On an index of housing conditions, using six measures (self-contained, bath, WC, central heating, housing density, tenure), households with lone parents or two or more families had the lowest mean scores, that is the worst housing conditions (Dale *et al.*, 1996).

Improvements in housing conditions over time

Generally, all surveys of housing conditions have shown a consistent trend for improvements over time. However, the level of improvements differ depending on which measure of house condition is examined (Leather and Morrison, 1997). For example, the provision of facilities and services to properties (central heating, double-glazing, security etc.) continued to increase between 1991 and 1996 in England (DETR, 1998) whereas the overall level of disrepair and number of unfit dwellings changed little. Nonetheless, on the DETR measure of 'poor housing' a drop from 18.2 per cent to 14.2 per cent living in poor housing was evidenced from 1991 to 1996, being accounted for by modernisation of dwellings.

The ONS Longitudinal Study using 1971, 1981 and 1991 census data (Dale *et al.*, 1996) examined changes in levels of housing deprivation over time. Housing deprivation was defined as overcrowding (less than one room per person), lacking amenities (sharing or lacking inside WC or bath/shower) and/or sharing accommodation. By these measures, housing deprivation had clearly reduced over the period 1971 to 1991 (see Table 7.1). The 1996 English House Condition Survey showed little change in the general level of overcrowding between 1991 and 1996 (DETR, 1998).

Those living in poor housing has also changed in recent years. In 1996, in England, lone parents and minority ethnic households, were proportionately more likely to be living in poor housing than in 1991, whereas those living on their own were less likely (DETR, 1998). The ONS study (Dale *et al.*, 1996) also found that, whilst a lower proportion of lone parents were overcrowded in 1991 than 1971 (15 per cent compared with 8 per cent), lone parents were twice as likely to be overcrowded when compared with *other* households in 1991 (1.5 times as likely to be overcrowded in 1971). Data showed little improvement in overcrowding rates for people from minority ethnic groups over the same period, despite significant improvements for *all* households.

Table 7.1 **Housing deprivation for residents in England and Wales**

	1971	1981	1991
No deprivation	74.9	87.7	94.4
Overcrowding only	9.3	6.6	4.2
Shared accommodation only	0.7	1.8	0.5
Not sole bath/ WC	9.7	2.2	0.4
> 1 indicator	4.9	1.4	0.4

Note: in 1981 shared accommodation was defined as shared access from the street. In 1971 and 1991 it is defined as self-contained accommodation (ie. with the household's accommodation behind its own front door)

Source: Dale *et al.* (1996), Table 9.4.

The effects of living in poor housing

As the recent Inquiry into Inequalities in Health stated, 'poor quality housing is associated with poor health' (Acheson, 1998). Numerous studies over the last two decades have asserted the link between poor housing and poor health (Furley, 1989; Smith, 1989; Ineichen, 1993; Burridge and Ormandy, 1993; Best, 1995; Marsh *et al.*, 1999). However, although there has been a considerable number of studies on health and housing generally there remains very little robust research on the causal relationship between poor housing and health. Studies on children's health have tended to concentrate on certain types of health problems more than others.

Health effects of damp and mouldy housing

The most prominent studies on the effects of poor housing on children's health were carried out in the late 1980s and were concerned with the link between damp and mouldy housing and asthma and other respiratory problems. A cross-sectional study of a random sample of 597 households with 1,169 children in social housing in Glasgow, Edinburgh and London, undertaken by Platt and colleagues (1989) in the late 1980s, showed that children had a greater prevalence of respiratory symptoms, fever and headaches when houses were assessed by a surveyor as damp and / or with mould growth. The greater the severity of the dampness, the worse the health of the children. Crucially, the researchers found that this correlation persisted after controlling for unemployment, household income, overcrowding and smoking in the household. An earlier, but much smaller study (101 households) in Edinburgh by the same team of researchers also found a relationship between diarrhoea and vomiting in children and dampness (Martin *et al.*, 1987). A second Edinburgh study by Strachan (1988) used a larger random sample of 873 primary school-children to examine the links between damp housing and health in all tenures. The study found that children living in damp housing were three times as likely to have experienced wheezing in the past year, even after controlling for housing tenure, overcrowding, smoking and gas cooking. The one weakness of this study, however, was that it relied on the self-reporting of parents and the author pointed out that the awareness of damp / mould might also have been a factor in parental reporting of health problems.

An ongoing project looking at health gains in housing is being carried out by Ambrose and colleagues at the University of Sussex. Preliminary data indicates that households in damp housing had twice as many illness days as those living in high quality social housing (Mahoney, 1997).

The effect of overcrowding

Associations between overcrowding and poor health have also been observed. A study in the 1970s using 1971 census data and child mortality rates (Brennan and Lancashire, 1978) found a relationship between overcrowding, lack of basic amenities, social housing and male unemployment and increased mortality rates for children, particularly in those under the age of five. Most studies, however, rely on common-sense observation; for example, that children are more likely to catch infectious diseases in overcrowded circumstances, an assumption which underpinned much public health reform in earlier decades (Ineichen, 1993).

Poor housing and the risk of accidents in the home

Home-related accidents are the most common cause of death in children under the age of one, with almost half of all accidents associated with design features of housing (DTI data cited in Best, 1995). The Child Accident Prevention Trust estimates that poor housing design is responsible for a quarter of a million home accidents a year (cited in Beishon, 1994). The risk of a fire in the home is greatest for those in poorest council housing and temporary accommodation (Home Office, 1994).

Poor housing and educational attainment

Poor health is undoubtedly the most obvious effect of poor housing on children. However a small number of studies have also pointed out a range of other effects on children; for example, the impact of living in poor housing on educational attainment. A recent poll by MORI of over 4,000 secondary schoolchildren for the National Housing Feder-ation found that one in three children cited housing-related problems, including having to share a room, having nowhere to do homework, cold and damp housing and noisy neighbours, as affecting their ability to study (*Inside Housing*, 18 September 1998).

Neighbourhoods and area disadvantage

> Where you live, as well as the kind of home you live in, may affect your health.
> (*Ineichen, 1993*)

The importance of area regeneration and neighbourhood renewal has been recognised within government policy for decades, but most recently with the announcement of the New Deal for Deprived Communities (Social Exclusion Unit, 1998b). However, defin-ing deprived and poor neighbourhoods has always been, and remains, problematic (Burrows and Rhodes, 1998). Most research has concentrated on identifying 'disadvan-taged' areas. This type of area definition is essentially problematic when attempting to look at the relationship between child poverty and poor environments, as almost all definitions of disadvantaged areas include measures of poverty in their construction. Any argument showing a correlation between disadvantaged areas (as a proxy for poor environment) and child poverty is therefore likely to overstate the relationship. In ad-dition, it has been pointed out that much research on disadvantaged areas classifies areas on the basis of the characteristics of those people who live there, often using cen-sus data, rather than on the characteristics of the area itself: in short they focus on people rather than places (Macintyre *et al.*, 1993). Such commentators argue that more research should be focused directly on the influence of the socio-environmental or cultural fea-tures of areas, particularly when examining the relationship between area and health.

The best, and most recent, study which centrally concerns itself with poor environ-ment is *Unpopular places? Area disadvantage and the geography of misery in England* (Burrows and Rhodes, 1998). The study used the 1994/5 Survey of English Housing (SEH) and specially commissioned data from the 1991 census to investigate the socio-economic characteristics of residents with the highest levels of dissatisfaction with their area. One of the main strengths of the study was that it allowed residents' subjective perception of their environment to be considered (issues considered included crime, poor leisure facilities, vandalism and litter). Households living in all tenures expressed some dissat-isfaction with their neighbourhood, but the highest level of dissatisfaction was in social housing (18 per cent, compared with 7 per cent of owner-occupied householders and 10 per cent of those living in the private-rented sector). Considering household compo-sition, the study found that lone-parent families were significantly more likely to be dissatisfied with the area than all other types of household, with over one-fifth (22 per cent) being dissatisfied compared with 9 per cent of couples with dependent children. A clear social class gradient of levels of dissatisfaction was observed. When controlling for all other variables in the model, households living in the social-rented sector were the only households significantly more likely to be dissatisfied with their area, a rela-tionship with class held (although slightly modified), and lone parents were the only type of household which had significantly higher levels of dissatisfaction. Burrows and Rhodes also found regional variations in area dissatisfaction with households in the North East, North West, Yorkshire and Humberside and London all significantly more likely to be dissatisfied with their area. Subsequent analysis of the 1995/6 SEH (Coles *et al.*, 1998) also showed that children aged between 10 and 15 in social housing were more than twice as likely (24 per cent to 11 per cent) to live in a home where the household was dissatisfied with the area compared with owner-occupiers.

The Burrows and Rhodes (1998) study is important as other work has shown that differences in area perceptions are associated with differences in self-reported health: in short those most dissatisfied with their living environment also report greater health problems. A study of four contrasting areas of Glasgow concluded that this correlation could not be fully explained by the differing social class composition of the neighbourhood, that is both social class and perceptions of area independently contributed to health differences between neighbourhoods (Sooman and Macintyre, 1995). Whilst this study was focused on the perceptions and health of adults, it is likely that such an association would hold for younger age groups, although further research is clearly required to confirm this.

The English House Condition Survey (DETR, 1998) also provides a useful measure of 'poor living conditions' concentrating on localities rather than solely on tenure or physical condition of the accommodation. A surveyor was used to assess areas with one or more of the following problems:
- over 10 per cent of dwellings seriously defective;
- serious problems with any of: vacant sites or derelict buildings; vacant or boarded up buildings; litter, rubbish or dumping; vandalism; graffitti or scruffy buildings, gardens or landscaping; neglected buildings;
- very poor visual quality of local area.

The 1996 Survey reported that 7 per cent of all households were living in poor conditions. Whilst 7 per cent of all couples with children were experiencing poor living conditions, twice as many lone parents were (13 per cent) and 10 per cent of households with infants. As with poor physical housing conditions, a much higher proportion (19 per cent) of minority ethnic households, and unemployed households (18 per cent) had poor living conditions, according to this measure.

A number of recent studies have specifically explored the spatial distribution of lone-parent families. As has been seen above, lone parents are more likely to live in social housing, and it is also known that lone parents are more likely to live in London, major cities and depressed industrial, often northern, towns (Forrest and Gordon, 1993). Bradshaw, N. *et al.*, (1996), using 1991 census data for England and Wales, found that 86 per cent of the spatial variation of lone parents in 115 areas could be accounted for by three variables: the level of male unemployment, the proportion of Black members of the population and the proportion of those living in social housing. Interestingly, although bivariate analysis confirmed the strong association between lone parents and social housing, and documented an increase in the relationship since 1981, multi-variate analysis revealed that most of the spatial patterning was explained by levels of male unemployment and for female lone parents social housing disappeared as an explanatory variable within the model. Further research by Webster (1997) has confirmed the link between high levels of male unemployment and lone parents through analysis of the 1991 census of all 459 local authority areas in Britain.

Social housing and poor neighbourhoods

Recent policy documents (Social Exclusion Unit, 1998b) have recognised that poor neighbourhoods are not necessarily synonymous with social housing estates. Lee and Murie (1997), through a mapping exercise of tenure against the Breadline Britain index,[1] concluded that 'housing tenure is not an adequate guide to the deprived status of areas', particularly in cities with high proportions of ethnic minorities. Nonetheless, the important spatial concentration of poor children in social housing needs to be considered.

Analysis of the 1995/6 Survey of English Housing showed that 28 per cent of residents in social housing were under the age of 16, compared with only 21 per cent in owner-occupation and 18 per cent in the private-rented sector (PRS) (Coles et al., 1998). In addition, two recent studies recorded much higher proportions of households with children recently entering social housing: analysis of the Housing Corporation Annual CORE returns from registered social housing landlords shows that new allocations to households with children increased from 29 per cent to 41 per cent over the period from 1989/90 to 1996/7 (Pleace et al., 1998). Analysis of the 1993/4 Survey of English Housing also demonstrated that new households entering social housing are more likely to be economically excluded and to have dependent children; in contrast those leaving social housing tend to have higher incomes and fewer children (Burrows, 1997). Dale et al., (1996) have shown how this process of residualisation has increased the odds of households in social class V being in public housing from 19:1 in 1971 to 27:1 in 1991. The odds of lone parents being in social housing over this period also increased, from 1.75:1 to 3:1 compared to the reference group (elderly single); however couples with children were less likely to be in public housing. Economic disadvantage and social housing are highly correlated. For example, over half (53 per cent) of 10- to 15-year-olds in social housing lived in a household where no adult was employed (compared with 7 per cent in owner-occupation) (Coles et al., 1998). Over a third of children (36 per cent) lived in a lone-parent household (compared with less than 10 per cent in owner-occupation).

Analysis of the British Household Panel Survey (Coles et al., 1998) found that young women living in social housing were much more likely than their male peers and young women in owner-occupation to experience confidence problems. Nearly half (44 per cent) of young women in social housing strongly agreed with the statement: 'I am inclined to feel I am a failure' compared with 27 per cent of young women in owner-occupation (young men have similar levels of self-esteem across tenures).

Environment and air pollution

Motor vehicle emissions are the main cause of air pollution (Royal Commission on Environmental Pollution, 1997). The volume of traffic on roads and in cities has continued to increase throughout the past three decades. Whilst a significant proportion of traffic is goods' vehicles and buses, the vast majority, and growing proportion, of traffic is composed of private vehicles (Royal Commission on Environmental Pollution, 1997). Despite the widespread use of the car, access to private vehicles shows a class gradient, with those from lower socio-economic groups being less likely to own a car. For example, the 1991 census showed that those living in social housing were nearly four times less likely to have access to a car compared with owner-occupiers, with owner-occupiers being six times more likely to have access to two or more cars (OPCS, 1993). Women, people from minority ethnic groups, older people and children are disproportionately less likely to have access to private vehicle transport (Acheson, 1998). However, as the recent Independent Inquiry into Inequalities of Health reported, inner-city areas, most likely also to be characterised by indicators of disadvantage, are most likely to experience high levels of traffic in their neighbourhoods, and therefore higher levels of air and noise pollution (Davis, cited in Acheson, 1998; London Research Centre, 1997). Evidence, therefore, would strongly suggest that poorer communities experience more air pollution, despite the fact that they contribute less to the creation of that pollution. The relationship between traffic and childhood accidents is a complex one as demonstrated in Micklewright and Stewart (1998) and discussed separately in Chapter 4.

The effects of air pollution

The Department of Health Committee on the Medical Effects of Air Pollutants (COMEAP) recently presented evidence (1998) which estimated that air pollution in urban areas contributes to 8,100 deaths a year and is responsible for, or contributes to, 10,500 hospital admissions for respiratory disease a year.

The most studied possible effect of air pollution is asthma amongst children. The prevalence of asthma amongst children, and adults, has increased steeply in many developed countries, with a national study showing 13 per cent of children having been diagnosed at some time with asthma (Strachan *et al.*, 1994). Whilst the prevalence of asthma *per se* has been found to vary little by socio-economic group, severity of symptom *is* associated with socio-economic group (Strachan *et al.*, 1994). In considering the evidence, Burr (1995) notes that many European studies have found a link between the prevalence of asthma and air pollution in urban areas, but other studies have not found such an association although higher rates of other respiratory problems like coughing and phlegm have been found. Burr points out that 'the results seem to be strangely conflicting', commenting that such research is susceptible to 'ecological fallacy' where the wrong factors are attributed as a cause (Burr, 1995). Wilson (1998), reviewing the research, also concludes that more research is required to disentangle cause and effect before the association can be proved. Nonetheless, the evidence does seem to point to an association between air pollution and respiratory problems (Burr, 1995), and exacerbation of existing asthma (Wilson, 1998). Less research has been undertaken in the UK, although one study of children under the age of five in Birmingham found an association between hospital admission rates for asthma and living in an urban area with high traffic flow, particularly when living within 500 metres of a main road (Edwards *et al.*, 1994).

Pollution obviously derives from other sources as well as motor vehicles, most notably power stations and other industrial sources. Despite the obvious effects of smog on health in past decades, evidence of whether industrial activity affects local communities is difficult to assess. A study in East Lancashire, of children living within 9km of a cement works, found no significant increased prevalence of respiratory problems in children compared with those living 20km or further away (Ginns and Gatrell, 1996). In contrast, a study of 1,872 schoolchildren in Merseyside found an increased prevalence of respiratory symptoms in those living within 2km of docks unloading large quantities of coal, in comparison with other areas of Liverpool. A higher proportion of children were also living in social housing, had parents who were unemployed and smoking members of the household, but differences remained after controlling for these factors (see also the discussion of respiratory illness in Chapter 3).

Conclusions

This chapter set out to answer four main questions. The first question was: are poor children more likely to live in poor environments? National surveys demonstrate that households on low incomes and unemployed households are much more likely to live in poor housing than other groups. Most surveys also show that certain 'types' of households are more likely to live in poor housing, most strikingly lone parents and minority ethnic households. This may be explained, in large part, by the association between lone parenthood and (male) unemployment, and because minority ethnic households are more likely to live in the private-rented sector, which is characterised by the highest level of disrepair and unfit dwellings. Households with children, overall, are over-represented in social housing which is only slightly more likely to be characterised by poor standards of accommodation than the owner-occupied sector, but there is increasing evidence that social housing is associated with higher levels of dissatisfaction with area or neighbourhood ie. the wider environment. Lone parents in particular, again, are significantly more likely to be dissatisfied with their neighbourhood compared with other households. A number of studies, (although not consistently), also suggest that poor children are more likely to live in areas with higher levels of pollution, mainly from traffic but also from industrial activities. In addition, children are more likely to be living in overcrowded households; overcrowding also being associated with lower social class, social housing and minority ethnic households.

Has the likelihood of children living in poor environments changed over time? Overall, all households, including those with children, are more likely to be living in better-quality housing, and in less overcrowded conditions, in the 1990s compared with the 1970s. However, importantly, lone parents and minority ethnic groups are now more likely to live in worse housing relative to other groups than in the 1970s, that is they have benefited less from overall housing improvements in comparison with other households. No studies exist which have explored household satisfaction with neighbourhood or area over time. However, survey data clearly demonstrates the process of *residualisation* in housing, as social housing accommodates increasing proportions of people who are economically excluded, as well as higher proportions of households with children.

Lone parents have also become more spatially concentrated within social housing over time.

The links between poor housing and poor health are generally accepted, although there are difficulties in proving a causal relationship. The effects of poor housing on children's health was most successfully demonstrated through studies on asthma in the late 1980s, which noted a relationship between increased levels of asthma and poor housing, even when controlling for other factors such as income levels and smoking. Air pollution is also associated with severity of asthma amongst children, and in some studies, although not consistently, with other health problems. Higher rates of accidents amongst children have been linked with poor housing, and increasingly studies are investigating other effects of poor housing on children's lives, particularly low educational attainment. Studies also show that people dissatisfied with their neighbourhood or environment are more likely to report health problems, although the data is presently confined to adults. Analysis of the British Household Panel has shown that young women living in social housing are much more likely than their peers in owner-occupied properties to have low self-esteem (although the association does not hold for young men).

How robust and reliable is the research on the links between child poverty and poor environment? Regular house condition surveys are conducted in England, Northern Ireland, Scotland and Wales but different measurement criteria make comparisons difficult. In addition, most survey data is presented as straightforward cross-tabulation of variables. More elaborate regression analysis is required to tease out associations, much as has been done, albeit in only one study to date, for neighbourhood dissatisfaction. More sophisticated measures of household satisfaction with locality and environment also need to be developed, measures which can be used to gauge children's feelings about their environment as well as adults'. Further research is also required to attempt to understand better the association between poor health and poor housing and environment.

Notes to Chapter 7

1   The Breadline Britain Index is based on an opinion poll of a representative sample of the population. Interviewees were presented with a list of items and asked which they thought were necessities that everyone should be able to afford. Items that were chosen by at least 50 per cent of the interviewees were then classified as necessities. People who lacked three or more necessities were defined as poor (Roll, 1992).

8 Child homelessness

Deborah Quilgars

Introduction

This chapter presents the research and statistical evidence on the incidence of home-lessness amongst children and young people in Britain, and its effects. The chapter evaluates the available data sources on child homelessness in Britain, looking firstly at the legislative framework and considering both statutory and non-statutory homeless-ness. The chapter then reviews what is presently known about the impact of homelessness on children and young people.

Homelessness: the legislative framework in England, Scotland and Wales

Protection for dependent children

Legislation to protect certain households from homelessness was introduced in the Housing (Homeless Persons) Act 1977, later incorporated into Part III of the Housing Act 1985 in England and Wales and Part II of the Housing (Scotland) Act 1987. This legislation placed duties upon local authorities to provide permanent accommodation for homeless households (and those threatened with homelessness) if they were con-sidered to be in priority need, were unintentionally homeless and had a local connection with the authority. Households with dependent children represent one of the main pri-ority need categories, along with households containing a pregnant woman, 'vulnerable' persons and those homeless in an emergency situation (for example, due to a fire). Where local authorities were unable to provide permanent accommodation immediately, they had a duty to provide temporary accommodation to the household until such time as they could discharge their full duties.

New legislation came into force in England and Wales on 20 January 1998, in Part VII of the Housing Act 1996, replacing the duty of the local authority to provide perma-nent accommodation with a lesser duty of assisting a household to obtain suitable private rented accommodation (must be available for two years) or secure accommodation for the household for at least two years if no suitable private accommodation is available. The same priority need categories and associated regulations apply. The household is entitled to be placed on the housing register along with other housing applicants to be considered for a full tenancy. The Scottish legislation remains unchanged.

The position of single 16- and 17-year-olds

Single homeless young people aged 16 and 17 have never been automatically accepted under the homelessness legislation in Britain, despite the removal of Income Support (then Supplementary Benefit) for 16- and 17-year-olds in 1988. The one exception to this is in Scotland, where young people under the age of 21 who are *looked after* by a local authority (formerly 'in care') at school-leaving age or later are accepted as being in priority need. The 1991 Code of Guidance for England and Wales suggested that local authorities might accept young people 'at risk' but that 16- and 17-year-olds should not be accepted as being vulnerable on the basis of their age alone (Section 6.13, Department of the Environment, 1991). Some local authorities have used their discretionary powers to accept young people, whilst others have interpreted their duties quite narrowly. Recent research by Anderson and Morgan (1997) showed that over a half of local authorities usually or always awarded priority to 16- and 17-year-olds leaving care and to young people referred under the Children Act 1989, but fewer than a quarter accepted young people on the basis of their age alone. The Children Act 1989 gave social service departments the duty, working alongside housing authorities and other agencies, to provide accommodation for 'any child in need in their area who has reached the age of 16 and whose welfare that authority considers likely to be seriously prejudiced if they do not provide him with accommodation' (Section 20(3)). However, as with the homelessness legislation, the definition of 'in need' has been interpreted differently and many social services department have not interpreted homelessness alone as sufficient to trigger their responsibilities (McCluskey, 1993). Since the recent Social Exclusion Unit report on rough sleeping (SEU, 1998b) the Department of Environment, Transport and the Regions (DETR) have issued guidance to local authorities. The code of guidance makes it clear that those leaving care and homeless 16- and 17-year-olds without 'back-up support' should normally be accepted as 'vulnerable' under the homelessness legislation (DETR, 2000). This represents an important policy shift, and something that has been argued for by housing and children's organisations for over a decade.

Statutory homelessness: incidence and trends

Measuring statutory homelessness: problems and limitations

The main statistical sources on the incidence of homelessness are the returns submitted by local authorities to the DETR and the Welsh and Scottish Offices on authorities' activities under the homelessness legislation (the PIE return in England and Wales and the HL1 and 2 returns in Scotland). Chiefly, the returns collect information on applications and acceptances under the homelessness legislation, the use of temporary accommodation and main reason for loss of last settled home, and are published on a quarterly basis.

Whilst the homelessness returns represent the best available dataset on the incidence of family homelessness, and the only data which allows trends over time to be observed, there are a number of considerable limitations associated with the statistics, and a particular problem in estimating the extent of child homelessness.

First, a general point needs to be noted. The statistics necessarily only measure the incidence of 'official' homelessness. The number of households who are homeless but do not apply to the local authority and are not therefore considered under the legislation is not known. Reasons may include a lack of knowledge of the legislation, a correct or misplaced belief that they will not qualify for assistance, and/or a desire not to rely on State support. The statistics therefore are an under-estimate of the extent of homelessness, both of those populations who would qualify for assistance and for the larger number of people who fall outside the legislation. Non-statutory homelessness, including self-placement by homeless families in temporary accommodation, is examined below.

The main limitation of the English and Welsh datasets when considering child homelessness is the fact that local authorities record the number of *households*, but not individuals, accepted under the legislation. It is therefore only possible to give figures for the number of households with dependent children accepted under the legislation (to be precise the number accepted as being in priority need), but not how many children this represents. It is also not possible to say whether these children are part of a two-parent or lone-parent family. In addition, no information is collected on the age or gender of applicants, and whilst information has been collected on ethnicity since the mid-1990s, this is only for total acceptances. Finally, the number of young people accepted under the legislation has only been recorded since 1992; unfortunately the age of the young people concerned is not recorded. More detailed information can only be found in special research studies undertaken in the area, as examined below. However, these usually provide snapshots, allowing only limited comparisons of trends, and are rarely conducted on a national basis.

In contrast, the format of the Scottish statistical return was improved in 1990, and since then information has been collected on type of household, age and size of household. Whilst it is not possible to count precisely the number of children accepted under the legislation, as the size of household only counts persons present without identifying their relationship to the head of household or age, the Scottish statistics do allow a better estimate of the extent of homelessness amongst children to be generated. These statistics, however, are not available routinely, and require a special request to the Scottish Office.

The homelessness datasets are also inflexible when it comes to cross-referencing between sections. For example, whilst information is collected on the *number* of households who have been placed into temporary accommodation by the local authority, this cannot be analysed by *type* of household. It is not possible, therefore, to give figures for the number of households with dependent children who are using temporary accommodation. The measure of use of temporary accommodation also represents the number of households in temporary accommodation at the *end* of each quarter, it does not give details on what has happened to the households accepted *during* the quarter, (who may no longer be in temporary accommodation). These two measures therefore cannot be correlated.

Trends over time

The major advantage of the homelessness returns is that statistics are available from when the homelessness legislation was introduced in the late 1970s for England, Scotland and Wales. It is therefore possible to examine trends for homelessness acceptances over the last two decades. Whilst English and Welsh statistics are produced on an annual basis, and Scottish statistics on a financial year basis, Wilcox usefully standardises these statistics in the annual Joseph Rowntree Foundation Housing Finance Review (Wilcox, 1998). The Housing Finance Review also contains statistics over time for acceptances by category of need and use of temporary accommodation in England.

A number of trends can be observed when looking at the homelessness statistics over the period from 1980 to 1997. The number of households accepted as homeless increased year on year for Britain (excluding Northern Ireland), from 76,342 in 1980 to a height of 178,867 acceptances in 1991 (Table 8.1). Since 1991, acceptances decreased year by year to 147,639 in 1996. English local authorities consistently accounted for over four-fifths of the acceptances, thus driving the overall trend, with acceptances reaching their height at 151,720 in 1991. Scottish and Welsh figures did not follow such a clear pattern although their acceptances also peaked in the early 1990s, at 19,176 in 1992 for Scotland and 11,125 in 1993 for Wales. The recent decline has not been uniform throughout all areas of Britain, in particular in England most of the decline was accounted for by the North West, North East, Yorkshire and Humberside and London, whilst the South West witnessed a continuing increase in acceptances (Pleace, Burrows and Quilgars, 1997).

The vast majority of households accepted for rehousing are assessed as being in priority need. In England, approximately three-fifths of priority need acceptances, over the two decades, have been households with dependent children, with a further one in seven being households with a pregnant woman. Since 1990 the proportion of households with dependent children has, however, slightly decreased, from 66 per cent in 1990 to 56 per cent in 1996, with an increase in the proportion of acceptances under the 'vulnerability' clause (Table 8.2). The proportion of young people being accepted as being in priority need has remained constant since 1992 at approximately 3 per cent of all priority need acceptances.

Whilst the legislation exists to house homeless households, and technically they are no longer homeless on acceptance, most households effectively remain homeless for a period of time as local authorities place people into temporary accommodation awaiting a (more) permanent placement. The use of temporary accommodation increased dramatically during the 1980s, broadly in line with increases in acceptances, reaching a height of 73,490 households in 1992 in England (Table 8.3). At the end of 1997, 53,150 households were in accommodation arranged by local authorities (Table 8.2). During the 1980s, the most prominent form of temporary accommodation in use was bed and breakfast establishments (B&Bs). However, following many reports on the bad conditions, along with high cost of B&Bs, the Government provided a subsidy to local authorities from 1990 to encourage the use of private sector leased accommodation. This stemmed the growth in B&B use (only 8 per cent of households in temporary accommodation were placed in B&B in 1997 compared with 42 per cent in 1987).

Table 8.1 **Local authority homeless acceptances**

Number of households

	1980	1981	1982	1983	1984	1985	1986	1987
Not held to be intentionally homeless								
England	60,400	66,990	71,620	75,470	80,500	91,010	100,490	109,170
+ Scotland[2]	7,038	7,332	8,360	7,770	8,787	10,992	11,056	10,417
+ Wales	4,772	4,779	4,896	4,314	4,382	4,825	5,262	5,198
= Great Britain	72,210	79,101	84,876	87,554	93,669	106,827	116,808	124,785
Held to be intentionally homeless								
England	2,520	3,020	3,180	2,770	3,050	2,970	3,070	3,270
+ Scotland[2]	938	773	847	808	977	980	1,144	1,030
+ Wales	674	683	715	694	617	546	703	485
= Great Britain	4,132	4,476	4,742	4,272	4,644	4,496	4,917	4,785
All homeless acceptances								
England	62,920	70,010	74,800	78,240	83,550	93,980	103,560	112,440
+ Scotland[2]	7,976	8,105	9,207	8,578	9,764	11,972	12,200	11,447
+ Wales	5,446	5,462	5,611	5,008	4,999	5,371	5,965	5,683
= Great Britain	76,342	83,577	89,618	91,826	98,313	111,323	121,725	129,570

Notes:

1   The 1990 figures for Wales include 2,000 households made homeless in Colwyn Bay by flooding in the February of that year.

2   Scottish figures are for priority need homeless and potentially homeless cases only.

3   '1996' figures for Scotland are for 1996/97; neither 1996 or 1997 figures were available at the time of compilation.

4   The England and Wales figures for 1997 reflect the changes in homeless legislation, and as a result no longer include 'non-priority acceptances'. In 1996 these accounted for 3,310 acceptances in England, and 3,501 acceptances in Wales.

				Number of households					
1988	*1989*	*1990*	*1991*	*1992*	*1993*	*1994*	*1995*	*1996*	*[4]1997*
113,770	122,180	140,350	144,780	142,890	132,380	122,460	121,280	116,870	103,340
10,463	12,396	14,233	15,508	17,062	15,462	16,100	15,000	[3]14,800	
6,286	7,111	[1]9,226	9,293	9,818	10,792	9,897	8,638	8,334	4,297
130,519	141,687	163,809	169,581	169,770	158,634	148,457	144,918	140,004	107,637
3,730	4,500	5,450	6,940	6,350	5,660	4,570	4,690	5,120	4,090
1,128	1,271	1,580	1,796	2,114	1,827	1,800	1,700	[3]1,700	-
532	694	737	550	452	333	396	362	815	343
5,390	6,465	7,767	9,286	8,916	7,820	6,766	6,752	7,635	4,433
117,500	126,680	145,800	151,720	149,240	138,040	127,030	125,500	121,990	107,430
11,591	13,667	15,813	17,304	19,176	17,289	17,900	16,700	[3]16,500	-
6,818	7,805	9,963	9,843	10,270	11,125	10,293	9,001	9,149	4,640
135,909	148,152	171,576	178,867	178,686	166,454	155,223	151,201	147,639	112,070

Source: Wilcox (1998) Table 86.

Table 8.2 **Homeless households in temporary accommodation under the provisions of the 1985 and the 1996 Housing Acts (England)**

	Number of households							
	1980	*1981*	*1982*	*1983*	*1984*	*1985*	*1986*	*1987*
Bed and breakfast	1,330	1,520	1,640	2,700	3,670	5,360	8,990	10,370
+ Hostels[1]	3,380	3,320	3,500	3,400	3,990	4,730	4,610	5,150
+ Private sector leasing	23,740	27,910	23,270	15,800	11,530	10,980	13,600	-
+ Other[2]	-	-	4,200	3,740	4,640	5,830	7,190	9,240
+ Homeless- at-home[3]	-	-	-	-	-	-	-	-
= Total	4710	4840	9340	9,840	12,300	15,920	20,790	24,760

Notes:

1   Includes women's refuges.

2   Other includes dwellings leased by local authorities from private landlords for years prior to 1991.

3   Figures for households accepted as homeless, but that remain in their existing accommodation pending rehousing, were not collected before 1991.

Number of households

1988	1989	1990	1991	1992	1993	1994	1995	1996	1997
10,970	11,480	11,130	12,150	7,630	4,900	4,130	4,500	4,160	4,230
6,240	8,020	9,010	9,990	10,840	10,210	9,730	9,660	9,640	9,320
-	-	-	-	-	-	-	-	-	-
12,890	18,400	25,130	14,050	16,690	15,200	15,970	18,450	17,410	17,210
-	-	8,700	10,420	8,640	8,370	8,890	9,500	8,690	-
30,100	37,900	45,270	68,630	73,490	62,220	54,000	53,030	51,690	53,150

Source: Wilcox (1998) Table 87.

Table 8.3 **Homelessness – categories of need (England)**

			Numbers of households:			
	1990	1991	1992	1993	1994	1995
Priority need households:						
Households with:						
Dependent children	84,120	88,950	85,300	76,390	68,620	66,290
Pregnant member	17,470	18,830	18,530	16,500	14,060	13,430
Vulnerable member:						
Old age	6,570	5,860	6,230	5,920	6,050	5,890
Physical handicap	3,950	4,430	5,440	5,400	6,050	6,550
Mental illness	4,220	4,750	6,070	6,490	7,100	7,430
Young[1]	-	-	4,460	4,470	4,090	3,760
Domestic violence[1]	-	-	6,470	7,060	7,370	8,430
Other	9,460	12,610	4,930	4,250	4,170	4,550
Homeless in emergency	2,300	1,820	1,270	1,150	980	1,160
Total priority need (A)	128,090	137,250	138,700	127,630	118,490	117,490
Non-priority need (B)	12,260	7,530	4,190	4,750	3,970	3,790
Total (A + B)	140,350	144,780	142,890	132,380	122,460	121,280

Notes:

1 Separate figures for domestic violence and young person cases are not available for 1991 or earlier years.

Percentages do not always add to 100 as a result of roundings.

996	1997	Percentages:							
		1990	1991	1992	1993	1994	1995	1996	1997
420	59,120	66	65	61	60	58	56	56	57
930	10,540	14	14	13	13	12	11	11	10
510	4,230	5	4	4	5	5	5	5	4
250	5,400	3	3	4	4	5	6	6	6
180	7,050	3	3	4	5	6	6	7	7
580	3,440	-	-	3	4	3	3	3	3
220	7,040	-	-	5	6	6	7	7	7
410	5,180	7	9	4	3	4	4	4	5
090	1,350	2	1	1	1	1	1	1	1
590	103,340	100	100	100	100	100	100	100	100
310	-	-	-	-	-	-	-	-	-
870	-	-	-	-	-	-	-	-	-

Source: Wilcox (1998) Table 89.

Use of temporary accommodation by families with children: evidence from research

A major study on temporary accommodation, conducted for the Department of the Environment in 1987 (Thomas and Niner, 1989) provided some information on the proportion of households with children placed in temporary accommodation by local authorities, as well as some broad characteristics of these households. Over three-quarters (78 per cent) of households placed in temporary accommodation contained children (40 per cent lone-parent and 38 per cent two-parent families) – higher than the two-thirds of households accepted as homeless which they represent. Just over half of the households (53 per cent) had one child, a quarter (25 per cent) two children and a fifth (21 per cent) three or more children. The average age of couples with children was 29, and that of one-parent families, 27; predominantly younger than childless couple and single-person households. A high proportion of households with children were from minority ethnic groups, particularly in London. Although bed and breakfast use was high for all household types, couples with children were more likely than other household types to be in short-life or other housing. Lone parents were more likely to be placed in refuges, whilst households without children were disproportionately found in bed and breakfast accommodation.

The same study found that couples with children spent an average of 70 weeks in temporary accommodation (including any time prior to approaching the local authority), slightly less than the average of 67 weeks. Lone parents spent on average 55 weeks in temporary accommodation. A study by the London Research Centre (1991) on length of stay found that the average length of stay in temporary accommodation from placement by a local authority for all households was 47 weeks, the average stay being higher at 65 weeks for short-life with homeless-at-home being shortest at 32 weeks (B&B being 39 weeks). The study found that families with four or more children experienced the longest average wait at 67 weeks (however this may have been associated with placement in short-life property offering larger accommodation). Most families do not stay in only one type of temporary accommodation, but are moved between different forms of accommodation whilst waiting for rehousing (Thomas and Niner, 1989; London Research Centre, 1991).

Non-statutory homelessness

No reliable statistics exist on the numbers of homeless families with children and young single people who have not applied or would not qualify under the homelessness legislation. It has been suggested that there has been a growth in the number of households containing children who have placed themselves in temporary accommodation (Carter, 1995), having been refused by local authorities for rehousing, excluded by the Asylum and Immigration Appeals Act or having not applied to the local authorities. However, no time-series data exists to either prove or refute this assertion. Nonetheless, two related studies have provided an estimate of the numbers of households, and those with children, who were 'self-placing' in the mid-1990s in England and Wales (Carter, 1995;

Carter, 1997). The total number of households was estimated at 67,665 (76,680 individuals). Whilst the vast majority of self-placements were by single people, and to a lesser extent childless couples, the 1997 study on self-placements outside London estimated that 6 per cent of the households were families with children, representing 4,910 children. A London figure was not given for children but it can be assumed that the total number of self-placed children living in temporary accommodation is somewhere between 5,000 and 10,000.

With respect to single youth homelessness, estimates produced by the voluntary sector range from 33,000 homeless 16- to 21-year-olds in the UK (London Research Centre, 1996) to 246,000 homeless 16- to 25-year-olds (Evans, 1996). These figures are not a result of systematic research and are, in essence, little more than guesses, which also do not allow a separate consideration of 16- and 17-year-olds. It is generally assumed that the incidence of youth homelessness has grown over the past two decades, particularly in the late 1980s, following changes in benefit rules, growth in youth unemployment and changes in housing policy and family formation. In 1991, 5 per cent of the single homelessness population using hostels and bed and breakfast accommodation in ten areas of England consisted of 16- and 17-year-olds (Anderson *et al.*, 1993). Young people sleeping rough have certainly become more visible and there has been a growth in hostel services catering for young homeless people (Quilgars and Pleace, 1999). However, the precise scale of the growth in homelessness amongst 16- and 17-year-olds is impossible to quantify.

A little more is known about the characteristics of young homeless people using hostels and bed and breakfast establishments, on a snapshot basis, from the 1991 survey of single homeless people (Anderson *et al.*, 1993). Young single homeless people, particularly 16- and 17-year-olds, are just as likely to be young women as young men, in great contrast to older single homeless people (particularly those over 25) where the great majority are men. A very high proportion of 16- and 17-year-olds (44 per cent) in 1991 were from minority ethnic groups, including some refugees (again in contrast to a generally white single homeless population). Very few young people (only 38 per cent) had any formal qualifications (compared with 58 per cent of 18- to 24-year-olds), with only 14 per cent in paid work. A particularly worrying finding was that over half of the 16- and 17-year-olds in the survey had some experience of institutional living; 39 per cent had lived in a children's home, 32 per cent with foster parents, 15 per cent in a penal establishment and 6 per cent in a psychiatric hospital. The survey showed that single homeless people under 18 are a particularly vulnerable and disadvantaged group of people.

Effects of homelessness on dependent children

A succession of reports has outlined the problems associated with temporary accommodation, and the effects of these problems, particularly as related to bed and breakfast provision. In Thomas and Niner's study (1989) professional surveyors judged 60 per cent of all accommodation, and 91 per cent of B&B accommodation, to be below standard and not providing tolerable accommodation due to lack of space, facilities, inadequate protection from fires etc. Over seven in ten (72 per cent) of families in B&B had no play space available for their children, and children commonly had to share bedrooms with adults. In addition, the location of temporary accommodation is often a problem, with many out-of-area placements, as well as movements between accommodation.

Health

Most early reports on the effects of homelessness on the health of families and children were based on information gathered by health visitors and other professionals, and centred on the use of bed and breakfast hotels (eg. HVA and GMSC, 1988; Taylor and Jones, 1990). A number of more rigorous studies have been undertaken since, often utilising comparison groups (see below); however they are usually very localised studies focusing on specific issues, mainly based in London. No robust national studies exist on the outcomes from homelessness on children. As Victor (1992) points out: 'Although there are many speculations and suppositions about the health status of homeless people living in bed and breakfast hotels, most of these data are derived from small-scale anecdotal surveys or relate to service utilisation. There have been few surveys which have attempted to compare the health of homeless and non-homeless populationss by means of a standardised survey instrument' (p.388).

Physical health

Reports have drawn attention to a number of possible outcomes for children living in temporary accommodation, including increased prevalence of infectious diseases, poor diet, low birth-weight and certain forms of accidents. An increased use of certain health services has also been documented, associated with problems of access to GP services.

A study that concentrated on the bed and breakfast hotels in London (Parsons, 1991) found a high proportion of children born in B&Bs had low birth-weights. Thirty per cent of homeless children were also considered not to be in normal health, although the relative poverty of the area meant that 20 per cent of children living in permanent housing (housed children) were also in this category. Recent research in Liverpool (Stitt et al., 1994) has shown that among homeless families in B&Bs in that city, diets are deficient in terms of the Department of Health nutritional guidelines.

Richman et al. (1991) conducted a study of paediatric admissions to St. Mary's Hospital, covering the Bayswater area of London, which has many bed and breakfast hotels, and found that children from B&Bs were more likely to attend with infectious diseases than other local residents, although there was no variation in the types of infection. In terms of injuries, although patterns were quite similar, children from B&Bs were twice as likely as others to attend with burns and scalding. For children under the age of five, the attendance rate of those who were homeless was almost twice that of other children.

Victor et al. (1989) conducted a study of the use of hospital facilities in the Parkside Health Authority area, which covers Paddington and North Kensington. This study also found that homeless people, mainly living in B&Bs, were high users of Accident and Emergency facilities, paediatric services and inpatient beds, although it qualified its results by stating that it was uncertain whether this greater use of hospital facilities was the product of greater morbidity or poor access to GPs.

Another study of the admission to hospital of homeless children in St. Mary's Hospital, Paddington Green Children's Unit, St. Leonard's Primary Care Centre and the Royal Free Hospital in London found that high admission rates among homeless children may not necessarily reflect the severity of their health problems. Examining the admission of 70 homeless children, it found that the decision to admit by doctors in 77 per cent of cases was influenced by 'social factors', which included family circumstances and accommodation, compared with 43 per cent for a control group (non-homeless children). Overall the homeless children had *fewer* pronounced health problems than children living in permanent housing who were admitted, but unlike any of the housed children, three homeless children (4 per cent) died of overwhelming infections (Lissauer *et al.*, 1993).

While it is important not to exaggerate the health problems of homeless families in comparison with the relatively poor housed population, this point is to some extent academic. Whether or not the general population has similar levels of need in terms of acute or long-standing illness, the problem of a high prevalence of such illnesses, in sections of either the housed or homeless populations, is still a matter of concern.

Mental health

Less research has been carried out on the mental health, psycho-social and behavioural effects of homelessness on children. Much anecdotal evidence exists which describes depression, disturbed sleep, over-activity, bed-wetting, toilet-training problems and violent mood swings. There is also evidence that children and their parents are subjected to isolation, boredom and loneliness that take a toll on familial relationships and on their general health (Barry *et al.*, 1991; HVA and GMSC, 1988). In one study in Oxford (cited in Royal College of Physicians, 1994), 55 per cent of homeless parents said that they were irritated by their children and 65 per cent said that they often lost their temper. One study has been undertaken specifically on the prevalence of behavioural problems amongst homeless primary schoolchildren in London, compared to a permanently housed control group from the same schools (Amery *et al.*, 1995). Using the Rutter Behavioural rating scale[1] some 49 per cent of homeless children's scores suggested a behavioural problem compared with only 11 per cent of the control group.

Vostanis and colleagues (1998) have recently undertaken a longitudinal study of rehoused families in Birmingham, utilising a comparison group of families in stable housing, examining children's (and mothers') mental health problems and children's levels of communication. Using the Child Behaviour Checklist,[2] homeless children were more likely to show clinical evidence of problems than the comparison group, and using another scale[3] revealed that homeless children were more delayed than the comparison group and remained so after rehousing. The mothers of homeless children, and the children, were found to have experienced high rates of abuse prior to homelessness. The authors raised the question of the extent to which these scores were related to previous experiences prior to homelessness or the experience of homelessness itself: 'Homeless families constitute a relatively heterogeneous population with complex health, social and educational problems which often precipitate the episode of homelessness. These are related to underlying psycho-social factors, and are likely to persist, even after rehousing'.

Education

Only four studies have specifically examined the effects of homelessness on children in Britain in any detail, all focusing on the impact of living in temporary accommodation on access to schools and educational attainment, as well as the response of schools in terms of policy and provision for these children. All have taken a case study approach with HM Inspectors of Schools (1990) examining 23 primary and five secondary schools in four areas of England; Power et al., (1995) looking at three case study areas, following a survey of local education authorities (LEAs); Stepien et al. (1996) concentrating on seven primary schools in Portsmouth, and Scottish Homes research (Study of Education and Society/Shelter (Scotland), 1998) focusing on three local authorities. Three of the studies relied mainly on interviews with key players and families, although educational social workers and psychologists provided information on individual children in the HM Inspectors of Schools' study and housing and educational records were examined in the Shelter study. Only the Stepien study attempted any standardised measurement of educational and behavioural progress using the British Picture Vocabulary Scales[4] (BPVS) and the Bristol Social and Behavioural Adjustment School Guides (BSAG), to look at development over time (following children aged from five to seven) and comparing their development with that of other children in the same schools.

The studies all highlight a range of educational effects of homelessness and living in temporary accommodation. Firstly, disruption in schooling is likely when families have to move area, sometimes involving frequent moves. Where families try to keep children in the same school, children often have long travelling distances with the associated costs of travel (Power et al., 1995). Secondly, children living in temporary accommodation may have gaps in schooling while awaiting a new school and/or often have poor attendance records when placed, sometimes related to caring for other family members (HM Inspectors of Schools, 1990). Arriving at school late is also sometimes a problem (HM Inspectors of Schools, 1990; Study of Education and Society/Shelter (Scotland), 1998). Thirdly, the nature of temporary accommodation often means that children have a lack of space and opportunity to study, as well as sometimes a lack of sleep and a poor diet to contend with, all of which may impact detrimentally on educational progress (HM Inspectors of Schools, 1990; Power et al., 1995). Fourthly, although one study pointed out that not all children had problems settling into new schools (Study of Education and Society/Shelter (Scotland), 1998), two studies cited cases of homeless children having problems with other children (HM Inspectors of Schools, 1990; Power et al., 1995). However the Stepien study (1996) indicated a stable level of social adjustment using the BSAG. Whilst the studies cite the above problems as explaining, at least in part, poor educational attainment of homeless children, only the Stepien study was able to quantify the educational effect. The study found evidence of a deficit in the educational development of children who were living, or had lived, in temporary accommodation, in terms of a vocabulary development score of between 9 and 20 months behind the national average compared with one between 6 and 17 months for other children in the primary schools under investigation, as well as language delays in pre-school children. The Scottish Homes study stressed that further research in this area needed to use clearer indicators to determine the relationship between social factors and educational attainment.

Effects of homelessness on young adults

Research has shown that single homeless people using hostels and B&Bs, and particularly those sleeping rough, suffer considerably worse physical and mental health problems than the general population (Bines, 1994). Two reliable sets of data exist which allow a consideration of the health effects of homelessness on young people although few studies have concentrated specifically on the health effects of homelessness on young adults.

The survey of single homeless people (Anderson *et al.*, 1993) found a particularly high rate of self-reported health problems for 16- and 17-year-olds in hostels and bed and breakfast accommodation. Whilst two-thirds (66 per cent) of all homeless people in the survey reported at least one health problem, over three-quarters (77 per cent) of 16- and 17-year-olds stated they had at least one problem, a much higher figure than that for 18- to 24-year-olds (54 per cent). Bines' study (1994) comparing the survey findings with the British Household Panel Study respondents also pointed out that, relative to the general population, younger people, especially those sleeping rough, appeared to be the most adversely affected by mental health problems in particular. Whilst the majority of young single homeless people were registered with a doctor (78 per cent of 16- and 17-year-olds), for a minority, access to a doctor or medical centre was still clearly problematic.

A recent longitudinal study conducted by Craig *et al.* (1996) examined the mental health of a representative sample of young homeless people (aged 16–21) compared with a group of young people taken from two inner-city GP practices, using the Composite International Diagnostic Interview for Psychiatric Disorder (CIDI). The study found that almost two-thirds (62 per cent) of homeless young people were suffering from psychiatric disorders, compared with only a quarter of the housed comparison group. Homeless people's health problems also tended to be more severe and more chronic. However, as with Vostanis' study (1997), the homeless young people had suffered a higher rate of childhood adversity (defined as the presence of parental indifference and/or abuse), with the onset of disorders having preceded the first episode of homelessness in the majority of cases. The authors conclude that childhood experiences strongly predict later homelessness, although other factors were also associated with high psychiatric disorder, particularly the experience of sleeping rough.

Explaining child and youth homelessness

Full discussions of the explanatory variables and causes of homelessness *per se*, and family and youth homelessness in particular, have been examined elsewhere and do not need repeating here (eg. Hutson and Liddiard, 1994; Carlen, 1996; Neale, 1997; Pleace and Quilgars, 1999). However, a number of broad points are worthy of mention.

There is no single cause of homelessness, rather homelessness is a result of a complex interaction between context, characteristics, experience and chance (Neale, 1997; Pleace and Quilgars, 1999). Much of the research discussed in this chapter clearly illustrates the importance of individual background and experience in explaining homelessness, particularly disruption to family life both in terms of relationship breakdown and problematic early childhood. However, the broader context of this, the low economic status or poverty of households experiencing homelessness, is also important in influencing life chances. The structural factors underlying these life chances need to be considered carefully in any explanation of homelessness, particularly policy changes over the last twenty years. An absolute shortage of affordable housing to rent, created and sustained by housing policy, including most prominently the policy of Right to Buy, and reduction in public spending in this area, has clearly influenced people's chances of being able to access and sustain their own housing (Anderson, 1994). In addition, social security changes, particularly for 16- and 17-year-olds, and high levels of unemployment, also represent structural factors over which families and young people have no effective control. The best explanation of homelessness is that some families and people, due to individual experience, are more vulnerable than others to the structural factors that precipitate homelessness than other people: that is, they have a heightened *risk* of becoming homeless (Jones, 1995).

Conclusions

This chapter has charted the increase in the incidence of homelessness amongst children and young people in the last twenty years, noting a slight decline in statutory homelessness in recent years. However, the datasets available on statutory child homelessness remain imprecise, and in need of improvement, whilst no reliable estimates exist on the extent of single youth homelessness and only rough estimates on the extent of non-statutory family homelessness are available.

Research studies show that children in certain types of families are more likely to experience homelessness, including children in lone-parent families, minority ethnic households and those with young parents. Similarly, young people from minority ethnic groups, with few formal qualifications, and experience of institutional living are most likely to be represented amongst single homeless 16- and 17-year-olds. More robust statistical analysis is required to more accurately identify the most important variables associated with homelessness.

Numerous reports have been produced on the effects of homelessness on children and families. Fewer systematic studies have been conducted, and those which exist tend to be very localised in focus. Nonetheless, poorer physical and mental health on a range of measures, as well as lower educational achievement have been documented for children living in temporary accommodation. Whilst two factors need to be borne in mind when drawing conclusions from these studies – the extent to which the findings are similar on some measures to other housed poor families and the extent to which families exhibit high scores on these measures prior to homelessness – overall the research clearly shows an association between homelessness and poor health and educational progress.

Even fewer studies have been conducted on the effect of homelessness on young single people. The few studies which do exist have allowed comparisons with the general housed population and if anything show a more striking association between poor physical, and particularly mental, health for young homeless people than for children. Whilst the caveat of cause and effect also needs to be noted when examining this data, there is no doubt that young single homeless people represent an extremely vulnerable group of people.

There is no simple explanation of homelessness, but it is clear that some children and young people have a heightened risk of experiencing homelessness. This risk is associated with multiple disadvantage, including structural factors among which are an inadequate supply of affordable housing, high levels of unemployment for certain groups and generally increased levels of poverty in Britain over the last twenty years.

Notes to Chapter 8

1   The Rutter Behavioural Rating Scale covers aspects of behavioural functioning within the past year.

2   The Child Behaviour Checklist describes symptoms of emotional and behavioural disturbance over the past six months.

3   The communication domain of the Vineland adaptive behavioural scales.

4   The Birth Picture Vocabulary Scale is a method of measuring language capability using pictures rather than text as stimulus.

Cognitive outcomes

Deborah Quilgars

9 Educational attainment

Deborah Quilgars

Introduction

This chapter centres on the possible impact of poverty on educational attainment or achievement, the most common measurement of cognitive ability. Whilst any link between poor educational progress and poverty may have a less immediate debilitating effect on children compared with measures such as child mortality and morbidity, a link between poor performance at school and future job opportunities (and therefore opportunities to earn and increase wealth) would effectively mean that poor educational achievement would heighten the chances that poor children would grow up to be poor adults.

In Britain, a (mainly) comprehensive schooling system over the last few decades has, in principle, attempted to offer the same educational opportunities to all children, regardless of background and educational promise. Yet one of the central features of any education system is the measurement of educational progress, and the differentiation of progress between pupils, chiefly through the taking of national examinations. This measurement of educational progress has occupied an increasingly high priority in the British school system over the last ten years. Most prominently, the Educational Reform Act 1988 made provision for all 7-, 11- and 14-year-olds in England and Wales to take standardised assessment tests (SATs) in English, maths and science at these three Key Stages.

Comparative tables of GCSE and A/AS level results have been published by the Department for Education and Employment (DfEE) since 1992, and league tables for progress at Key Stage 2 (age 11) have been published for the last few years. This information indicates that levels of educational attainment rose during the 1990s (presuming standards have remained the same which is a debated issue): for example, there was an improvement of 2.8 points in those attaining 5 GCSEs at grades A–C over the period 1993–1997 (Sparkes, 1999).

League tables of results have provoked much debate, as they do not allow a 'value added' assessment to be made of the achievements of pupils and schools; that is they do not take account of differences in intake (prior attainment and pupil characteristics) between schools. An investigation into the possible link between poverty and educational attainment is even more critical when it is known that recent educational improvements have not been across the 'ability' range. West and Pennell (1999, cited in Sparkes 1999) have shown that the top decile improved by 4.4 points whilst the bottom decile had a 0.1% fall. In short, the gap between those with higher and those with lower 'ability' has actually increased over this period.

This chapter seeks to answer two main questions: firstly, does a link exist between poverty and educational attainment?; and secondly, has this link changed over time? The substantive part of the chapter reviews the evidence of the link with educational achievement across the school career, looking at primary and secondary school levels as well as staying-on rates. The links between other factors closely related to poverty and educational attainment, and evidence of change over time, are reviewed. Finally, the relative importance of individual or school effects in affecting performance is considered.

The link between poverty and poor educational attainment

The available research has consistently demonstrated the existence of significant differences in educational attainment for children from different social backgrounds, at all levels, over the last twenty years. Most of this evidence comes from specific studies on pupil performance at either the primary or secondary school level. As the DfEE has not collected data on pupil background (although to some extent this is now changing with the introduction of a new National Framework for Baseline Assessment), studies have tended to take one of two approaches: analysis of school results on a local education authority / local authority level (and sometimes school level) looking at local socio-demographic indicators, or collecting specific individual-level data on children in a sample of schools. The latter approach obviously has a major advantage over the former by virtue of being able to link individual data on poverty and educational progress rather than simply looking at aggregate details of performance and assuming links with area characteristics.

Evidence at primary school level

A number of studies have undertaken an analysis of the link between social class and educational attainment at a local, but aggregated level. McCallum (1993) examined 1991 and 1992 SAT data for 7-year-olds for 107 LEAs and found a clear relationship with type of LEA and the social class of households with children under 16. McCallum estimated that between a quarter and a half of variance in SAT scores is associated with differences in the proportion of households in social classs I and II in any given area. Similarly, Smith and Noble (1995) found that the higher the proportion of children from partly-skilled and unskilled households in the LEA, the lower the proportion of children reaching level 2 (the expected level) for reading at Key Stage 1. In addition, a National Union of Teachers (NUT) and University of Leeds study (1993) used school-level data (89 schools in 52 LEAs) and found marked differences between children from different neighbourhoods, with over a quarter of children from 'low status' neighbourhoods, but only 10 per cent from 'high status' areas scoring at or below level 1 (that is, below the expected level 2) at Key Stage 1.

The first, and arguably most detailed, study to provide individual level data on the educational attainment of children at primary school was the *School Matters* study (Mortimore *et al.*, 1988). This study involved a sample of 50 schools in inner-London (randomly selected from the 636 in the Authority) consisting of 2,000 pupils. The longitudinal study followed children from ages 7 to 11. It collected information on three main aspects of school life: (i) measures of pupil intake (detailed individual data on social characteristics and child's attainment on entering junior school including assessments of reading, mathematics, visual spatial skills and teachers' rating of behaviour); (ii) measures of educational outcomes (standardised reading and maths tests, primarily the Edinburgh Reading Test and National Foundation for Educational Research Basic Mathematics Test, as well as tests on practical maths, creative writing and verbal reasoning, and teachers' assessment of children's behaviour and pupils' attitudes to school); and (iii) measures of classroom and school environment (including school policies, class organisation, teacher strategies etc).

Multilevel modelling meant that background factors such as social class could be looked at whilst controlling for all other factors. The study found that, in reading tests at age 7, social class was highly related to reading level with a gap of 14 raw score points representing a difference of ten months in reading age between children from professional backgrounds compared with children with parents in semi- or unskilled occupations. By age 11, the differences by fathers' occupation had become more pronounced. In maths tests, a similar difference of nine months gap in progress was found between social classes. Here, the difference remained at each year, but did not appear to increase over time, which suggested that home factors were less important for maths (although eligibility for free school meals (FSMs) did have an impact on maths progress). Difference by social class was also found for creative writing, but not for some aspects of non-verbal performance, which signals the importance of incorporating oral elements into teachers' assessments of ability. Interestingly, whilst differences by mothers' social class were also pronounced for most measures, there was not a significant increase in the gap between classes over time for many subjects, although missing data might have accounted for some of this.

A number of more recent studies have also looked at pupil progress at primary school, especially between the new tests at Key Stages 1 (age 7) and 2 (age 11). Sammons *et al.* (1997) focused on the progress of 2,404 pupils in 62 inner-London schools at the end of Key Stage 1 in the early 1990s. This study collected information on pupil background characteristics, school compositional variables (eg. number of pupils with free school meals, number of children from lone-parent families etc.), and a head-teacher survey on teaching and school processes. It found that children eligible for free school meals (FSMs) (as well as younger children, those not fluent in English and boys) had poorer results at Key Stage 1 (KS1). In addition, the proportion of children from lone-parent families also had a significant effect on attainment. However, the proportion of pupils receiving FSMs did not have an impact, in contrast to Thomas's study (1995) in a shire-county context: the authors suggested that this may have reflected the greater incidence of disadvantage in the inner-city study. Schagen (1994) and Thomas (1995) also analysed KS1 against concurrent measures of pupils' backgrounds, including FSMs, and found strong correlations with KS1 results.

Strand (1999b) examined educational progress from the younger age of four to the end of Key Stage 1 (age 7) for a sample of 5,160 pupils in 55 inner-London schools (covering three cohorts) in Wandsworth LEA over the period 1992–1994 (baseline) to

1995–1997 (KS1). Unlike the previous study, this study incorporated a baseline assessment in the first term of reception class (aged 4–5) which included a combination of structured teacher observations, standardised assessment of early literacy skills, and background characteristics. This made it possible to compare this baseline with the KS1 assessment tests in reading, writing and maths (the author used an average across the three tests). *At baseline,* pupils entitled to FSMs had lower attainment than others, but the author noted that the performance gap associated with those receiving FSMs was significantly smaller for most ethnic groups than for the ESWNI group (English, Scottish, Welsh and Northern Irish). *At KS1,* again pupils entitled to FSMs had significantly lower attainment. Looking at progress *from baseline to KS1,* pupils eligible for FSMs made significantly less progress than their peers. However, again there was an interaction with ethnic group, with African, Caribbean and Indian children entitled to FSMs making significantly more progress that ESWNI pupils on free school meals. This study pointed to the importance of looking at variables in an interaction model to take account of other factors. Overall, the study found that low family income was the most significant factor affecting progress, although the size of the effect (when controlling for all other factors) amounted to 'only' 3.5 months progress.

Strand (1999b) also looked in more detail at baseline assessment results at age four against pupil background factors for the same schools in Wandsworth, but over a five year period (1993–1997: total 11,121 pupils). Again pupils eligible for FSMs scored significantly lower than those not eligible. Factorial analysis of variance revealed that the main effects were age, terms of early education, English as a second language and FSMs. Again, a clear interaction effect was found between ethnic group and FSMs, with the performance gap being greater for white children than others. And once more, when looking at the difference from baseline to KS1, pupils receiving FSMs continued to fall further behind their peers.

Other studies, including Bondi (1991) and Hutchinson (1993), also report that pupils from disadvantaged backgrounds remain behind their peers or fall further behind over the primary school years. Overall, the available research consistently reveals a clear link between a range of poverty indicators and educational attainment and progress in primary school.

Evidence at secondary school level

The research evidence on the links between educational attainment and poverty indicators for secondary school reaches very similar conclusions as that on primary schools: children from low-income families fare much worse at school than their better-off peers, and if anything, their progress relative to their peers is likely to become worse over their school career.

Shuttleworth (1995) analysed the impact of socio-economic status on academic attainment of GCSEs in Northern Ireland, looking at the results of 1,600 pupils who left school in 1990/91 and using FSMs as the main indicator of deprivation, as well as looking at government data on the percentage of pupils per school in receipt of FSMs. The model showed that FSMs, at the individual level, had a small but statistically significant effect on individual success at GCSE; similarly there was a small contextual effect at school level of the proportion of pupils receiving FSMs. Other things being equal, the results suggested that pupils in schools with 75 per cent of pupils receiving FSMs would score 10 points less than pupils in schools where no children received FSMs (equivalent to two grade Cs); and that pupils receiving FSMs in a school with 75 per cent FSMs would be expected to score 13 points less (about three grade Cs), than pupils ineligible for FSMs in schools with no children eligible for FSMs. The inclusion of other socio-economic indicators, including number of siblings and parental labour-market position, improved the explanatory power of the model. Shuttleworth concluded that some pupils attending secondary schools as opposed to grammar schools (which still exist in Northern Ireland) may suffer the double disadvantage of both low personal socio-economic status and low contextual socio-economic status.

Jesson *et al.* (1992) looked at GCSE performance in Nottinghamshire in 1991 and found pupils in receipt of FSMs were also much less successful at GCSE, achieving a mean score of 10 points less than their peers. A multivariate model found gender, parental occupation, FSMs and school attended accounted for around 30 per cent of the difference. The model suggested that FSMs accounted for pupils obtaining 4.4 fewer points than their peers.

Patterson (1992c) in a study of Fife pupils between primary 7 and 4th year at school in the mid-1980s found that all dimensions of socio-economic status had independent influences on the progress of children over this period. In another study, Patterson (1992b), identified the most influential factors affecting children as parental education (accounting for a gap of one O grade); followed by father's occupational class (gap of three-quarters of O grade); mother's occupation (one-quarter of a grade); and family size (one-quarter of a grade). This study indicated that 'a class schema that described only father's occupation would be inadequate for summarising the effect of social circumstances on children's progress' (p12), a theme returned to below.

Evidence across both primary and secondary school levels

Few studies have succeeded in tracking children's educational progress over their school career, across both primary and secondary school. The one study that stands out in this area was undertaken by Sammons (1995). Here, Sammons looked at attainment in maths and reading in years 3, 5, 6 (secondary transfer) and 11 (GCSE) using the *School Matters* (see above, Mortimore *et al.*, 1988) Junior School Project dataset of detailed individual level data, followed up at secondary transfer (using London Reading Test and Verbal Reasoning) and at GCSEs. Following a cohort over such a long time inevitably meant a loss of sample size (the research team only had GCSE information for 49 per cent of the junior school intake), nonetheless the sample remained broadly representative. The author found that differences by socio-economic factors remained consistent and increased over time. At age seven, 20 per cent and 18 per cent of variance in reading and maths was accounted for by background variables, and socio-economic factors (social class and eligibility for free school meals) were found to 'have a pronounced effect'. At age ten, background effects remained fairly stable (though accounting for 21 per cent of reading variance but only 11 per cent of maths); however looking at the relative progress (between ages 7–10), it was found that those from poorer backgrounds had made less progress given prior reading attainment (as reported earlier). In short, the gap between the attainment of working-class children and those on low incomes had increased over time. Those on low family income were also found to have made less progress in maths, although there were no significant differences over time by social class. By GCSE, Sammons (1995) found that the effects of social class and low family income were relatively larger than those identified at transfer: the gap in attainment between non-manual and other social classes (which was particularly marked), those with unemployed parents and those receiving free school meals increased steadily throughout the school career.

On an aggregate level, McCallum (1993) looked at GCSE at LEA level and showed that the correlation with social class, unemployment and car ownership was higher for GCSE results than for SATs for 7-year-olds, indicating a worsening of educational attainment of children from poorer backgrounds.

Finally, McNiece and Jolliffe (1998) undertook an investigation into regional differences in educational performance using the National Child Development Study (which follows the lives of those born in one week in 1958). Whilst the dataset is slightly outside of the time period in which the present study is interested, as the children would have been 16 in 1974, it is worth noting that multilevel modelling found that those from professional backgrounds (by father's occupation) consistently scored higher than other groups in both reading and maths at ages 7, 11 and 16, whilst those from skilled backgrounds scored more highly than those from semi/unskilled backgrounds (apart from maths at age 7). Again, the relative progress of the 'higher' classes was also greater than the other groups over the school career. The study concluded that, when controlling for social class, gender and ethnicity, differences between regions and LEA areas in educational attainment only accounted for three per cent of variation.

Staying-on rates and poverty indicators

School staying-on rates have risen considerably over the last two decades, although they have continued to show a class gradient, albeit a diminishing one. For example, 65 per cent of young people with parents in classes I and II stayed on after school-leaving age in 1980, a figure which had risen to 73 per cent in 1990. In comparison, only 17 per cent of young people with parents in classes IV and V stayed on in 1980, although this had doubled to 34 per cent in 1990 (Paterson, 1992a).

Gray *et al.* (1993) looking at post-16 participation in full-time education found that those most likely to stay on came from non-manual and well-educated backgrounds. A linked study by Jesson *et al.* (1991) also pointed to the importance of looking at a mix of post-16 provision, for example, a higher proportion from high social background stayed on at school rather than going to a further education college, and vice versa.

Patterson (1992c) found that of those pupils with the same levels of attainment in the fourth year, those with well-educated parents had higher staying-on rates than those from less well-educated backgrounds. The pattern was the same for those in the fifth and sixth years with regard to application rates to higher education, especially university.

Other factors related to poverty and poor educational achievement

Some of the above studies (Jesson *et al.*, 1992; Paterson, 1992c; Shuttleworth, 1995) have pointed to the fact that a number of factors interrelate in a child's background to explain poor educational attainment and that a combination of factors improve the explanatory power of models in this area. Another good example of this is research by Sammons *et al.* (1993) which found that 92 per cent of those children affected by the following factors – eligibility for free school meals, large family size, lone parent, semi or unskilled manual parental occupation or unemployed, behaviour, fluency in English, ethnic family background – were in the lowest verbal reasoning band, as compared with only 11 per cent of those not affected by any factors.

Many studies have shown there to be an association between tenure, housing conditions and educational attainment. Chapter 8 looks at this issue in detail, in particular reviewing the evidence of the link between homelessness, poverty and educational difficulties. A link between neighbourhood and environment may also have an effect over and above individual factors or school (Garner and Raudenbush, 1991, cited in Paterson, 1992c), suggesting, perhaps, that pupils draw on resources in neighbourhoods and/or that teachers' expectations are influenced by the character of the neighbourhood as well as housing.

There appears to be a weak link between family structure and educational attainment, but this is not pronounced and in some studies does not appear to be significant. When controlling for other factors, lone-parent status has little effect, although the effect is slightly more for lone fathers than lone mothers (Gregg and Machin, 1997; Bosworth, 1994, cited in Patterson, 1992c). Being a member of a large family may also have a slight effect, but this, like lone parenthood is more dependent on income levels than family structure *per se*. However, one group of children fares particularly badly: those children who have been in care. Surveys show that over 75 per cent of these young people gain no qualifications on leaving school, compared with 11 per cent of the general population and that this is worse the more care placements they experience in childhood (Biehal *et al.* 1992, cited in Patterson, 1992c).

The link between ethnic origin, poverty and educational attainment is a complex one. The Committee of Inquiry into the Education of Children from Ethnic Minority Groups (the Swann Committee) (1985) reviewed educational performance by minority ethnic groups and detailed the under-achievement of Afro–Caribbean young people, and the somewhat varied achievement for other groups. Some research suggests that minority ethnic groups exceed majority groups in value added analyses of GCSE results and the research by Strand (1999a) shows ethnic groups receiving FSMs may make better progress than their white peers.

Changes over time?

Overall, there is little high-quality research available on changes in the relative educational achievement of different groups of pupils. Whilst, as shown above, some quite robust longitudinal research exists which allows the progress of the same pupils to be followed over time, there is much less research which allows comparisons of subsequent cohorts of pupils passing through the educational system.

Paterson's (1992c) review of the evidence concluded that differences in educational achievement by socio-economic group appeared not to have changed in the preceding decade. This was in contrast to changes that had been seen during the development of comprehensive schooling (McPherson and Willms, 1987, cited in Paterson, 1992c) which showed that average SCE attainment rose for all social groups but more rapidly for children of fathers in manual occupations.

Smith and Noble (1995) have looked at trend data on GCSEs at LEA level since 1988 using Department for Education Annual GCSE Statistics, 1988–94 and 1991 census data. They split LEAs into three groups: the most disadvantaged LEAs (25 per cent of LEAs with the highest proportion of children from semi or unskilled manual backgrounds), the most advantaged LEAs, and the rest, and found that the GCSE results of all areas increased at about the same rate. They pointed out that this meant that the actual rate of progress diverged, with more advantaged areas ending up further ahead than less disadvantaged areas.

There is also some evidence of changes in educational progress for minority ethnic groups since 1985. A relatively recent review of this area (Gillborn and Gipps, 1996) concluded that African–Caribbeans (especially boys) had not shared equally in increasing rates of educational achievement, with Indian children achieving more highly than pupils from other South Asian backgrounds (and higher than whites in some areas); and no single clear pattern for Pakistani children who achieve less well in many areas than whites. Some studies still show gaps in early and middle schooling (eg. Smith and Tomlinson, 1989, cited in Smith and Noble, 1995) but the gap seems to be closing in the final stages of schooling. If anything, data suggest that the poorest *rate of progress* is being made by white children (AMA data cited in Smith and Noble, 1995) .

School or background: which is more important?

> The problem for researchers is how to tease out the effects of families from the effects of schools. (Mortimore *et al.*, 1988, p1)

It is clear that both the type of school and the background of pupils have a profound impact on the educational progress of children. Some studies have concluded that non-school factors are more important than the type and quality of schooling (Sparkes, 1999). For example, one study (Thomas and Mortimore, 1996, cited in Sparkes, 1999) claims that 70–75 per cent of school variation in 16-year-olds' attainment at GCSE is explained by intake factors. Other studies (eg. Mortimore *et al.*, 1998) conclude that the school makes a far larger contribution to the explanation of educational progress than background factors. Yet another (Sammons *et al.,* 1997) concluded that school process factors were about equally as important as background factors.

However, whichever is the more important, one main point is clear. Most studies have found that schools which have a negative effect on the educational progress of higher social classes also have a negative effect for lower classes and vice versa. Sammons *et al.,* (1993) undertook further analysis of the *School Matters* dataset to investigate differential school effectiveness in more depth and confirmed their original finding that there was no evidence of differential school effectiveness for different groups of pupils, including those from different social classes, free school meal eligibility, gender and ethnicity. They did find some evidence of differential effectiveness of individual schools for pupils with different prior attainments, but in general effective schools raised performance for all groups. Mortimore *et al.'s* (1988) study commented: 'Our results show, therefore, that effective schools tend to 'jack up' the progress of all pupils, irrespective of their social class background, while ineffective schools will usually depress the progress of all pupils' (p208–9).

The suggestion is that if all schools became more effective they are likely to improve standards for all children more or less equally. By implication, this means that, although disadvantaged children will do better in some schools than others, differences by social class and low income are likely to remain.

Similarly, Strand (1999b) looked at school effects, finding they were large, with pupils of same baseline data doing much better in some schools than others. However they also found that, in general, schools most effective for pupils with low baseline assessment were also most effective for those with higher attainment. This held specifically for children eligible for free school meals. However, Strand (1997) has also undertaken a value added analysis of school effects (as distinct from individual background effects) looking at educational progress of children from baseline to KS1. Strand found that the 'value added' by the school (school compositional effects) meant that pupils made less progress in schools with a high proportion of pupils eligible for free school meals and where the school average on the baseline was high. He concluded that the composition of schools' intake can have a substantial effect on pupil outcomes over and above effects associated with individual prior attainment or background. Differences between school scores at KS1 were reduced when account was taken of school intake but still left differences, which means that some schools are better at facilitating progress than others during KS1. 'It can be hypothesised that schools with a low proportion of socially disadvantaged pupils may have some benefits associated with their context: they may receive greater help from parents, have fewer disciplinary problems or an atmosphere more conducive to learning' (Strand, 1999b:484–5).

Conclusion

All the research evidence clearly demonstrates a strong, and enduring link, between poverty and educational attainment. Whilst trend data for subsequent cohorts is limited, longitudinal research following the same children through their schooling career provides relatively robust data which suggests that children living in low-income families start off at a disadvantage compared with other children, and that this disadvantage not only endures but increases over the schooling career. Whilst data on links between other factors like gender and ethnicity is complex, the link between low family income and poor educational attainment is clear. Other factors such as living in a disadvantaged area, poor housing, and factors such as family structure and ethnic group may compound this effect (although not always in the way expected).

It is important to point out a number of limitations which are evident in the research evidence. Firstly, most of the influential studies in this area have been undertaken in inner-London schools. A number of authors (for example, Strand, 1999) have noted that care needs to be taken in generalising findings of school progress of children in inner-London schools to the national context. Secondly, whilst the Qualifications and Curriculum Authority (QCA) has recently introduced the National Framework for Baseline Assessment which schools will have to administer within the first seven weeks of primary school, relatively little information has been collected over time which allows a measurement of pupils' progress using a value added approach (that is, taking account of prior attainment). Thirdly, a lack of national time-series datasets is still evident. And finally, whilst the last ten years has seen a growth in the amount of research into educational attainment, there is still a lack of insight into the process by which poverty and other factors lead to poor educational attainment. Research is still required to demonstrate causal links rather than the associations, which are now well known (Sparkes, 1999).

Behavioural outcomes

Francis McGlone and Paul Higate

10   School exclusions

Francis McGlone

Introduction

The objective of this chapter is to evaluate critically the existing data sources on school exclusion and the link with poverty and social deprivation.

Sources of data

Data on permanent exclusions[1] from school have only been collected by the Department for Education and Employment (DfEE) since January 1996, although local education authorities (LEAs) have provided data on a voluntary basis for a number of years. Since 1999, schools have also been required to provide figures on fixed-term exclusions over 15 days in total, but these have not been collated.

The only other source of national data on exclusions is provided by the Audit Commission. For their report *Missing Out* (1999), the Audit Commission carried out two national surveys of LEAs into unauthorised absences and exclusion from schools.

In addition, both OFSTED (1996) and the Social Exclusion Unit (1998) have published reports reviewing the research evidence on school exclusions, and there have been a number of small specialist studies and reports.

Permanent school exclusions

There were 12,298 permanent exclusions from primary, secondary, and special schools in England in 1997/98, a decrease of 3 per cent compared with the previous year. Of those permanent exclusions, 13 per cent were of pupils permanently excluded from primary school, 83 per cent from secondary schools and 5 per cent from special schools (Table 10.1).

The permanent exclusion rate[2] in 1997/98 for primary schools, secondary schools and special schools was 0.03 per cent, 0.33 per cent and 0.58 per cent, respectively.

Fixed-term exclusions

Since 1999, schools have had to report fixed-term exclusions[3] over 15 days in total, but these are not collated by the DfEE. OFSTED estimates that there are around 100,000 a year, but some of these may be repeat exclusions of the same child. The Audit Commission, on the other hand, puts the figure as high as 150,000. An unknown number of children are also excluded from school 'informally' each year.

Table 10.1 **Number and percentage of permanent exclusions by type of school. 1996/97 and 1997/98, England**

	1996/97		1997/98	
	Number of permanent exclusions	Percentage permanent exclusions[1]	Number of permanent exclusions	Percentage permanent exclusions[1]
Primary[2]	1,573	12	1,539	13
Secondary[2]	10,463	83	10,187	83
Special[3]	632	5	572	5
All schools	**12,668**	**100**	**12,298**	**100**

1 The number of permanent exclusions expressed as a percentage of the total number of permanent exclusions

2 Includes middle schools as deemed

3 Includes both maintained and non-maintained special schools

Source: DfEE, 1999.

Trends

The number of permanent exclusions appears to have risen very sharply in recent years. Figures collated by the Social Exclusion Unit show that there were 3,000 exclusions in 1990/91, rising to 4,000 in 1991/92. However, as the figures for these years were gathered on a voluntary basis, they are almost certainly under-estimates. There are no figures for 1992/93 and 1993/94. For 1994/95 and 1995/96 the figures were 11,100 and 12,500, respectively.

Gender

Boys are about six times more likely than girls to be permanently excluded from school (Table 10.2). DfEE published data for 1997/98 does not break this down by type of school, but in 1996/97 girls formed a much larger proportion of the total number of exclusions in secondary school than in primary schools (Social Trends, 1999).

Age

The highest rate of permanent exclusions is among pupils aged 13, 14 and 15. Two-thirds of permanent exclusions in England in 1997/98 were of pupils aged 13, 14 or 15 (at the start of the school year); 19 per cent were aged 13, 27 per cent were aged 14, and 20 per cent were aged 15 (Table 10.3).

Table 10.2 **Permanent exclusions by gender. 1997/98, England**

	Number of permanent exclusions	Percentage of permanent exclusions[1]	Percentage of school population
Boys	10,270	84	0.26[2]
Girls	2,028	16	0.05[3]
All schools[4]	12,298	100	0.05

1   The number of permanent exclusions expressed as a percentage of the total number of permanent exclusions

2   The number of permanent exclusions expressed as a percentage of the number (headcount) of full-time and part-time boys of all ages in primary, secondary and special schools (excluding dually-registered pupils in special schools) in January 1998

3   The number of permanent exclusions expressed as a percentage of the number (headcount) of full-time and part-time girls of all ages in primary, secondary and special schools (excluding dually-registered pupils in special schools) in January 1998

4   Includes maintained primary, secondary and special and non-maintained special schools

Source: DfEE,1999.

Ethnic group[4]

In 1997/98, the overall permanent exclusion rate was 0.18 per cent. The highest exclusion rate, at 0.76 per cent, was among Black Caribbean pupils, followed by Black Other (0.57 per cent) and Black African (0.29 per cent). The lowest rates were among Chinese and Bangladeshi pupils (0.05 per cent and 0.09 per cent, respectively). The permanent exclusion rate among White pupils was 0.17. In other words, Black Other and Black Caribbean are, respectively, about three and four times more likely to be permanently excluded from school than other pupils (Table 10.4).

The Social Exclusion Unit cites research which found that African–Caribbean children who had been excluded had different characteristics from other excluded children: a higher proportion lived with a lone parent, and they also tended to be of higher or average ability (although the schools said that they were under-achieving). Moreover, they had not usually shown disruptive behaviour from early in their school career, and showed less evidence of deep-seated trauma. The Unit also notes that statistically, African–Caribbean children are not more likely to be persistent truants, which suggests that they are not disaffected from education.

OFSTED points to a relatively high level of tension, and even conflict, between white teachers and African–Caribbean pupils. Examples quoted by OFSTED range from complaints by teachers about 'troublesome' black pupils, negative stereotypes, and a 'stimulus–response' situation where pupils identified and responded to expectations of low ability and disruptive behaviour.

Table 10.3 Number of permanent exclusions by age. 1997/98, England

Age[1]	Number of permanent exclusions	Percentage of permanent exclusions[2]	Percentage of school exclusions[3]
5	81	0.7	0.01
6	131	1.1	0.02
7	176	1.4	0.03
8	254	2.1	0.04
9	368	3	0.06
10	616	5	0.1
11	703	5.7	0.12
12	1,564	12.7	0.28
13	2,385	19.4	0.44
14	3,351	27.2	0.61
15	2,447	19.9	0.46
16	192	1.6	0.11
17	24	0.2	0.02
18	5	–	0.04
19	1	–	0.09
All ages	**12,298**	**100**	**0.16**

1 Age at 31 December 1997

2 The number of permanent exclusions expressed as a percentage of the total number of permanent exclusions

3 The number of permanent exclusions expressed as a percentage of the number (headcount) of full-time and part-time pupils of each age in primary, secondary and special schools (excluding dually registered pupils in special schools) in January 1998

– Less than 0.5

Source: DfEE, 1999.

Table 10.4 **Number of permanent exclusions of pupils of compulsory school age by ethnic group. 1997/98, England**

Ethnic Group	Percentage	Number of exclusions	Percentage permanent exclusions[1]	Percentage of school population[2]
White	88.6	10,132	83.9	0.17
Black–Caribbean	1.5	753	6.2	0.76
Black–African	1.0	198	1.6	0.29
Black other	0.7	282	2.3	0.57
Indian	2.5	106	0.9	0.06
Pakastani	2.5	209	1.7	0.13
Bangladeshi	0.9	58	0.5	0.09
Chinese	0.4	11	0.1	0.05
Any other ethnic group	1.9	321	2.7	0.26
All pupils	**100**	**12,076[3]**	**100**	**0.18**

1 The number of permanent exclusions of compulsory school age expressed as a percentage of the total number of permanent exclusions of compulsory school age

2 The number of permanent exclusions of compulsory school age expressed as a percentage of the number (headcount) of pupils of compulsory school age in each ethnic group, in primary, secondary and special schools (excluding dually-registered pupils in special schools) in January 1998

3 Includes six permanent exclusions of pupils classified according to ethnic group

Source: DfEE, 1999.

Special Educational Needs (SEN)

DfEE's data show that pupils with statements of SEN[5] were about seven times as likely to be permanently excluded as pupils without statements of SEN in 1997/98 (Table 10.5).

The Audit Commission's research suggests that the percentage of permanently excluded pupils with SEN statements could be even higher; as much as 25 times greater than their incidence within the pupil population as a whole.

Children in care

There is very little data on school exclusions among children in the care of local authorities, but estimates suggest that it is significantly higher than average. The National Foster Care Association estimates that it is ten times higher than the average (Social Exclusion Unit, 1998), while the Audit Commission estimates that, in some LEAs, it could be as much as 30 times higher.

Table 10.5   **Number of permanent exclusions by special educational needs. 1997/98, England**

	Number of permanent exclusions	Percentage of permanent exclusions	Percentage of school population
Pupils with statements of SEN	2,252	18	0.96[2]
Pupils without statements of SEN	10,046	82	0.14[3]
All pupils	**12,298**	**100**	**0.16**

1   The number of permanent exclusions expressed as a percentage of the total number of permanent exclusions

2   The number of permanent exclusions expressed as a percentage of the number (headcount) of full-time and part-time pupils of all ages with statements of SEN in primary, secondary and special schools (excluding dually-registered pupils in special schools) in January 1998

3   The number of permanent exclusions expressed as a percentage of the number (headcount) of full-time and part-time pupils of all ages without statements of SEN in primary, secondary and special schools (excluding dually-registered pupils in special schools) in January 1998

Source: DfEE, 1999.

Regional and socio-economic differences

Inner and Outer London had the highest permanent exclusion rates in England in 1997/98; the lowest was Eastern region (Table 10.6). However, differences within regions are much more marked than differences between regions, even after taking into account socio-economic differences. For example, the Hammersmith and Fulham rate in 1997/98 was nearly three times that of Newham, 0.33 per cent compared with 0.12 per cent.

Despite this, there does appear to be some link between social deprivation and school exclusions. Using free school meals as an indicator of poverty, OFSTED found a correlation between the socio-economic background of the school and its exclusion rate. But, as OFSTED points out, there are schools in very disadvantaged areas with very low rates of exclusion.

Part of the problem is that schools' practice on exclusion varies enormously, and in many cases it is at odds with DfEE guidance. DfEE guidance states that exclusion should only be used in response to serious breaches of a school's policy on behaviour or the criminal law, and that it should only be used as a last resort. Nevertheless, pupils in some schools are being excluded for very minor offences. The Social Exclusion Unit cites press reports of exclusion for issues such as wearing trousers not bought from the nominated supplier and breaking a school rule about using a subway to cross a road. Other schools, it notes, seem to veer in the opposite direction and are too slow to use exclusion where it is necessary.

Table 10.6 Number of permanent exclusions by region. 1997/98, England

	Number of permanent exclusions	Percentage of the school population[1]
North East	677	0.16
North West and Merseyside	1,889	0.17
Yorkshire and Humber	1,262	0.15
East Midlands	1,008	0.15
West Midlands	1,544	0.17
Eastern	1,020	0.12
London		
Inner London	756	0.21
Outer London	1,271	0.19
South East	1,822	0.16
South West	1,049	0.15
England	**12,298**	**0.16**

1   The number of permanent exclusions expressed as a percentage of the number (headcount) of full and part-time pupils of all ages in primary, secondary and special schools, excluding dually-registered pupils in special schools in January 1998

Source: DfEE, 1999.

Family and social background

One small intensive study of 11 cases of permanently-excluded primary schoolchildren (all boys) found that most were from families experiencing a range of difficulties. Five of the children in the sample had experienced the divorce of their parents. Six of the children were living in one-parent families, two of whom were never-married mothers, three divorced and one a widow. Eight of the children were living in what the author of the study called 'chaotic' families. Social services were providing support in six of the families.

The researcher concluded that there was a strong suggestion, both informally, and from the evidence of the involvement of other agencies, that depressed parents, poor role models and experience of forms of rejection leading to low self-esteem can all play a part in making unmanageable behaviour at school in young boys more likely (Parsons, 1994).

Other research indicates that social and family factors play a role in social exclusion. OFSTED highlights poor acquisition of basic skills, particularly literacy, limited aspirations and opportunities, poverty, and poor relationships with pupils, parents or teachers. It also notes that: 'what appears to be happening is a degree of polarisation between the great majority of children who appear orderly and a small minority who are becoming increasingly intractable'.

However, others attribute the increase in school exclusions to the publication of league tables and performance targets. The Social Exclusion Unit points out that in such a competitive climate, some schools might exclude the less able pupils or those who cause disruption in class. Another possibility discussed by the Social Exclusion Unit is the lack of specialist staff, time and expertise within mainstream schools to deal with behavioural difficulties.

Conclusion

Beyond the headcount figures, we know very little about school exclusions. It appears that the numbers of pupils being excluded has increased rapidly since the early 1990s, but the reasons are far from clear. It is possible that a small minority are becoming increasingly intractable, but it could also be because of changes in the educational climate. What is clear is that some groups are more likely to be excluded than others, in particular African–Caribbean children, pupils with SEN statements, and children in the care of local authorities.

The link with poverty and social deprivation is also unclear, although there is some evidence that pupils living in the most socially-deprived areas are more likely to be excluded. But, there are schools in very disadvantaged areas with very low rates of exclusion. A complication is that some schools appear to exclude pupils for very minor offences, while others are slow to use exclusion where it is necessary. An element that clearly needs further investigation is the connection between exclusion and 'chaotic' families, and, in turn, the factors that lead to 'chaotic' families, such as social deprivation.

Notes to Chapter 10

1   Permanent exclusion results in the removal of a pupil from the roll of a particular school.

2   The number of permanent exclusions expressed as a percentage of the number (headcount) of full-time and part-time pupils of all ages.

3   Fixed-term exclusions can be anywhere between 1 and 45 days. The excluded pupil remains on the roll of the school and returns to that school at the end of the period of exclusion (Audit Commission, 1999).

4   Data on pupils by ethnic group have only been collected from schools since January 1997.

5   A child is deemed to have special educational needs if he or she has learning difficulties and needs special help. A child has learning difficulties if he or she finds it much harder to learn than most children of the same age, or if he or she has a disability which makes it difficult to use the normal educational facilities in the area. Emotional and behavioural problems are considered to be one kind of learning difficulty (Audit Commission, 1999).

11 Youth crime

Francis McGlone

Introduction

The objective of this chapter is to evaluate critically the existing data sources on crime and young people in Britain, in particular the link between youth crime and poverty.

Methodological problems

Research into youth crime is dogged with methodological problems. There are problems both of measurement and definition. For example, official statistics only measure recorded crime ie. the numbers found guilty or cautioned for indictable offences. This means that children under the age of criminal responsibility (age ten in England and Wales and eight in Scotland and Northern Ireland) do not appear in official data as they cannot be said to have committed a crime.

Problems with causality

Further problems arise with causality. For example, early researchers focused only on individual differences, ie. why some people commit crimes and others do not. But, as Rutter *et al.*, (1998) point out, this is a misleading over-simplification of the causal process as distinctions need to be drawn between individual differences in the liability to engage in anti-social behaviour, the translation of that liability into the actual committing of illegal acts, differences over time, or between places, in the overall levels of crime, situational variations in delinquent activities; and persistence or non-persistence of anti-social behaviour as individuals grow older.

Despite these methodological and causal difficulties, research has come to a common set of conclusions on the major risk factors for youth offending. Before examining this research, the chapter looks at the main measures of crime: official statistics, including trends over time, victim studies and self-report data.

Recorded crime

Official statistics show that over 300,000 young people under 21 were found guilty or cautioned for an offence in England and Wales in 1997, just under one-third of all offences that year. As can be seen from Tables 11.1 and 11.2, young men and women under 21 tend to commit more of certain types of offences than they do of others. Theft is particularly significant among young people, especially those aged 14 and under 18.

Table 11.1 **Male offenders found guilty at all courts or cautioned by type of offence and age group**

England and Wales *thousands*

	Aged 10 and under 14	Aged 14 and under 18	Aged 18 and under 21	Aged 21 and over	All ages
Indictable offences					
Violence against the person	1.8	10.3	7.6	30	49.6
Sexual offences	0.2	0.9	0.4	4.8	6.4
Burglary	3.3	11.9	7.6	16.4	39.2
Robbery	0.3	2.2	1.2	1.9	5.6
Theft and handling stolen goods	9.7	33.9	23.3	81.9	148.9
Fraud and forgery	0.2	1.4	2.4	13.5	17.5
Criminal damage	1.0	2.7	2.0	6.4	12.0
Drug offences	0.3	10.4	19.5	56.1	86.2
Other (excluding motoring offences)	0.3	4.7	8.2	32.2	45.4
Motoring offences[1]	0.0	0.4	1.2	7.3	8.9
Total	**17.0**	**78.7**	**73.6**	**250.5**	**419.8**
Summary offences (excluding motoring offences)	7.0	37.6	46.8	297.3	388.8
All offences (excluding motoring offences)	**24.0**	**116.3**	**120.4**	**547.9**	**808.6**

1 Offenders found guilty only; motoring offences may attract written warnings.

Source: Home Office, 1998.

Gender differences

Most marked in the recorded crime figures is the large gender imbalance in young people's offending (Tables 11.1 and 11.2). Of the 314,000 young people cautioned or found guilty between the ages of 10 and 20 in England and Wales in 1997, 83 per cent were male. Theft and handling stolen goods formed a far higher proportion of offending by the young women than it did among the young men (45 per cent compared with 26 per cent). Young men, on the other hand, had relatively larger proportions of offences involving violence, burglary and drug offending.

Table 11.2 Female offenders found guilty at all courts or cautioned by type of offence and age group

England and Wales   *thousands*

	Aged 10 and under 14	Aged 14 and under 18	Aged 18 and under 21	Aged 21 and over	All ages
Indictable offences					
Violence against the person	0.6	2.8	1.0	4.2	8.6
Sexual offences	0.0	0.0	0.1	0.1	0.1
Burglary	0.2	0.7	0.3	0.6	1.9
Robbery	0.1	0.4	0.1	0.1	0.6
Theft and handling stolen goods	4.6	12.3	6.8	28.7	52.4
Fraud and forgery	0.1	0.6	0.9	5.0	6.7
Criminal damage	0.1	0.3	0.1	0.7	1.3
Drug offences	0.0	0.9	1.8	7.7	10.4
Other (excluding motoring offences)		0.7	0.9	4.3	5.9
Motoring offences[1]	-	0.0	0.0	0.5	0.5
Total	**5.7**	**18.7**	**12.0**	**51.9**	**88.3**
Summary offences (excluding motoring offences)	1	7.2	8.3	101.7	118.2
All offences (excluding motoring offences)	**6.7**	**25.9**	**20.3**	**153.6**	**206.5**

1 Offenders found guilty only; motoring offences may attract written warnings.

Source: Home Office, 1998

Peak age for offending

Official data show that the peak age of known offending for both males and females in 1997 was 18. This has remained the same for males since 1987. However, for females the peak age has previously been at 14 or 15 since at least 1987. The change in 1997 has been attributed to falls in the number of females cautioned aged 17 or under (Home Office, 1998).

Social background of known offenders

Unfortunately, official statistics provide very little information on the background of known offenders. Nevertheless, there is some evidence in official data that youth crime is connected to unemployment. A survey of convicted youths aged 16 or 17 found that nearly 60 per cent were unemployed on the date of their conviction; the figure for those who were employed or in full-time education was nearer 20 per cent (Home Office, 1997).

There is also compelling evidence that crime in general is connected to changes in economic circumstances. Home Office research has found that property offences increase when the rate of growth in personal spending slows (Field, 1990).

Trends over time

The main source of information on time trends are official statistics but, as noted above, they can be distorted by factors other than crime. Nevertheless, they remain a useful indicator of underlying trends. Reviews of official data show that crime has been on a steady increase since the Second World War. Notifiable offences per 100,000 of the population quadrupled between the early 1950s and the late 1970s, and then doubled again by the early 1990s (Rutter et al., 1998). Since then rises have been less dramatic, and in some cases show a decline.

The focus on youth crime is relatively new and tends to be concentrated on the last 15 years. Consequently, it is not possible to be entirely clear what part juvenile crime has played in the overall rise in crime, but given the sizable proportion of crime committed by young people it seems unlikely that juvenile offending has fallen in the last 50 years. Indeed, studies of behaviour problems in young people suggest that they are rising rather than falling (Rutter et al., 1998).

Recorded crime figures for England and Wales show that the number of young people found guilty or cautioned for an indictable offence has fallen substantially since the mid-1980s. For example, between 1987 and 1997 it fell by a half among males aged 10 to 13 and a fifth among males aged 14 to 17. Over the same period, there was an increase of 6 per cent for male offenders aged 21 or over (Home Office, 1998). However, the decrease is almost certainly due to changes in court and police procedures and not because young people are committing fewer offences. Recorded crime statistics and victim studies both agree that the types of offence that young people are most likely to commit have continued to rise over this period, despite falls in the numbers of juveniles formally processed or convicted (Farrington, 1996; Rutter et al., 1998).

Victim studies

Another important measure of crime is victim studies. These suggest that crime is far more widespread than indicated in officially recorded figures. The latest British Crime Survey (BCS) for 1998 shows that just under a quarter of the BCS crimes that can be compared to recorded offences ended up in police records (Mirrlees-Black et al., 1998). Like recorded offences, the 1998 BCS shows a fall between 1995 and 1997 in nearly all the offences it measures. This is the first time the survey has recorded a fall. Given that the age of the perpetrator of the crime is not known and in most cases would be unknown, it is not possible to say if the fall in offences extends to youth offending.

The BCS has, however, identified young people as one of the groups most at risk of crime. Other groups at risk are: the unemployed, single parents, private renters, those living in inner-city areas, and in areas of high physical disorder, ie. the most socially disadvantaged.

Self-reported offending

The limitations of official statistics have led to growing interest in self-report studies of crime, which typically record the usual forms of delinquency, as well as non-personal and victimless crimes. Results from self-report studies tend to show that most young people have committed a delinquent act at some time, and that offending by young women is much higher than the officially-recorded figures would suggest. For example, one in two males and one in three females admitted to having committed an offence at some time in a self-report study carried out by the Home Office (Graham and Bowling, 1995).

There are, however, a number of major problems with self-report studies, in particular the over-reporting of minor offences and under-reporting of serious offences. Another is that respondents may exaggerate or understate their involvement in crime (Pitts, October 1996 – April 1997). Minority ethnic groups also tend to report fewer delinquent acts than their national counterparts (Rutter *et al.,* 1998). Despite these difficulties, the results from a range of self-report studies generally concur with regard to the frequency of offending and the differences between delinquents and non-delinquents (Rutter and Giller, 1983).

Home Office self-report study

An important advantage of self-report studies is that they can make use of background information about the informants. A Home Office self-report study carried out in 1993 (Graham and Bowling, 1995) used the data to explore the reasons why young people start to offend and why some stop whilst others do not. The results revealed that the strongest influences on starting to offend were low parental supervision, persistent truancy and associating with others involved in offending, all of which (the researchers note) are strongly related to the quality of relationship with parents.

Females offenders who had completed the transition to adulthood, ie. completed full-time education, left home and formed a new family unit, were found to be significantly more likely to stop offending than those who do not. For males, this development process made little difference. However, males who continued to live at home into their mid-twenties, were successful at school, avoided heavy drinking, drug use and associating with other offenders were more likely to stop offending.

The association with poverty and offending was not explored in the study, although social class and family size were. Nevertheless, only a weak association was found between social class and offending and this relationship disappeared after controlling for family and other variables. Similarly, young people living in larger families were no more likely to offend than those living in small families. This latter finding is at variance with other research but, as the researchers point out, an effect for family size is more likely to be found in studies using recorded conviction than self-report data. Taking up stable full-employment also had no effect on the likelihood of either males or females desisting from offending.

Longitudinal surveys

The development of longitudinal surveys which monitor children's progress from an early age has made it possible to identify the major risk factors for youth offending. These include poor parental supervision and discipline, family breakdown, low educational achievement, relatives and friends involved in criminal behaviour, and social and economic factors. Three of the most informative longitudinal surveys are reviewed below.[1]

The National Survey of Health and Development (The 1946 cohort)

The National Survey of Health and Development which investigated the health, growth and development of over 5,300 children born in March 1946 (Wadsworth, 1979) found that the sons of unskilled manual workers were three times more likely to have a criminal record before they were 21 than those of professional and salaried workers. Male recidivists, ie. those with two or more convictions, were more likely to come from large families, and there was evidence that broken homes were related to delinquency. Attitudes to school work and conduct at the age of ten were also found to be of significance in identifying later offenders, as was a lack of parental interest in children's education.

The Newcastle 1,000 Family Study

The Newcastle 1,000 Family Study (Kolvin *et al.*, 1990) which looked at children born in Newcastle upon Tyne in May and June 1947 found that delinquency was closely correlated with family deprivation. One in three children living in the poorest neighbourhoods became delinquent compared with one in six living in the more affluent districts. Six in ten boys and one in ten girls who came from what were classified as 'multiply-deprived' backgrounds acquired a criminal record. Those receiving poor maternal and domestic care before the age of ten were also more at risk of becoming delinquent.

Delinquent children who came from homes which were not classified as deprived were found to be more likely to have experienced emotional stress and, in some cases, to have been raised by an unmarried, relatively young mother. Teenagers from non-deprived backgrounds who became involved in criminal activities took noticeably less part in shared, family activities, and their parents maintained less contact with school and were more likely to have been classified as 'ineffective personalities' by the researchers.

The Cambridge Study in Delinquent Development

One of the most detailed longitudinal investigations ever undertaken into adolescent crime was the Cambridge Study in Delinquent Development (Farrington and West, 1990). This followed the fortunes of over 400 working-class boys in South London, the majority of whom were born in 1953. The boys were interviewed and tested by psychologists in their schools at ages 8, 10 and 14. Teachers completed questionnaires about the boys and, while at primary school, classmates were questioned about the boys' popularity, daring, dishonesty and troublesomeness. Parents were also interviewed annually by social workers until the boys were aged 14–15, and information was collected about their incomes, living conditions, family circumstances and child-rearing practices. In addition, details of convictions were collected and the boys, themselves, were asked to keep a self-report account of any offending. They were surveyed up until the age of 32.

The Cambridge researchers found that one of the best predictors of later offending was the rating of boys' troublesomeness at age 8–10 by teachers and classmates. However, they also identified four other important predictors of offending:

- economic deprivation
- family criminality
- parental mishandling
- school failure.

A significant precursor of delinquency was coming from a large family but essentially this was because such families tended to be poorer and less well housed. The risk of later delinquency was effectively doubled for children coming from a low income family, a large family or having a parent with a criminal record. This was the same for boys with below average IQs or who had unsatisfactory parenting. Of those boys who combined three or more of these risk factors, nearly a half became juvenile delinquents.

Risk factors

Based on these findings, augmented by more recent research, the Director of the Cambridge study, David Farrington (1996) has suggested that there are literally thousands of factors that point to an increased risk that children and young people will become criminally involved in the future. The most significant, he maintains, are:

- **Pre-natal and perinatal factors:** early child-bearing increases the risks of outcomes such as low school attainment, anti-social behaviour, substance use and early sexual activity. An increased risk of offending among children of teenage mothers is associated with low income, poor housing, absent fathers and poor child-rearing methods.
- **Personality:** impulsiveness, hyperactivity, restlessness and a limited ability to concentrate are associated with low attainment at school and a poor ability to foresee the consequences of offending.
- **Intelligence and attainment:** low intelligence and poor performance in school are important statistical predictors of offending but are difficult to disentangle from

each other. One plausible explanation of the link between low intelligence and crime, Farrington notes, is its association with a poor ability to manipulate abstract concepts and to appreciate the feelings of victims.

- **Parental supervision and discipline:** harsh or erratic discipline and cold or rejecting parental attitudes have been linked to delinquency.
- **Parental conflict and separation:** parental separation or divorce is more strongly related to delinquency than when the disruption has been caused by the death of a parent. However, it may not be the divorce or separation that creates an increased risk of offending so much as the parental conflict that led to the separation.
- **Socio-economic status:** social and economic deprivation are important predictors of delinquency but low family income is a better measurement than the prestige of parents' occupations.
- **Delinquent friends:** delinquents tend to have delinquent friends but it is not certain whether membership of a delinquent peer group leads to offending or whether delinquents simply gravitate towards each other, or both.
- **School influences:** the prevalence of offending by pupils varies widely between secondary schools but it is not clear how far schools themselves have an effect on delinquency or whether it is simply that delinquent children tend to go to high delinquency-rate schools.
- **Community influences:** the risks of becoming criminally involved are higher for young people raised in inner city areas, characterised by physical deterioration, over-crowded households, publicly-subsidised renting and high residential mobility.

Farrington points out that most of these factors coincide and are interrelated and therefore it is very difficult to explain the development of offending. For example, he notes that: 'adolescents living in physically deteriorated and socially disorganised neighbourhoods tend, disproportionately, to come from families with poor parental supervision and erratic discipline, and to display a high level of impulsiveness and low intelligence.'

Criticisms

In a critical review of Farrington's work, Pitts (April 1997 – October 1997) argues that the Cambridge study (and by association other criminal longitudinal investigations) emerges from a particular school of criminal research rooted in developmental psychology. This, he says: 'presupposes that the origins of crime are best sought within the development histories of individual criminals and, more contentiously, that this research is best conducted in accordance with the protocols of the natural sciences'. For example, the research transforms crime into a static 'effect' of development anomalies, in that it lumps together diverse phenomena like low birth-weight, unemployment and 'anti-establishment attitudes', as if they were a single phenomena, and then ascribes them an arbitrary numerical value.

Pitts also questions the Cambridge study's scientific neutrality and contemporary relevance because of its description of divorce and unemployment as 'anti-social'. And, he points out, that 'social factors' are assigned a secondary importance in the study:

'simply serving to exacerbate developmental anomalies originating in the family, the first few weeks of life or, indeed, the womb'.

He further notes that the offences examined in the study were committed in the 1960s and 1970s (as with the other longitudinal surveys) in low-income, high-crime neighbourhoods when a high proportion of apprehended young offenders were processed by the courts and incarcerated. This, he says: 'makes it very difficult to disentangle the effects of developmental anomalies from the impact of culture, neighbourhood, social stigma and institutionalisation'. Nor, as he points out: 'can we draw hard and fast conclusions of young offenders from this 30-year-old data'.

Rutter *et al.*, (1998) also raise a number of general concerns about longitudinal studies. First, echoing the point made by Pitts, individuals will have gone through their childhoods in a much earlier period, when social circumstances were very different. Second, it needs to be recognised that longitudinal studies are heavily reliant on retrospective recall. Research shows that people can remember a great deal about their past behaviour and major life experiences but there are problems. For example, accurate recall will depend on skilled interviewing, and recall is better for more concrete, easily defined behaviours and events than it is for ones that require relative judgements, such as feeling states or parenting qualities.

The research reviewed

In a major review of international research evidence on anti-social behaviour by young people, Rutter *et al.*, (1998) argue that the rise in crime, and other psychological disorders of young people, since the Second World War is due to environmental influences but research findings give us no more than plausible leads at this stage. They believe that the most likely contenders are demographic and social changes, such as increased rates of family breakdown, changes in the meaning and experiences of adolescence, and situational changes in surveillance and opportunities for crime. Individual characteristics also appear to play a role, including genes.

Worsening living standards do not, however, directly account for the rise in overall rates of disorder. As Rutter and his colleagues point out, soaring crime rates between the 1950s and 1970s were associated with a marked increase in the standard of living, low unemployment and steady or slightly reducing levels of inequality. Nevertheless, the weight of research evidence suggests that social disadvantage and poverty increase the risk of delinquency but the research to date (all from the United States) indicates that the effects are indirect and are mediated by parental depression and family conflict. These mediating factors, in turn, derive from family stresses brought about by the adverse effects of prolonged economic and associated stresses on family functioning.

Conclusion

The existing data sources on youth crime are all subject to different problems and distortions. Most crime is not recorded and therefore is not reflected in official statistics. Victim and self-report studies suggest that crime is far more widespread than indicated in officially-recorded figures, but most of this conduct is less serious than that reported in official statistics.

The development of longitudinal surveys has made it possible to identify the major risk factors for youth offending, but most of these factors coincide and are interrelated, thus making it very difficult to explain the development of offending. It is also not clear if the existing longitudinal data – which are now over 30 years old – can help us to draw any firm conclusions about the causes of youth offending in the 1990s.

Poverty is clearly one of the risk factors associated with youth offending but this risk appears to be indirect and mediated by other factors such as parental depression and poor parental discipline, though these in turn derive from stresses brought on from an adverse social situation.

Although there has been a considerable amount of work done in the last two decades into youth offending, there is a clear need for further research, in particular into gender differences. More research is also required which attempts to disentangle the various risk factors for youth offending. This includes investigating biological influences, including the influence of genes, but also exploring the impact that adverse social and economic circumstances has on good parenting.

Notes to Chapter 11

1   The review of longitudinal surveys draws upon the Family Policy Studies Centre Occasional Paper 16, *Crime and the Family,* (Utting *et al.,* 1993).

12 Children's smoking behaviour

Francis McGlone

Introduction

The objective of this chapter is to evaluate critically the existing data sources on smoking behaviour and children in Britain, in particular the link between smoking and poverty.

Surveys of smoking among children

Since 1982, the Social Survey Division has carried out biennial surveys of smoking among 11- to 15-year-old schoolchildren in England and Scotland for the Department of Health and the Scottish Office Department of Health. An additional survey, conducted only in England, was used to measure progress towards the 1994 *Health of the Nation* target for children's smoking in England. The most recent published survey in the series, the ninth, was carried out in 1996.

The Health Education Authority (HEA) commissioned eight surveys of children's attitudes to smoking in England between 1989 and 1994, and since 1996 has, with the Department of Health, commissioned three Teenage Smoking Attitudes surveys. The Teenage Smoking Attitudes surveys and the Social Survey Division surveys for the Department of Health (henceforth called the Department of Health surveys) use the same sampling design and same group of core questions, though the two surveys maintain different focuses. The Department of Health surveys are, however, regarded as the official source of smoking prevalence for 11- to 15-year-olds (Jarvis, 1997a).

The General Household Survey[1] (GHS) and the Health Survey for England also ask a series of questions about cigarette smoking, although interviews are only conducted with people aged 16 and over.

In addition to these surveys, health education authorities and boards in England and Scotland regularly commission surveys of the health behaviours of school children, including the prevalence of smoking, as part of a health promoting environment. Unfortunately, because of the different questions asked about smoking behaviour in these various surveys, it is not always possible to compare results.

The prevalence of smoking among secondary schoolchildren

The 1996 Department of Health survey of smoking among secondary schoolchildren in England found that 13 per cent of those aged 11–15 were regular smokers (defined as usually smoking at least one cigarette a day). This represents an increase of one per cent since 1994 and, although not statistically significant, continues a recent upward trend in smoking among this age group (Table 12.1).

The results of the 1996 survey also show that girls continue to be more likely than boys to be regular smokers (15 per cent compared with 13 per cent). The proportion of girls who smoke regularly is now at its highest level since the survey began in 1982 (Table 12.1). However, other research suggests that the gender difference in smoking among schoolchildren is transient (Acheson, 1998)

The likelihood of a boy or girl smoking grows with age. The 1996 Department of Health survey found that very few children were smokers when they started secondary school, but by the age of 13, one in ten children smoked regularly and by 15, three in ten children smoked regularly (Jarvis, 1997b).

Table 12.1 Regular smokers* among 11- to 15-year-old pupils by sex. 1982–1996

Year	Boys	Girls	Total	Year	Boys	Girls	Total
	%	%	%		%	%	%
1982	11	11	11	1992	9	10	10
1984	13	13	13	1993	8	11	10
1986	7	12	10	1994	10	13	12
1988	7	9	8	1996	11	15	13
1990	9	11	10				

* Defined as usually smoking at least one cigarette a week.

Source: Jarvis (1997b).

Inconsistency in findings

The increase in prevalence of children's smoking identified by the 1996 Department of Health survey is inconsistent with the trend in adult smoking monitored by the GHS, which showed a decrease in the proportion who smoked between 1990 and 1994 – from 30 per cent to 27 per cent. The same decrease to 27 per cent was also found among those aged 16–19 in the GHS, although the difference was not statistically significant.

The 1995 Health Survey for England, on the other hand, suggests an upward trend among those aged 16–24. In 1993, 32 per cent of men and women in this age group were smokers, compared with 36 and 37 per cent, respectively, in 1995 (Jarvis, 1997b).

The results of the 1996 Department of Health survey are also inconsistent with the findings of the 1996 HEA survey of children's attitudes to smoking. Although the HEA survey was carried out at about the same time, and used the same sampling methodology, question wording and ordering as the Department of Health's survey, the HEA's prevalence rates were lower (10 per cent of children aged 11–15 were regular smokers, compared with 13 per cent in the Department of Health's survey). Moreover, the HEA survey found no statistically significant difference in the prevalence of smoking among boys and girls (Jarvis, 1997a).

Regional variations

Unfortunately, the 1996 Department of Health survey and the earlier surveys of children's smoking behaviour are not able to provide regional data because of the small sample size in each region. The problem has been partly overcome by grouping the regions into four larger regions. Nonetheless, no consistent pattern of regional variation was found, nor has it been found by any of the previous surveys in this series. The only statistically significant change found was an increase in the North of England from 10 per cent of pupils in 1994 to 15 per cent in 1996 (Jarvis, 1997b).

An HEA-commissioned survey of English children aged 9–15 years did, however, find regional differences in smoking behaviour. Children from the South East and Inner London were more likely than other children to have tried smoking (classified as ever smoked) and to be regular smokers (classified as smoking more than one cigarette a week). Those from the East Midlands and East Anglia were the least likely (HEA, 1992).

Surveys carried out in Scotland and Wales have found similar prevalence rates to those in England, though secondary schoolchildren in Scotland were found to smoke more cigarettes on average per week than their English and Welsh counterparts (CSO, 1994).

The GHS has regularly found that a higher proportion of adults in Scotland smoke (classified as smokes at all) than in England and Wales. For England, the highest prevalence rates in 1996 were in the North and North West and the lowest in East Anglia (OPCS, 1998).

The influence of family and friends

Studies have consistently shown that children are much more likely to smoke if other people in their family smoke. For example, an HEA-commissioned survey among English children aged between 9 and 15 found that those who came from a household where at least one parent smoked were twice as likely to become regular smokers (6 per cent) than those who came from non-smoking household (3 per cent). The highest rates of smoking (16 per cent) occurred in households where an older brother or sister smoked (HEA, 1992).

The 1996 Department of Health survey found that those who lived with two parents who smoked were more than twice as likely to smoke as were those who lived in households where neither parent smoked: 21 per cent compared with 8 per cent. Children living in lone-parent families, as with children living with both parents, were more likely to be smokers if that parent smoked than otherwise: 20 per cent compared with 13 per cent. Overall, 17 per cent of those children who lived with a lone parent smoked, compared with 12 per cent of those who lived with both parents. However, brothers and sisters appear to have more influence than do parents. Children who had at least one brother or sister who smoked were over four times as likely to be smokers themselves as those who said none of their brothers or sisters smoked. As with previous surveys in the series, the 1996 survey also found a clear association between children's smoking behaviour and that of their friends: 79 per cent of regular smokers said that all or most of their friends smoked, compared with 5 per cent of children who had never smoked (Jarvis, 1997b).

Social factors

The content of the 1996 Department of Health survey was similar to that of previous years' surveys with the addition of some questions to the children about consumer durables, the number of cars in the family, and whether their parents own or rent their home. These were used to indicate the family's socio-economic position. Compared with GHS figures for households containing children aged 11–15, the children appear to have over-reported the availability of consumer goods and cars. Consequently, the results need to be treated with caution (Jarvis, 1997b).

As with previous surveys in the series, no attempt was made in the Department of Health survey to collect information on parents' occupations from the children as it was thought that, even if they knew their parents' occupations, it was unlikely that they would provide enough details for an accurate classification of their parents' socio-economic group to be made.

The only significant difference found by the Department of Health survey was for home computers: 15 per cent of those who live in families that do not have a computer were regular smokers, compared with 11 per cent of those in households with home computers. No association was found for car and dishwasher availability, which might also indicate a higher socio-economic group (Table 12.2).

When the sexes were looked at separately an association was found between car availability and smoking prevalence for girls: 19 per cent of those whose do not have a car were regular smokers, compared with 14 per cent of those whose families do have a car (Table 12.2). Nevertheless, the difference was not statistically significant.

Pupils who said that their families rented their home were more likely to be regular smokers than those who said that their families were owner-occupiers (15 per cent compared with 12 per cent), but again the difference was not statistically significant. Boys were more likely to be more regular smokers if their families rented rather than owned (15 per cent compared with 9 per cent). No significant difference was found for girls (Table 12.3).

The 1996 HEA survey, which asked the same questions as the 1996 Department of Health survey, similarly found few statistically significant differences between the availability of consumer durables and tenure and children's smoking behaviour. One unexpected result was that children from families with two cars (presumably the most affluent) were more likely to be regular smokers than those from families with one car (11 per cent compared with 8 per cent). As with the findings of the Department of Health survey, these results must be treated with caution because the children over-reported the availability of consumer goods and cars (Jarvis, 1997a).

Other surveys have also failed to find socio-economic differences in children's smoking behaviour. An HEA-commissioned survey among pupils in primary, middle and

Table 12.2 Proportion of pupils who were regular smokers, by sex and whether pupil's family has a car, a home computer or a dishwasher

	Boys %	Girls %	Total %
Number of family cars			
Two or more	11	14	13
One	9	14	12
None	10	19	14
Whether family has a home computer			
Yes	9	13	11
No	12	17	15
Whether family has a dishwasher			
Yes	11	14	13
No	9	15	12

Source: Jarvis, 1997b.

Table 12.3 Proportion of pupils who were regular smokers, by sex and their families' housing tenure

	Boys %	Girls %	Total %
Whether family owns or rents where they live			
Owns	9	15	12
Rents	15	16	15
Don't know	8	16	12

Source: Jarvis, 1997b.

secondary schools in England (HEA, 1992) found no significant difference for the number of regular smokers, though children from the higher socio-economic groups smoked on average fewer cigarettes per week than those from the lower socio-economic groups, while those from the higher socio-economic groups were most likely to have ever tried smoking. Green *et al.*, (1991) did, however, find a social class gradient in smoking in their 1987 longitudinal study of young people and their parents, resident in the west of Scotland. Even controlling for parental smoking and gender, young people from manual families were over one and a half times more likely to smoke than those from non-manual families.

Moreover, surveys and studies have consistently found a social class gradient in smoking behaviour among adults and older teenagers. The 1996 GHS, for example, found that a third (35 per cent) of men in manual households smoked, compared with 21 per cent in non-manual households. The figures for women that year were 33 per cent and 22 per cent, respectively (OPCS, 1998). Other GHS data show that by the age of 16–19 the prevalence of smoking is highest amongst semi-skilled and unskilled manual groups (Botting, 1995)

Research has also shown that smoking is far more common among the poorest groups in society. Marsh and McKay (1994) found that the least well-off were twice as likely to smoke compared with the better-off, and that reductions in smoking prevalence in recent years have been confined to higher income groups.

A 1995 infant feeding survey found that of women in all age groups who had recently given birth, teenage mothers were the most likely to have smoked before and during pregnancy (Foster *et al.*, 1997). This finding needs to be seen in the light of other research which shows that teenage pregnancy rates tend to be higher in deprived areas than affluent areas (Botting *et al.*, 1998), and that a major risk factor associated with becoming a teenage parent is having parents whose socio-economic status is low (Kiernan, 1995, and see also Chapter 6).

One possible reason for the dissimilar results between surveys is that socio-economic factors only begin to have a potentially strong influence in later teenage years. A study carried out by the Office for Population Censuses and Surveys (OPCS) concluded that at least up to the age of 14 or 15 smoking is erratic and probably opportunistic, because attitudes and behaviour are generally unstable during this period (Botting, 1995).

Educational factors

Questions were asked in the 1996 Department of Health survey about the educational expectations of the children. This was to provide a rough guide to educational ability, which has been shown to be related to socio-economic group.

When asked whether they would stay in full-time education after year 11 (16 years of age), a third (34 per cent) of all the children in the survey did not know if they would. Those who thought that they would not stay on were twice as likely to be regular smokers as those who thought they would (22 per cent compared with 11 per cent). This difference was especially marked among boys: 23 per cent of those who did not expect to stay on at school were regular smokers compared with 9 per cent of those who expected to stay on (Table 12.4). Because of the high proportion who did not know whether they would stay on, these findings must be treated with caution (Jarvis, 1997b).

Questions were also asked about expected GCSE results (Table 12.5). Children who thought that they would take GCSEs, but not get as many as five passes, were nearly three times as likely to be regular smokers as those who thought that they would pass at least five (29 per cent compared with 11 per cent). There was little difference in smoking prevalence among the other categories of expectation of GCSE results. Because nearly half of the children (47 per cent) said that they did not know whether they would take

Table 12.4 **Proportion of pupils who are regular smokers, by sex and whether they think they will stay in full-time education**

Whether staying in full-time education after year 11	Boys	Girls	Total
	%	%	%
Staying on	9	14	11
Not staying on	23	19	22
Don't know	9	16	13

Source: Jarvis, 1997b.

GCSEs or pass five or more of them, these findings must again be treated with caution (Jarvis, 1997b).

Children in the 1996 HEA survey were also asked whether they expected to stay in full-time education after the end of year 11, whether they expected to sit GCSEs and, if so, whether they expected to pass more than five Grades A, B or C. The findings were very similar to those obtained in the Department of Health survey. For example, children who did not expect to stay on were more likely to be regular smokers than those who did (16 per cent compared with 10 per cent). Also, children who were planning to sit GCSEs but thought they would not pass five of them were twice as likely to be smokers as were those expecting to do well in their exams, and those not expecting to take any (21 per cent compared with 10 per cent and 9 per cent).

Table 12.5 **Proportion of pupils who were regular smokers, by sex and expectation of GCSE results**

Whether expects to take GCSEs before leaving school	Boys	Girls	Total
	%	%	%
Thinks will take GCSEs			
Expects to pass five or more	8	14	11
Does not expect to pass five or more	29	29	29
Not sure about likely results	12	14	13
Thinks will not even take GCSEs	12	17	13
Not sure if will take GCSEs	9	13	11

Source: Jarvis, 1997b.

Conclusion

Despite the large number of major surveys into the subject, it is difficult to come to any firm conclusions about the smoking behaviour of children, in particular the link with poverty. First, due to inconsistent findings, it is not clear if the prevalence of smoking among schoolchildren is increasing or decreasing, or if prevalence rates are higher among girls than boys. Second, because of small survey sample sizes, there are no area or locality data which can be compared, for example between poor and affluent areas and localities. Third, the surveys failed to find any socio-economic differences. This may be because of methodological difficulties in accurately measuring children's socio-economic position, but, more likely, it is because socio-economic factors only begin to have a potentially strong influence in later teenage years – an age group outside the scope of all the major surveys, except the GHS.

Such pointers as there are suggest that socio-economic factors are linked to the smoking behaviour of children. Research has consistently found that there is a social class gradient in prevalence of smoking among adults and young people, with those from lower socio-economic backgrounds more likely to smoke than those from higher socio-economic backgrounds. There is also a clear association between educational expectations and smoking, which has been shown to be related to socio-economic group. Finally, studies have consistently found a clear association between children's smoking behaviour and the smoking behaviour of other family members who, of course, share the same socio-economic background.

Notes to Chapter 12

1   The GHS is a continuous survey which has been running since 1971 and is based each year on a sample of the general population resident in private households in Great Britain.

13 Adolescent alcohol use

Francis McGlone

Introduction

The objective of this chapter is to evaluate critically the existing data on alcohol use by children and adolescents in Britain, in particular the link with poverty.

Surveys of adolescent alcohol use

There are very few surveys into adolescent drinking, and scarce national data from which to establish trends. For example, the Office for National Statistics (ONS) has only been monitoring the drinking habits of adolescents since 1988, and prior to 1996 the questions asked were very limited. Also, it was not until 1988 that the General Household Survey (GHS) provided any data on the drinking habits of 16- to 17-year-olds (Botting, 1995).

The only other major sources of information on the drinking habits of young people were a Health Education Authority (HEA) survey carried out in England in 1989 (HEA, 1992), and a separate survey carried out by the Office of Population Censuses and Surveys (OPCS) in 1984 (Marsh et al., 1986).

A difficulty with these various surveys is that the questions asked were often different and therefore it is not always possible to compare results.

Consumption of alcohol

The most recent data on the smoking habits of adolescents comes from the 1996 ONS survey of schoolchildren aged 11–15 in England (Goddard, 1997). This found that 27 per cent of children aged 11–15 had had an alcoholic drink in the previous seven days, with no significant difference between boys and girls: 27 per cent and 26 per cent, respectively (Table 13.1).

Not surprisingly, the proportions who reported that they had had a drink in the previous week increased with age: only 7 per cent of 11-year-olds had done so, compared with 53 per cent of 15-year-olds (Table 13.1).

Of those who said that they had had a drink in the previous week, the average weekly amount drunk was 1.8 units (slightly less than a pint of beer). Boys drunk, on average, more than girls: 2.1 units in the previous seven days, compared with 1.5 units. These average amounts conceal wide variations in the amounts children of this age drink. The vast majority drank very little or nothing in the previous week, and most of the remainder had drunk only modest amounts. However, 5 per cent of boys and 3 per cent of girls had drunk 15 or more units in the previous week (Goddard, 1997).

Table 13.1	**Percentage of children aged 11–15 who said they drank 'last week', by sex and age. 1996, England**		
Age	Boys	Girls	Total
	%	%	%
11 years	7	6	7
12 years	12	9	11
13 years	27	22	24
14 years	37	35	36
15 years	50	55	53
Total	27	26	27

Source: Goddard 1997.

Drinking frequency

Nearly two-fifths (37 per cent) of the 1996 ONS survey sample said that they had never had a proper alcoholic drink, and a further 4 per cent said that they had done so, but did not drink at all now. Older children were more likely than younger children to have had a proper alcoholic drink: 72 per cent of 11-year-olds said that they had never had a proper drink, compared with 12 per cent of 15-year-olds.

One in five 11–15 year olds (20 per cent) said that they usually drank at least weekly. This is consistent with the proportions who said that they had a drink in the previous week, as you need to add half of the 9 per cent who said they drank once a fortnight, one quarter of the 9 per cent who said they drank monthly and so on, giving a total of around 27 per cent who might be found drinking in a typical week – the same proportion who said that they did drink in the previous week (Goddard, 1997).

Trends

A comparison of the results of the 1996 ONS survey with previous surveys in the series shows that there has been no clear rise in the proportion of secondary schoolchildren who drink at all, but there has been a rise in the frequency with which those who do drink, do so. As Table 13.2 shows, the proportion of children aged 11–15 who had a drink in the previous week increased from 20 per cent in 1988 to 27 per cent in 1996.

The average weekly consumption of alcohol of those who do drink has also increased: nearly doubling between 1990 and 1996 from 0.8 to 1.8 units. The increase has been fairly steady, and has occurred to a similar degree among boys and girls.

Unfortunately, the GHS does not provide trend data for 16- to 17-year-olds. Nevertheless it does show that since 1984 alcohol consumption levels (units per week) have remained fairly constant for adult men, while for adult women there has been a gradual rise, with the largest rise among the youngest women (18–24). Despite the increase in

Table 13.2 Percentage of children aged 11–15 who said they drank 'last week', by age. 1988–1996, England

Age	1988 %	1990 %	1992 %	1994 %	1996 %
11 years	5	6	6	6	7
12 years	9	8	10	9	11
13 years	16	18	13	19	24
14 years	22	32	29	30	36
15 years	40	40	45	50	53
Total	20	21	21	24	27

Source: Goddard, 1997.

levels of alcohol consumption by women, it is still much lower that of men (GHS, 1998).

The GHS also shows that alcohol consumption is higher among younger age groups than older age groups. In 1996, 35 per cent of men aged 16–24 were drinking more than 21 units per week (the recommended weekly maximum for men), compared with 18 per cent of those aged 65 and over. The equivalent figures for women drinking more than 14 units per week (the weekly recommended level for women) were 22 per cent and 7 per cent (GHS, 1998).

Regional variations

The 1996 ONS survey did not provide a regional breakdown of its results, but it did compare them with a companion survey carried out in Scotland in 1996. However, the comparison must be treated with caution because the populations covered were not quite the same (Goddard, 1997). The comparison shows that average consumption per pupil was similar in both countries: 1.8 in England and 1.9 in Scotland: although the proportion of pupils who drank alcohol in the previous week was lower in Scotland than in England: 23 per cent compared with 27 per cent. Those in Scotland who did drink, however, drank significantly more: the average number of units consumed by those who had drunk in the previous week was 11.1 units in Scotland compared with 8.4 in England. Girls in Scotland were less likely than boys to drink at all, but among those who did drink, consumption was not much lower than it was among boys. It was also clear that alcohol consumption among schoolchildren in both countries is increasing, as is the average amount drunk per pupil.

The 1996 GHS found similar alcohol consumption levels for adult men in England, Scotland and Wales, but adult women in Scotland were less likely than women elsewhere to drink more than 14 units per week. Consumption levels showed a North–South divide in England with higher levels for men in the North, Yorkshire and Humberside and North West, and lower levels in the South East and South West. For women, it was highest in the North West and fairly even distributed throughout the rest of the country.

The 1989 HEA survey of alcohol use among 9- to 15-year-olds also found a North–South divide with alcohol experimentation highest in the North of England and lowest in Inner London. Children in the South West, however, were the most likely to be regular drinkers (those who claimed to consume alcohol at least once a week), while those in Outer London were the least likely.

Socio-economic factors

As with previous ONS surveys of children and alcohol, the 1996 survey did not ask for details of parents' jobs as it was felt that children would not be able to provide enough details for an accurate classification of their parents' socio-economic group to be made. The 1996 survey did, for the first time, ask a series of questions designed to identify the family's socio-economic position: cars, home computers, dishwashers, and whether their parents owned or rented their home. However, the results need to be treated with caution as a comparison with GHS figures for households containing children aged 11–15 suggests that the children over-reported the availability of consumer goods and cars. Moreover, a significant proportion of the children (12 per cent) could not say whether their family owned or rented their home (Goddard, 1997).

As Table 13.3 shows, the ONS survey found no consistent association between children's drinking behaviour and the family's socio-economic position. If anything, the results indicated that it is children from better-off families who are most likely to drink. Almost a quarter (23 per cent) of the children who said that their families had two or more cars usually drank at least once a week, compared with only 15 per cent who said that their family had no car.

Other surveys have obtained similar results. The 1989 HEA survey found that children from the top two social classes were more likely than those from the bottom two to have experimented with alcohol and to be regular drinkers. A West of Scotland cohort study found that young people from non-manual households were more likely to drink than those from manual households (Green et al., 1991). However, the HEA survey also found that children from higher social classes tended to consume slightly fewer units of alcohol than those from lower social classes, and were less likely to exceed safe adult limits. They were also far more likely to drink regularly with their parents.

One suggested reason for these differences is that social class differences in alcohol consumption, like smoking, only begin to develop in later teenage years and early adulthood (Dennehy et al., 1997). But, as the GHS shows, adults in the highest household income groups are more likely to exceed the recommended weekly maximum levels for sensible drinking than those in the lowest household income groups (GHS, 1998).

Table 13.3   **Percentage of children who usually drink at least once a week, by sex and socio-economic indicators. 1996, England**

Socio-economic indicators	Boys %	Girls %	Total %
Number of family cars			
Two or more	25	21	23
One	20	15	17
None	14	17	15
Whether family has a home computer			
Yes	22	18	20
No	20	18	19
Whether family has a dishwasher			
Yes	25	20	22
No	19	17	18
Whether family owns or rents where they live			
Owns	22	19	20
Rents	23	17	20
Don't know	18	13	15
All pupils	**21**	**18**	**20**

Source: Goddard, 1997.

Educational factors

The 1996 ONS survey asked children if they thought that they would stay on at school after the end of year 11 (the fifth year of secondary education), and whether they thought they would get any GCSEs. The reason these questions were asked is that research has shown that educational expectations are related to social class and have been shown to be associated to smoking: those with higher educational expectations being less likely to smoke (Goddard, 1997).

However, the results were somewhat confusing as the highest proportions of frequent drinkers were among, on the one hand, those from better-off families, but on the other, from among those with lower educational expectations (Goddard, 1997).

As can be seen from Table 13.4, the highest proportion of frequent drinkers (45 per cent) was among the relatively small number of children from families with two or more cars who do not expect to stay on at school after year 11. Similarly with GCSE results: the highest proportion of frequent drinkers was among children who expect to sit GCSEs but not to get good results, and whose families have two or more cars.

Table 13.4 **Percentage of children who usually drank at least once a week, by whether they expect to continue in full-time education after year 11 and number of family cars. 1996, England**

	Number of cars		
Whether expects to continue in full time education after year 11	*More than one* %	*One or none* %	*Total* %
Yes	23	17	20
No	45	25	33
Not sure	19	16	17
Total	23	17	20

Source: Goddard, 1997.

The survey concludes that these results suggest that the group most likely to drink frequently may be children from better-off families who do not expect to do well at school, but because of the reservations about the quality of the data, the findings are only tentative at present.

Conclusion

Data on adolescent drinking in Britain is limited, and therefore it is very difficult to establish trends, or to confirm any link with poverty. The available evidence suggests that a substantial proportion of older children drink regularly, though the amounts consumed are small. However, those who do drink are drinking more than their contemporaries did a decade or so ago. There is also some evidence of a North–South divide in drinking behaviour with children in the North of England more likely to experiment with alcohol than those in the South. Where the evidence is less clear is on the socio-economic background of young drinkers, but it appears that children from better-off families are more likely to drink than those from poorer families, though this finding is tentative at present.

14 Drug use among children and young people

Francis McGlone

Introduction

The objective of this chapter is to evaluate critically the existing data sources on drug use among children and young people, in particular the link between drug use and poverty.

Surveys of young people's drug use

Since the early 1990s there have been a number of attempts to quantify the degree of illicit drug use among adults and young people in Britain. The most important is the biennial British Crime Survey (BCS) for England and Wales which has included a self-completion questionnaire on drug use for 16- to 59-year-olds since 1994. The latest in the series was carried out in 1998 (Ramsay and Partridge, 1999).

As there was no equivalent survey for younger age groups, the Office for National Statistics (ONS) included for the first time in 1998 a series of questions on drug use in its biennial survey series on smoking and drinking among secondary school children aged 11–15 in England and Scotland (Goddard and Higgins, 1999). These questions were very similar to those included in the BCS, as was the list of drugs used, thus making it possible to draw comparisons between the two surveys.

In addition to the BCS and ONS surveys, there are a number of other relevant surveys, in particular those carried out by the Health Education Authority (HEA, 1992; HEA/BMRB, 1996) and Leitner's 'Four Cities' study (Leitner *et al.*, 1993). However, the prevalence rates of these surveys are now rather dated. Another important source is the work of Exeter University's Health Education Unit (eg., Baldwin, 1997; Baldwin 1998;), although these surveys are not strictly representative of England (Aldridge *et al.*, 1999). Consequently the main focus of this chapter is the 1998 BCS and 1998 ONS surveys.

The 1998 ONS survey

The results on the 1998 ONS survey for England (the results for Scotland were published in a separate report) show that about one-third (34 per cent) of 11- to 15-year-olds had been offered at least one of a list of illegal drugs. Not surprisingly, the likelihood of being offered drugs increased with age: 15 per cent of 11-year-olds had been offered drugs compared with 61 per cent of 15-year-olds. Boys were slightly more likely than girls to have been offered drugs: 36 per cent compared with 32 per cent. The most likely drug to be offered was cannabis.

Although a third of 11- to 15-year-olds had been offered drugs, just 13 per cent had ever used drugs. As Table 14.1 shows, the prevalence of drug use increases very sharply with age: 33 per cent of 15-year-olds had used drugs compared with only 1 per cent of 11-year-olds. Again, boys were slightly more likely to have used drugs than girls: 14 per cent compared with 12 per cent.

Table 14.1 **Percentage of children who had ever used drugs, by sex and age. 1998, England**

Age	Boys %	Girls %	Total %
11 years	1	1	1
12 years	4	4	5
13 years	10	9	9
14 years	18	16	18
15 years	33	30	31
Total	**14**	**12**	**13**

Source: Goddard and Higgins, 1999.

Cannabis was the drug that the highest proportion of children had used (12 per cent), followed by amphetamines (3 per cent), poppers (2 per cent), magic mushrooms (2 per cent) and glue (2 per cent). The proportion using opiates (heroin and methadone) or stimulants such as cocaine and ecstasy was roughly one per cent. Over half (52 per cent) of the 13 per cent of children who had ever taken drugs had only taken cannabis, 40 per cent had used cannabis and other drugs, and 9 per cent had used other drugs only.

The ONS survey collected no information on frequency of drug use, although the children were asked about the last time each drug was used. As Table 14.2 shows, of the 13 per cent of children who had ever used drugs, only about half (7 per cent) had done so in the last month, another 4 per cent had done so in the last year, and 2 per cent had last used drugs more than a year ago.

Roughly similar proportions of boys and girls had used drugs in the last month, although among those aged 15, slightly more boys than girls had done so: 19 per cent compared with 16 per cent. Overall, 28 per cent of 15-year-olds had used drugs in the last year.

Results showed that the likelihood of having ever used drugs was strongly related to smoking: 63 per cent of regular smokers had used drugs compared with only 1 per cent of those who had never smoked. Drug use was also related to drinking frequency, but less strongly than to smoking: 44 per cent of those who drank at least once a week had used drugs compared with just one per cent of those who had never had a drink. Virtually no children in the survey who had never smoked or drunk alcohol had ever used drugs, but three-quarters (75 per cent) of regular smokers who also drank at least once a week had done so.

Table 14.2 **When last used drugs, by sex and age. 1998, England**

	11 years %	12 years %	13 years %	14 years %	15 years %	Total %
Boys						
In the last month	0	2	4	10	19	7
In the last year	1	2	3	6	10	5
More than a year ago	0	1	3	2	4	2
Never used drugs	99	96	90	81	67	86
Girls						
In the last month	0	2	3	9	16	6
In the last year	1	1	3	5	10	4
More than a year ago	0	1	2	2	4	2
Never used drugs	99	96	91	84	70	88
Total						
In the last month	0	2	4	10	18	7
In the last year	1	2	3	6	10	4
More than a year ago	0	1	2	2	4	2
Never used drugs	99	96	91	82	69	87

Source: Goddard and Higgins, 1999.

Comparison of drug use in England and Scotland

Comparison of the results for England and Scotland[1] found that children in Scotland were more likely than children in England to have been offered drugs: 41 per cent compared with 34 per cent. They were also more likely to have tried drugs: 18 per cent compared with 13 per cent. The types of drugs the children used in the two countries were similar, albeit that Scottish children's use was higher. For example, 16 per cent of children in Scotland had used cannabis compared with 12 per cent of children in England.

Regional variations

Apart from the comparison with Scotland, no regional data was provided by the ONS survey. Nonetheless, earlier surveys have found very little variation between regions. For example, the 1989 Health Education Authority (HEA) survey of 9- to 15-year-olds found similar rates of experimentation with Class A drugs (acid, cocaine, ecstasy, crack and heroin) across England, though exposure to such drugs was significantly higher in Inner London and the South East (HEA, 1992).

Socio-economic differences

The ONS survey did not provide any information on socio-economic differences, possibly because past attempts by ONS to classify children's socio-economic backgrounds have not been entirely successful. ONS's 1996 enquiry into the prevalence of smoking among secondary schoolchildren, for example, found that respondents tended to over-report the availability of consumer goods and the number of cars in their families (Jarvis, 1997, and see also Chapter 12).

Results from the 1989 HEA survey of drug use among 9- to 15-year-olds (HEA, 1992) found that experimentation with drugs was fairly evenly distributed across socio-economic groups, although children from higher socio-economic groups were less likely to have tried Class A drugs (HEA, 1992)

British Crime Survey (BCS)

The BCS is a large biennial survey representative of the general public aged 16 and over in England and Wales. Since 1992, it has carried a drugs self-report component, and because the same self-report method and identical sampling techniques were used in 1994, 1996 and 1998, it is possible to make comparisons between the surveys.

Results from the 1998 BCS show that drug misuse among the young is relatively widespread: half (49 per cent) of young people aged 16–29 have used an illicit drug. However, it is important to bear in mind that this is *ever* used an illicit drug, and most illicit drug use simply involves cannabis. If the focus turns to the two recall periods in the BCS, the last year and the last month, reported rates of drug use fall considerably. For example, among the age group 16–29, it falls to 25 per cent and 16 per cent, respectively.

Results for the age group 16–19 are reproduced in Table 14.3. As can be seen, as with the 16–29 year old age group, reported rates of drug consumption drop considerably as between ever, the last year and the last month: 49 per cent, 31 per cent and 22 per cent, respectively.

Other research shows that roughly three-quarters of last month users can be deemed regular users (Ramsay and Spiller, 1997). Consequently, we can estimate that about 16 to 17 per cent of 16- to 19-year-olds are regular users. We can also estimate from the ONS survey that approximately 5 per cent of 11- to 15-year-olds are regular users.

Table 14.3 further shows the clear gender gap in drug consumption among older teenagers, with males generally more likely to report drug use than females.

As with all other age groups, cannabis is considerably more popular among 16- to 19-year-olds than any other prohibited drug. As Table 14.4 reveals, it has been tried by 40 per cent in this age group. Only one per cent have ever tried heroin or crack.

Table 14.3   **Percentage of 16- to 19-year-olds who had used drugs, ever or in the last year or month, by gender. 1996, England and Wales**

	Boys %	Girls %	All %
Ever/lifetime	55	42	49
Last year	35	27	31
Last month	25	19	22

Source: Ramsay and Spiller, 1997.

Table 14.4   **Percentage of 16- to 19-year-olds who used four different drugs, ever or in the last year or month. 1996, England and Wales**

	Cannabis %	Amphetamine %	Heroin %	Crack %
Ever	40	18	1	1
Last year	28	9	*	*
Last month	19	6	*	0

*   Less than 0.5 per cent

Source: Ramsay and Partridge, 1999.

Trend data

As the 1994, 1996 and 1998 BCS all included the same self-report component, it is possible to compare the results in order to detect changing patterns in drug use among the adult population in England and Wales. The published results, however, only provide figures for the full 16 to 59 age range, the 16 to 29 age group and, in a special analysis at the end of the 1998 BCS report, 16- to 24-year-olds.

A comparison of the three BCS sweeps show that drug use among the full 16 to 59 age range is fairly stable. For the 16 to 29 age group, there was a small increase from 23 per cent to 25 per cent between 1994 and 1996 for any drug use, but this was not statistically significant. There were some small changes in the use of drugs by 16- to 29-year-olds, in particular cocaine, the use of which increased from one to three per cent. The use of cannabis also increased from 20 per cent in 1994 to 23 per cent in 1998, but again this was not statistically significant.

Some significant changes were found when the patterns for young men and young women were looked at separately. While use of any drug by young women was the same in both 1994 and 1998, for young men the prevalence rate increased from 28 per cent to 33 per cent. And, while female use of cannabis increased by just one per cent across the four years, male use of cannabis increased from 25 per cent to 29 per cent.

The analysis of the narrower 16 to 24 age group also showed very little change in any drug use since 1994. As Table 14.5 shows, use within the last year, which is probably the best indicator of changing trends, remained the same at 29 per cent between 1994, 1996 and 1998. Last month prevalence rates increased slightly from 17 per cent in 1994, to 18 per cent in 1996, and to 19 per cent in 1998. Ever/lifetime use did, however, increase from 45 per cent in 1994, to 48 per cent in 1996, and then to 52 per cent in 1998. But, as the BCS acknowledges, ever/lifetime use of drugs is not a very useful prevalence indicator.

Table 14.5 **Percentages of respondents aged 16 to 24 in the 1994, 1996 and 1998 British Crime Surveys who used any drug ever, or in the last year or month**

	1994 BCS %	1996 BCS %	1998 BCS %
Any Drug			
Ever	45	48	52
Last year	29	29	29
Last month	17	18	19

Source: Ramsay and Partridge, 1999.

Figures for cannabis use among the under-25s changed in a broadly similar pattern to that for any drug use, only edging up one per cent over the four years. Rates of heroin use remained extremely low throughout the four year period with ever/lifetime rates constant at one per cent, but lifetime, last year and last month prevalence rates for cocaine all increased significantly, particularly between 1994 and 1998. Ever/lifetime use of cocaine increased from 3 per cent in 1994 to 7 per cent in 1998.

Other research suggests that ever drug use among schoolchildren increased substantially between the late 1980s and early 1990s. Exeter University's Health Education Unit (Baldwin, 1996) found that the proportion of 15- and 16-year-olds reporting having tried an illicit drug more than tripled between 1989 and 1999 to over 30 per cent, although the Exeter survey also noted some tailing-off of 'ever tried' rates (cited in Aldridge *et al.*, 1999).

Regional variation

The 1994, 1996 and 1998 BCS have consistently found regional variations in the use of drugs, with rates for any drug use generally higher in London. The only significant increase in the use of any drug use for the 16 to 29 age group between 1994 and 1998 was in the combined Midlands / North.

Socio-economic variables in the BCS

A number of social, economic and lifestyle factors were used to analyse the BCS data, including household income, social class, employment status, and ACORN – A Classification of Residential Neighbourhoods.

Unfortunately, the published social and economic analysis of the BCS data combines the respondents into just two age groups (16–29 and 30–59) and therefore it is not possible to ascertain the socio-economic characteristics of just those aged 16–19. Nevertheless, the analysis does provide some illuminating perspectives on the topic.

According to the ACORN classification, last year and last month drug users, regardless of age, were more likely to live in households located in relatively affluent 'Rising' areas, ie., those with a preponderance of affluent urbanites, prosperous professionals and better-off executive households. There was very little difference in drug use between those living in affluent 'Thriving' areas and those living in hardship in the 'Aspiring' and 'Striving' areas. Young people in the 'Thriving' areas were marginally more likely to have used illegal substances in the last year, but for the over-thirties drug use fell below the average rate of use (Table 14.6).

A comparison of the three sweeps of the BCS showed that only those young people aged 16 to 29 living in 'Thriving', 'Rising' and 'Striving' neighbourhoods experienced any growth in drug use over the last four years (Table 14.7). Collectively, they represent roughly half of all young people – the very poor, the very rich and the much smaller 'Rising' category, whose rates are the highest of all. Drug use has stayed the same, or even declined, for the remaining young people, living in, what the BCS calls, 'middle of the road' types of areas (Ramsay and Partridge, 1999)

Household income, social class and employment status

Analysis of the BCS data by household income found that income was only a modest indicator of differential rates of drug use. Rates of use in the last year among 16- to 29-year-olds in the poorest and richest households were not exceptionally different at 33 per cent and 26 per cent, respectively. Nor was social class a useful indicator. Rates of drug use in the last year among 16- to 29-year-olds who lived in manual and non-manual headed households were 23 per cent 26 per cent, respectively.

Analysis of the BCS data did, however, find a clear association between unemployment and drug use. As Table 14.8 shows, 40 per cent of 16- to 29-year-olds unemployed during the week before their BCS interview, reported using drugs in the previous year, which is nearly double the rate of those in employment.

Table 14.6 **Drug use in the last year and month, by ACORN classification and age group**

ACORN Category	16–29 age group %	30–59 age group %	16–59 age group %
Last year			
Thriving	27	3	8
Expanding	16	4	7
Rising	43	12	24
Settling	20	4	8
Aspiring	24	6	11
Striving	24	6	12
Average	25	5	11
Last month			
Thriving	17	1	4
Expanding	10	2	4
Rising	26	6	14
Settling	14	2	5
Aspiring	16	3	7
Striving	14	3	7
Average	16	3	6

Source: Ramsay and Partridge, 1999.

Table 14.7 **Percentage of respondents in the 1994, 1996 and 1998 British Crime Surveys, aged 16 to 29, in neighbourhoods with different ACORN classifications, who used drugs in the last year**

ACORN Category	1994 BCS %	1996 BCS %	1998 BCS %
Thriving	23	27	27
Expanding	19	18	16
Rising	40	32	43
Settling	20	21	20
Aspiring	25	24	24
Striving	21	24	24
Average	23	24	25

Source: Ramsay and Partridge, 1999.

Table 14.8 **Percentage using any drug in the last year, by employment status and age**

	16–29 %	30–59 %	All 16–59 %
Employed	25	5	10
Unemployed	40	9	24
Economically inactive	23	5	11
Average	**25**	**5**	**11**

Source: Ramsay and Partridge, 1999.

Ramsay and Partridge (1999), the authors of the BCS report, argue that these results support Leitner's proposition that some of the highest rates of drug use are found in the highest socio-economic groups, although the most problematic use is mainly found among low-status groups (Leitner *et al.*, 1993). However, the extent to which the BCS results actually do confirm this is questionable.

The BCS data further found that marital status and responsibility for young children appeared to influence the prevalence of drug use. The highest prevalence rate for the last year was among single people, of all ages. Divorcees and separated respondents were also more likely to have used drugs than married or cohabiting couples.

This, the BCS believes, points to the salience of drug use in some people's lives, when they are actively pursuing leisure activities, typically outside the home. It points out that research indicates that being away from the parental environment increases the likelihood of drug consumption among young people. Indeed, the BCS's own data found that young people spending three or four nights out during the previous week had rates of drug use in the last year 57 per cent higher compared with those young people going out less than three times a week.

Finally, the 1998 BCS found a clear association between alcohol and increased drug taking. Young heavy drinkers were almost three times more likely to have used prohibited substances in the last year compared with light drinkers: 44 per cent compared with 16 per cent. While frequent evening pub-going was associated with increased drug taking, a more powerful indicator was frequent lunchtime drinking: doubling the likelihood of drug taking in the last year.

Under-reporting

There are number of methodological difficulties with both the 1998 BCS and the 1998 ONS surveys, in particular with under-reporting. The drug component element of the 1998 BCS lost 21 per cent of its originally targeted sample (which already excludes the homeless and those in institutional setting, ie. those most at risk of drug use) and 3 per cent refused to answer the drugs question. ONS's response rate was only 62 per cent. The BCS's findings also show that current drug users are more likely to be out of the home a great deal, making their capture more difficult (Aldridge *et al.*, 1999).

A general problem with household surveys of young people is that parental permission must be sought (usually for the under-18s), and the young subjects must then undertake the interview in the parental home, possibly with parents in the same room or near by. This, Aldridge *et al.,* (1999) believe, will inevitably reduce disclosure.

These problems do not, however, appear to apply to the 1998 BCS or the 1998 ONS survey. The BCS does not say if it asked parental permission to interview those under 18, but since 1996 it has allowed respondents to enter answers directly into a laptop computer which may have improved self-disclosure rates considerably (Ramsay and Percy, 1997).

ONS's survey was school-based and parental permission was requested. Each school in the survey was given copies of a letter from ONS to be sent to parents of the children, asking them to reply only if they wished their child not to take part. The sampled pupils completed a questionnaire in a classroom under the supervision of an interviewer, but with no teacher present. Moreover, extreme care was taken to protect the confidentiality of pupils' answers and to make them aware that the answers would not be identified with them personally, or with the school (Goddard and Higgins, 1999).

Despite some under-reporting by most surveys of drug use, they do come up with consistent results. Nevertheless, a major shortcoming of drug use surveys is the problem of defining drug use (ie. ever, last month or last year) and, as a consequence, problems with use and problem use. For example, a significant proportion of young people have tried, but will not have had further or recent drug-taking episodes (Aldridge *et al.,* 1999).

Also missing from present research, as Aldridge *et al.,* (1999) point out, is an understanding of the drugs pathways and journeys young people take right through adolescence and on into young adulthood. Social surveys, they argue, have been excellent for describing offer and trying rates and contextualising these by gender, age, ethnicity and region, but because we have almost no longitudinal work and very little substantive qualitative work, 'we still have some way to go in developing a more comprehensive picture of youthful drug use in the 1990s'.

Conclusion

The most recent survey-based evidence suggests that around a half of young people have tried an illicit drug by the time they are 19, although most of this illicit drug use involves cannabis. Only about 16 to 17 per cent of 16- to 19-year-olds and 5 per cent of 11- to 15-year-olds could be considered regular drug users.

There is very little trend data on drug use by young people under 16. However, research suggests that between the late 1980s and early 1990s use by 15- to 16-year-olds increased substantially, although this may now have tailed off. Certainly, evidence for older age groups suggests that it is now fairly stable. There is also very little regional data on illicit drug use by children, but exposure appears to be higher in Inner London and the South East. Among adults and young people, surveys have consistently found higher prevalence rates in London.

Due to a scarcity of evidence, it is not possible to be entirely accurate about the link between drug use and poverty. The available research suggests that use by children is fairly evenly distributed across socio-economic groups. Among the general public, it is the most affluent who have the highest rates of use, although the most problematic use may be among low-status groups. There is, however, evidence of a clear association between unemployment and drug use.

A problem with many drug use surveys is under-reporting. Difficulties also remain over defining drug use and problem drug use, and in understanding the drugs pathways and journeys young people take right through adolescence and on into young adulthood.

Notes to Chapter 14

1   The comparison of results for England with those for Scotland need to be treated with caution as the populations surveyed were not quite the same. Children in Scotland transfer to secondary school a year later than in England, and transfer is usually based on the child's age on 1 March, rather than at the beginning of the school year as in England (Goddard and Higgins, 1999).

15 Suicide

Paul Higate

Introduction

Concern has been expressed about the growing numbers of suicides amongst young people (aged 15 to 24). The *Health of the Nation* document (1991) has recognised this worrying trend by setting targets to reduce the number of deaths through suicide, though young people do not represent a particular focus. Further, it does not make any mention of improving the economic conditions of those who may be more vulnerable to the series of risk factors that underlie suicide (Maynard, 1994). One explanation of this is the inconclusive links between suicide and socio-economic position. As Maynard (1994:185) states:

'The exploration of links between suicide and economic and social trends, is contentious. Do unemployment, poverty, increasing inequality in the distribution of income and wealth, poor education and other socio-economic influences such as increases in divorce and single households create the feelings of isolation and hopelessness which induce depression and suicide? Are these factors the cause of depression and suicide, or does the depressed state lead to unemployment of vulnerable groups and enhanced suicide risk? The direction of causation and the problems of compounding factors are neither well understood or adequately researched.'

With these problematic methodological issues in mind, the aim of this chapter is to illuminate:

- the *complex nature* of the relationship between poverty and suicide amongst young people;
- *trends over time* within the context of this relationship;
- the *linkage* of these trends with other factors.

In addition, the *robustness* of the literature will be considered in terms of research design, and operationalisation.

Estimations: suicide and young people

The focus of this study is young people. Clearly, there are a range of competing definitions of what constitutes a young person: child, adolescent, young adult and so forth. For the purpose of the estimation, many statistics consider only those aged 15 years and over (Madge, 1998); although work from the age of ten upwards is unusual, it has featured in research (see Gunnell *et al.*, 1995). Importantly, suicide for those aged under 12 is noted to be extremely rare (Hawton, 1986; Hill, 1995). Most studies tend to work with the 15 to 19 age cohorts (Kerfoot, 1996), and tend to draw on the parameters utilised by a variety of agencies that are involved in suicide, from hospitals to coroners.

Suicide is a complex business. Dead bodies do not talk and therefore one can *never* be utterly sure of the original motives leading to death. Suicide does not occur in a social vacuum. The meanings brought to an act that leads to death are mediated by a number of agencies working with differing agendas and organisational philosophies. For example, coroners – in recognising the stigma of suicide – may be reluctant to pass this particular verdict. This is important within the context of young people, where stigma and trauma may well be exacerbated amongst bereaved parents (Madge and Harvey, 1999). Social class, circumstances of death, availability of a suicide note, the risk-seeking pursuits of young people (particularly within the context of road traffic accidents and drug use), intent to die and so forth combine in complex ways. In Britain a 'burden of proof' (Madge and Harvey, 1999) dictates the suicide verdict. Similarly, young people (under 12) have been noted to be 'unable' to understand the 'irreversibility' of death, thereby problematising the intent to commit suicide. Questions have, however, been raised around the complexities of a child's motivation in respect of intentional death (Hawton, 1986). These social-contextual or 'ecological' factors also serve to problematise the comparability of data at the cross-national level, as suicide 'gets made within the context of differentiated cultural contexts'. Official statistics, however, are said to under-estimate the actual numbers of young people who have taken their own lives. As a consequence of the noted difficulties facing coroners there is said to be a systematic under-reporting of suicide amongst young people. It is thought that as many as two in three of suicides in Britain for those under 20 go unreported (Madge and Harvey, 1999). Despite the numerous difficulties, which make the accurate quantification of youthful suicide a problematic exercise, mortality statistics compiled by the Office for National Statistics can reveal trends in youthful suicide, and a tentative indication of suicide rates for England and Wales. Table 15.1 illustrates the marked increase in suicide rates of those aged 15–24 since the early 1970s.

Table 15.1 Suicide rates by age, 1991–1997 (selected years)

Suicide rates amongst young people aged 15–24 (per million of the population)

	1971	1976	1981	1986	1991	1996
15–24	9.9	14.2	14.0	16.1	19.9	20.4

Source: Dataset Name: ST30707 – Office for National Statistics: General Register Office for Scotland, Northern Ireland Statistics and Research Agency, 1971–1997 (selected years).

Paradigms in which suicide has been studied and subsequently reported

Questions linking poverty with suicide have been difficult to address as a consequence of the nature of the literature more generally. The bulk of the literature operates within a medicalised framework which tends to focus on individual 'pathology' (ie. mental health issues), rather than environmental or social issues. Thus poverty is often reduced to socio-economic indicators such as (un)employment or social class. Indeed, seminal work by the sociologist Durkheim was informed by a considerably greater consideration of the links between social context and suicidal act, resulting in the expression 'anomie' (Diekstra, 1989). This term captures the ways in which individuals come to define themselves in relation to others. Here, 'normlessness' could arise within the context of unemployment, as individuals struggle to reconcile ('deviant') activity (ie. not working) with the central significance or perceived value of paid employment in society (see Levitas (1999) on the neglect of paid employment from the debate and policy around social exclusion). These insights around anomie are not without limitations, and have been questioned, for example, against the (anomalous) backdrop of high suicide rates amongst Black Americans who were presumed to be characterised by high degrees of social cohesion (Maynard, 1994). Although it is difficult, if not impossible, to establish causal links between unemployment and suicide, the rate of attempted suicide has been shown to be at least ten times higher for the short-term unemployed compared with those in work. (Gunnell *et al.*, 1995). At a greater level of abstraction, anomie captures the dynamic of suicide within the context of the links with poverty. The following attempts to explore the 'social' characteristics of suicide, within the context of a somewhat limited literature.

Gender

There is overwhelming evidence in the literature for the increase in suicide amongst young males (Pritchard, 1992), a trend that tends not to have affected young women (Hawton, 1986:61). The central explanations for this growth are linked to patterns of employment amongst young men (Platt, 1984; Platt and Kreitmann, 1984; Pritchard, 1992). According to official data, between 1971 and 1997 the suicide death rate for men aged 15–24 rose from 6.9 per million of the population to 16.4 per million of the population. For women in this age group there was a fall in the decade between the mid-1970s and mid-1980s (see Table 15.2).

Table 15.2 **Suicide rates by gender and age, 1971–1997 (selected years)**

	1971	1976	1981	1986	1991	1997
Males: 15–24	6.9	9.6	10.6	12.7	15.9	16.4
Females: 15–24	3.3	4.6	3.4	3.4	4.0	4.0

Source: Dataset Name: ST30707 – Office for National Statistics: General Register Office for Scotland, Northern Ireland Statistics and Research Agency, 1971–1997 (selected years).

Young women make more 'attempts at suicide' (parasuicide) (Hawton, 1986:61), but men tend to be more successful on account of their methods which are considerably more aggressive (Hill, 1995). Women are more likely to take overdoses (self-poisoning), whilst men use carbon monoxide poisoning (car exhaust fumes), hanging and extreme alcohol use (Hawton, 1986), together with jumping off buildings, bridges and so on

(Madge, 1996). Whilst young women remain most likely to attempt suicide, usually by overdose, the attempted suicide rate amongst young men aged 15–24, has doubled since 1985. Follow-up studies of teenagers who take overdoses show that 11 per cent will succeed in killing themselves within the next two to three years (Hawton in *Handbook of Affective Disorders*). Attempted suicide by young women and girls aged 15–24 increased by 42 per cent between 1992 and 1995. In terms of attempted suicides females outnumber males by a ratio of 1.26:1 (Hawton *et al.*, 1995). Much of the recent research has been in response to the increase in (young) men's suicide, which has been implicitly (though less explicitly) linked to the economic downturns during the 1980s (Coleman, 1997).

Employment/unemployment

We have already noted that the explanatory frameworks turn on individual factors in the bulk of the studies. Here, 'risk factors' are routinely identified that are most frequently grounded in non-environmental factors. However, the work of Pratt and Pritchard considers, in some depth, the links between unemployment and suicide. For the purposes of commentary for this chapter, unemployment is understood as a prime poverty indicator. In an extensive review of the literature in this area, Platt (1984:108) states: 'Results from all but one of the individual longitudinal studies point to significantly more unemployment, job instability and occupational problems among suicides compared with non-suicides … we can confidently state that there is an association between unemployment and suicide but we cannot specify with the same degree of confidence the nature of this association.' (emphasis added).

The incidence of mental illness is invoked in this study, but the complex links between mental health–unemployment–suicide are such that individual causal factors cannot be highlighted as decisive (Maynard, 1994), but rather contributional in terms of suicide. Figure 15.1. captures this:

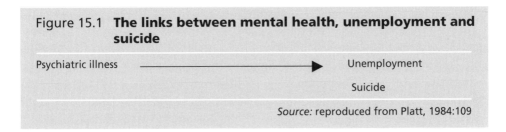

Figure 15.1 **The links between mental health, unemployment and suicide**

Psychiatric illness ——————————————▶ Unemployment

Suicide

Source: reproduced from Platt, 1984:109

Pritchard (1992) compares the links between suicide and young men cross-nationally with other EU countries. The findings are framed thus: '[Y]outh suicide rates in the UK correlated positively with young adults' (18–24) unemployment rates; (Pritchard, 1992:752). He continues: 'The association between increased male suicide rates and unemployment should not be surprising in view of the known 'depressive' reaction and poorer health associated with being jobless.' (Pritchard, 1992:755).

The evidence from these studies points to the complex relationship between mental health and employment. How might we make sense of this relationship? Is it the sense of hopelessness engendered by unemployment that undermines mental well-being, or might poor mental health influence success in the labour market? While individual cases will differ in terms of their particular dynamic, it is important to reflect this complexity theoretically. For many individuals driven to suicide in these contexts, unemployment and mental health problems are likely to be experienced as mutually constitutive; neither unemployment nor mental health can be accorded primacy. Rather than working with a one-sided model of cause and effect, more illuminating accounts of suicide should assimilate this 'recursive' understanding (Giddens, 1984), and in doing so recognise the sophistication of the human actor within disadvantages contexts. Here, asymmetries between job aspirations and rapidly-changing labour markets render the 'psychologically vulnerable' early victims of recession (Pritchard, 1992:755). This finding, though not focusing on poverty *per se,* raises other issues linked to the 'cumulative' social forces resulting in the suicidal act (Martunnen *et al.*, 1991). Kerfoot (1996:238) understands poverty in terms of its influence in producing 'psycho-social stressors'. Suicide's linkage with poverty is contingent on the way in which poverty is conceptualised, though in these three studies, poverty has a stronger relationship with the mental health dimension.

Socio-economic deprivation

The study by Gunnell *et al.,* (1995) uses data from those aged from 10 to 75 years of age. It makes the point that suicide is a 'rare event' and may be a poor indicator of the overall incidence of mental illness. Once again, close links are made between psychiatric admission rates and unemployment. Clearly, younger people (children) are not available for paid employment on the same scale as the adult population, though this (and other) studies tend to neglect this important point (along with the resonance amongst other family members of unemployment amongst parents), with the statistical being grouped together. The key findings of this study point to the links between 'psychiatric morbidity' and 'mortality', within the context of socio-economic deprivation. Strategies to resist suicide should be addressed at the level of social policy rather than attempting to tackle the more obvious and highly visible incidence of suicide (Gunnell *et al.*, 1995) which may come at the end of a long endurance of difficulty (Martunnen, 1992). Other high-profile suicides amongst young people that might be aligned with relatively low economic status concern those who experience prison; here disproportionately large numbers of individuals (mainly young men) attempt and complete suicide in the punitive setting.

Social class

Roberts *et al.,* (1998:465) focus on 'intentional injury and death' measurements amongst 10- to 19-year-olds (referred to as 'teenagers'). Whilst these figures include homicide and parasuicide, nevertheless they do find (after controlling for homicide) that 'there is a steep social class gradient in intentional injury death rates' which has widened over the period 1980–83 and 1992–1995. A more explicit focus on the linkage between suicide and children under 15 is problematic because of the relatively low numbers of deaths amongst this group (in addition, see above).

Conclusion

Maynard (1994), whilst recognising the complex cause and effect influences that render positivist framing as largely inappropriate, nonetheless cites unemployment, increasing inequality and poverty, as likely contributory factors within the context of suicide more broadly. To extrapolate, similar resonance may well be found amongst young people (particularly males) *vis-à-vis* access to paid employment as commentators have invoked the notion of 'troubled men' within the context of rapidly changing labour and housing markets, and the concomitant shifts in the 'breadwinner role' of the man (Hearn, 1998). Issues around mental health clearly warrant further research, and may contain the seeds of confounding factors in which poverty is somewhat downplayed. In this way, the relatively strong links between suicide and depressive illness (*The Guardian*, 6 July 1998) may lie partly in the ways in which mental health problems contain a genetic component emphasising individual rather than environmental factors. Diekstra (1989:22) invokes the nature of the 'constellation of social factors' in helping to explain 'prevailing trends amongst adolescents and young adults'. He expands, stating that 'the search for one single responsible agent, a 'suicidococcus' as it were, has proven to be unfruitful' (Diekstra, 1989:30).

The paucity of work examining the links between suicide, poverty and young people represents a somewhat surprising shortcoming in the literature. Clearly, the complexities of suicide render analysis problematic from a statistical point of view, for reasons outlined above. Most studies have turned to secondary data analysis, working with pre-existing poverty indicators, many of which have limited utility within the context of the particular focus on suicide. Finally, a focus on quantitative material has tended to undermine deeper issues, perhaps more suitably elicited through qualitative study design. Future work (could) for example, develop ways of interrogating both subjective and objective understandings of the experience of poverty. For example, to conflate 'poverty' with 'social exclusion' is to infer, rather than explore analytically, the ways in which shared hardship may fuel a degree of community spirit, that in turn erodes the likelihood of suicide. During the 1980s the individualisation and fragmentation of society (and its particular corollary, the decimation of traditional working-class male occupations, (Connell, 1995)) speaks as much about individual atomisation as it does about poverty. In addition, there is evidence to suggest that suicide's 'acceptability' rises as the number of suicides grow, fostering 'copy-cat' acts (Hill, 1995:94–110). There appears to be a 'critical point' at which rapidity of change can no longer be assimilated into a particular biography giving rise to irreconcilable tensions in the relationship between self and society. One clear manifestation of this conflict is suicide.

16 Child labour

Paul Higate

Introduction

In this chapter the literature exploring the relationship between children's involvement in paid employment and poverty is outlined. The extent of children (or young people's) paid employment is considered first. Next, we consider the forms of employment taken up by children and young people, before turning to rates of pay, hours worked, and the ways in which child labour has been framed analytically. Poverty and child labour is then considered, together with issues linked to the deeper motivation for young people to work. We conclude with a look at the relationship between the generation of income and the household budget.

Background

Analyses of child labour are far from straightforward on account of the contested nature of the central concepts. For example, what is meant by the term 'labour' in this context? Child labour is complex in terms of both the nature of the labour at the centre of analyses, and the attitude of (usually adults) towards it. Some see it as the simple acquisition of pocket-money, whilst others understand its close alignment with the worst forms of exploitation; prostitution and 'drug running' are two cases in point (Pettit, 1998). The extent to which the linkage of poverty can be made with child labour is therefore problematic, as is any statistical comparison. For example, unpaid work and babysitting are frequently excluded from considerations of child labour, and are understood as 'grey areas' (Pettit, 1998).

What is clear, however, is that a significant number of young people are currently involved in employment of some kind. Pole *et al.*, (1998:4) frame it in the following way: 'Translated into 'hard' numbers, between 1.1 and 1.7 million school-age children are estimated to be currently working ... the large parameters of these estimates in part reflects the definitional confusion and dispute surrounding what can be said to constitute a legitimate form of paid work.'

Other commentators flag the high numbers of children involved in work of one or other kinds. For example, Hobbs and McKechnic (1998:8) estimate that 'over half of young people (13–18 years of age) had worked at some time during the last year'.

One source of data on the employment of young people that has not been fully exploited is the British Household Panel Survey (BHPS). Bradshaw and Williams (1999) undertook an analysis of BHPS data as a contribution to this review. Since 1994 the BHPS has collected data from young people aged 11–15 living in respondent households. The youth questionnaire covers a range of topics and includes questions on employment, hours worked, earnings and the amount of pocket-money young people receive. To undertake the analysis the authors combined the youth data regarding income from four waves (1994–1997). Any young people occurring in more than one wave were dropped and the most recent response from the young person was then linked to the data on their parents/carers and the household within which they lived. In the analysis Bradshaw and Williams (1999) found that around 38 per cent of young people aged 11–15 had some income from paid employment at the time of interview.

It should be noted that the number of hours worked by the young people included in the BHPS may not be representative of the true extent of child labour in Britain. The participation rates proffered by the work of both Pole *et al.*, (1998) and Hobbs and McKechnie (1998), may also be subject to under-estimation. It can be said that the sampling strategies used by these studies may fail to include young people involved in the 'hidden' side of work – as already indicated in terms of sex work, the illicit-drug economy and other closely-linked employment. Despite the problematic nature of definition and comparison, Pole *et al.*, (1998:2) believe that 'the paid employment of children in contemporary Britain is a normative aspect of childhood'.

Forms of employment

It is not possible to provide an extensive list of employment in this brief overview. Typically, however, employment covers the following: distribution, hotel work, catering and repairs, newspaper and other deliveries, shopwork, cleaning, modelling and manual labour on building sites (Hobbs and McKechnie, 1998:12; O'Donnell and White, 1998). Whilst the majority of this work fits with the somewhat idealised notions of the young person finding their way in the world of employment (consider for example, the fresh-faced newspaper boy providing a 'community service' through his efforts), a note of caution should be sounded. Children's employment not only involves large numbers of young people, but in addition is usually unskilled, poorly paid and repetitive (Pole *et al.*, 1998:2). Indeed, young people tend to be involved in paid work that is typically carried out by adults, pointing to a purely economic employer motive, as young people tend to work for relatively less pay (O'Donnell and White, 1998). In addition, young workers tend to be more compliant, ready to accept very low wages – in essence more 'flexible' in an increasingly competitive labour market. Here, flexibility can be equated with 'cheapness, disposability, and relative tolerance of boring and unrewarding tasks' (Pole *et al.*, 1998:9). Expectations of 'high' wages are less likely, and willingness to work irregular hours at short notice renders this cohort increasingly attractive to employers. The theme of pay and hours worked is touched on in the next section.

Rates of pay and hours employed

There appears to be relatively little analysis centering on pay for young people involved in various forms of employment. However, Hobbs and McKechnic (1998), in reporting a number of studies including their own (targeted on northern England and Scotland), found wide variation. They recorded wages of 10 pence per hour in one instance, and cite another study in which one young person earned £8.33 per hour (Pond and Searle,

1991). Their own study found an average hourly wage in the range £1.79 to £2.34 which amounted to weekly figures between £11.85 and 13.97. Secondary analysis of BHPS data by Bradshaw and Williams (1999) also found a wide variation in the amount of money earned per week. Young people's earned income varied from less than £1.00 to £70 per week with a mean value of £12.54. The mean hourly rate of pay of respondents was £2.91 and 69 per cent of young people aged 11–15 were earning less than £3.00 per hour. It is clear from these analyses that young people have little protection from low wages and the potential to organise collectively to improve conditions is less than likely amongst this group (Pole *et al.*,1998). A number of factors influence the range of hours worked, in particular the extent to which employment is considered 'heavy' or 'light' (Hobbs and McKechnie, 1998:14). In one study cited by Hobbs and McKechnie it was noted that: '51 per cent of 13- to 15-year-olds worked up to five hours per week, 33 per cent worked between six and twelve hours and 16 per cent over twelve hours' (extract from Hibbet and Beatson, 1995).

The study of Hobbs and McKechnie (1998:14), found that for those young people involved in paid employment, their average working week amounted to around eight hours, though around a fifth worked in excess of ten hours per week. Bradshaw and Williams (1999) found the hours worked by young people in the BHPS Youth Survey was on average six hours a week. The most common number of hours worked was two per week. However, there was considerable variation in the number of hours worked, with one young person working for 58 hours in the previous week. Hobbs and McKechnie (1998:14) point out the ways in which long working hours detract from time spent with 'family, friends, leisure and homework'. Whilst legislation prohibits children and young people from working before 7am and after 7pm, the nature of employment (for example, delivery of milk and newspapers) frequently necessitates the early starts that are noted to be a widespread feature of current young people's employment patterns. These practices are in clear breach of the legislation which has been devised to protect young workers from exploitation (Lavalette, 1998:36). There appears to be little enforcement, and, in line with comments made earlier around the 'culturally normative' aspect of child employment, a high degree of tacit acceptance proliferates with child labour being understood as a largely positive experience. As Lavalette (1998:38) states: 'By the early years of the twentieth century child labour was viewed as a decreasing problem and increasingly viewed as a healthy and beneficial pastime. It set in stream a way of thinking about child workers which remains dominant today.'.

Child labour – a problem? Contemporary paradigms

Given the large numbers of children involved in employment, studies have been slow to develop, and previous analyses in the UK have tended to turn on 'defining and cataloguing' the phenomenon (Pole *et al.*, 1998:2). It is only recently that studies have engaged with broader social forces that constrain and limit the lives of young people and their subsequent involvement in the labour market.

The agenda – work as 'normal'?

The US paradigm, informed by social psychology and childhood development, whilst considerably more developed than work in the UK, remains limited. The ways in which it frames young people's involvement in paid work as a normalised element of development necessarily 'leads to a denial of work as a rational response on the part of many children to the specific and changing social conditions of childhood' (Pole *et al.*, 1998:3). Indeed, there has emerged a degree of consensus in the US that 'moderate' levels of work are broadly beneficial, with similar sentiments being echoed by children themselves in the UK context in terms of the homework (school) work / paid work interface. For example, in a study commissioned by the charity Save the Children, a 14-year-old young woman who worked as a cleaner and waitress stated: 'Sometimes I did have quite a lot of homework but I just fitted it in. I'd probably just end up lazing about if I didn't go anyway.' Another female, aged 15, who worked as a campsite receptionist, stated that: 'You get to know how to work in a team, like with other staff there, and it's something to write down when you're going for another job ... like experience.' (quotes taken from Campbell *et al.*, 1998:66–74). These sentiments should be balanced by others that portray the highly exploitative and pressured environments that children are employed in (see Campbell *et al.*, 1998). The rationale for including these two more positive extracts is linked to what might be deemed the 'common sense' view of child labour invoked earlier. Thus, it is to the 'changing material conditions of childhood' (Pole *et al.*, 1998) that we should turn to make better sense of social forces that may illuminate the spurious linkage of 'choice' with young people's participation in labour.

Poverty and childhood labour

Relatively little is currently known about the characteristics or motivations of children who enter work (Pole *et al.*, 1998:10). According to Pole *et al.*, (1998) a view has emerged from the so-called 'Paisley Group' (researchers include Sandy Hobbs and Jim McKechnie) – we can call this the 'normal view' in line with comments made above – that children's involvement in work may not be linked to 'need' and 'cannot be simply explained by poverty' (Pole *et al.*, 1998:19) . A variation of the normative view is echoed by Morrow (1994) who sees young people's employment as far from exploitative, rather, that these individuals are 'enterprising' partly on account of their middle-class origins in which parents, and perhaps siblings participate in the labour market. However, Pole *et al.*, (1998:11) argue that the 'Paisley Group' and others have prematurely rejected the influence of economic conditions *vis-à-vis* children's involvement in work. This oversight, rooted in a methodological flaw, follows from the apparent similarity in numbers of young people employed across regions characterised by differing wealth levels. The neglect of competing evidence: for example, that which points up local difference, may be compounded by the difficulties linked to comparing contested categories such as 'work' and 'poverty'. For example, O'Donnell and White (1998:Executive Summary, not numbered) in their study of child employment in North Tyneside state that: 'The motivation for children to work is overwhelmingly financial ... one child in fifteen gives some of their earnings to their parents (and) one in ten children who have a part-time job is the only member of their household in employment.' (1,146 questionnaires returned).

Bradshaw and Williams' (1999) analysis of the national BHPS data found no evidence to suggest that the poverty of parents had an impact upon young peoples' participation rates in paid employment. The odds of having earnings/pocket-money and, for those working, the level of earnings/pocket-money and the number of hours worked were compared across households with varying socio-economic circumstances. The authors developed four separate indicators of socio-economic status: equivalent household income, dependence on means-tested benefits, the number of adults within the household in employment and a measurement of the number of household durables lacking within the household. In their subsequent analysis, Bradshaw and Williams (1999) found no statistically-significant relationships between household socio-economic status – as measured on all four indicators – between the number of hours worked by young people, or their earnings. The same conclusion holds for pocket-money; there was no significant variation in the proportion of young people receiving pocket-money by any of the indicators of family resources. The authors note the possible interaction between the indicators of living standards and other characteristics of the young person and the family. Using logistic regression, Bradshaw and Williams (1999) explored what factors influenced the odds of young people's involvement in paid employment. The only variable found to be significant – in both bivariate and multivariate analysis – was the age of the child. The authors conclude that the older the child, the more likely he/she is to be in paid employment.

Perceived inequality and pressures to work

Whilst it is likely that relatively few children are directly pressured into employment to meet basic levels of sustenance, or to assist their households in this most fundamental of ways, nevertheless the increases in relative poverty in the UK is likely to impact disproportionately on children in the 'two-thirds of all families ... existing on an income less than the national average' (Pole et al., 1998:13).

In attempting to understand the deeper 'push' factors that underpin children's involvement in work, a broader context that considers external pressures should be outlined. Firstly, children's leisure time has become increasingly dependent upon possession of economic resources. 'Megabowls', amusement arcades and fashion consciousness, for example, typify their vulnerability to consume, which is contingent on income of one or other sorts. Secondly, it is important to see these pressures in terms of the 'need' to acquire membership of particular and unique (youth) lifestyles. Exclusion follows inability to 'enlist' and increasing inequality compounds the elusiveness of membership as a disproportionate number of children experience economic disparity. White (1996:830–831) states:

> 'All over the world ... it is increasingly important for children not only to have sufficient food and clothing ... [but] to consume certain kinds of foods and beverages, and to engage in certain kinds of recreational activity which are

considered attributes of 'proper' people ... We can thus speak of a new kind of child labour: alongside cases that are better known and publicised ... there are children all over the world, who simply decide that they need to earn cash' (quoted in Pole *et al.*, 1998:14).

Thus, understandings that turn on the simple 'choice' to be 'enterprising', to earn cash that is not 'needed' represent ideological positions in which relative poverty is given little weight. The analytical limitation of the normative view comes into sharp focus here with an undeveloped notion of 'need'. These assumptions – traditionally championed by the New Right – pivot on more absolute notions of poverty through which, for example, acquisition of material goods is equated with 'well-being'. However, young people are increasingly pressured, as has been suggested above, to conform to the norms of their social milieu. We could suggest that many children are caught within a pincer movement characterised by increasing inequality on the one hand, and on the other, the convergence of identity with market place activity. The 'powerlessness' of children in many areas of their lives imbues leisure time with particular importance such that involvement in exploitative employment may be seen as a 'price worth paying' and in turn, as a pathway to inclusion, or 'normality' (Pole *et al.*, 1998:15).

Children's income and family budget

We have already considered the broader context of children's work in terms of inequality / pressure to consume and the likelihood that young people from poorer backgrounds may be relatively excluded 'from part-time paid jobs outside the home' (Middleton *et al.*, 1998:57). However, that is not to say that individuals who originate from households drawing means-tested benefits do not work, or do not want to work. Bradshaw and Williams (1999) note that although the BHPS data does not lend itself to an exploration of young people's motivations to work, it may be that young people from poor families might be keener to work than their more affluent counterparts. However, because they live in the labour markets that are partly responsible for their parents not being in employment they also cannot find jobs. In a recent Joseph Rowntree Fund commissioned study 1,239 children provided information linked to a number of facets of their working lives (Middleton *et al.*, 1998). Analysis of the data suggested that, when poorer children work they earn more than their affluent counterparts, as they tend to spend relatively more hours in employment. The authors also found evidence that the earning of many of the young people made some contribution to total household income. Overall the contribution of the children represented between 2 and 6 per cent of the household budget, with the latter figure originating from children of lone parents, or households in receipt of Income Support (Middleton *et al.*, 1998:57). Similar findings, in which children from poorer households provided a relatively larger proportion of the household budget than their affluent working cohort were produced by Leonard (1998) within the context of a study commissioned by Save the Children in Northern Ireland.

Conclusion

There is no evidence from this that the poverty of the parents has an impact on whether young people are earning, the hours they work or their total earnings. Furthermore, there is no evidence to suggest that a young person's membership of an impoverished household has an impact on whether pocket-money is paid or the amount of pocket money received. Nor is there evidence of a trade-off between pocket-money and earnings. Pocket-money does not seem to be a factor affecting earnings once the age of the young person has been taken into account. Young people tend to work more hours and earn more as they grow older. In spite of the tentative nature of the relationship between household income and young people's employment this relationship has tended to influence the trajectory of earlier study and debate. Pole *et al.*, (1998:11) frame this trend in the following way: '[T]o suggest that the very poorest children might actually face particular barriers to work is one thing, but to replace this with the claim that paid work is more likely to be the preserve of children from more affluent families is another.'

Cultural and historical conditions through which young people's employment has been received relatively unproblematically, together with contemporary discourse (for example, notions of 'enterprise') have served to shift the focus to young people for whom access to employment is considerably more straightforward. In turn, these better-resourced children are seen to be making a 'free choice' to earn money over and above their 'need'. In addition, Morrow's (1994) study (see above), linking relative affluence with part-time paid work for young people neglects 'social class, family [and] ethnic composition' (Pole *et al.*, 1998:11); these variables may be consequential in terms of young person employment patterns. Finally, conflicting evidence pervades geographical variation – a measure used by the 'Paisley Group' to (prematurely) sever the links between economic conditions and employment take-up. There are, however, at least two key issues that remain under-explored. First, the contested nature of what constitutes part-time paid employment renders comparison somewhat problematic. Second, and closely related, is young people's potential involvement in the 'hidden economy'. Without adding weight to an already stigmatised population through asserting their role in criminal activity, it may well be the case that, for example, small-turnover drug dealing, car and shop-theft and domestic–dwelling burglary represent income generation activities for young people. In areas of employment inaccessibity, involvement in these activities represents a more rational pathway to inclusion, albeit of groups described as 'subcultural'.

Many of the issues raised in these discussions pivot on moral questions. Is it right for young people to be involved in paid employment? At what point does this involvement impinge on issues of education or development? It is important to set these questions in the broader social context. Here, increased commodification of the private sphere, together with greater pressure on those that do work should alert us to the worrying pervasiveness of the market. Given that current legislation linked to young people and work is largely ignored, the increasing numbers of economically active young people represents a retrograde step, as ultimately their development is embedded into wage labour and consumption, leaving little room for lives outwith pressures that are likely to intensify as they move into the highly competitive adult world of paid employment.

Emotional outcomes

Deborah Quilgars

17 Mental health

Deborah Quilgars

Introduction

This chapter reviews critically the evidence on the links between poverty and poor mental health in childhood in Britain over the period of the last 20 years. Our hypothesis was that children living in poverty would be more likely to experience a range of emotional and behavioural problems than children in more affluent homes. The chapter demonstrates the complexity of the issue, finding evidence of a link between poverty and some measures of mental disorders, at the same time as finding little evidence of the link between poverty and the broader mental well-being of children. The chapter also presents evidence of a link between young people's own emerging socio-economic status and their mental health, as well as indirect effects of poverty on the mental health of children.

The chapter begins by considering the difficulties surrounding the definition and measurement of mental health, before introducing the discussion about causes of mental ill-health and considering the evidence for a link between poverty and children's mental health. Here, firstly the association between children and young people's mental health and the social class/socio-economic status of their parents is considered. Secondly, associations between young people's own socio-economic status and mental health are discussed. Thirdly, the chapter examines the evidence for an indirect link between children's mental health and poverty mediated through other factors such as family type. Finally, trends in children and young people's mental health are considered, together with any possible links with increasing poverty in Britain in the last two decades.

Definitions of mental health

Defining mental 'health' or 'well-being' is a difficult task. There are no universally accepted definitions of which states of mind should be included within 'mental health' or 'mental illness'. It is acknowledged that ideas about mental health are inevitably culturally determined and specific. The Western medical model, which tends to dominate discussions of 'mental illness', generally classifies mental disorders into psychotic illnesses (such as schizophrenia, manic depression), neurotic disorders (including depression, eating disorders, panic attacks), organic disorders (caused by brain damage, illness or drugs) and personality disorders (Drew and King, 1995). Table 17.1 details a more helpful, and slightly broader, categorisation of the range of children's mental disorders which has been used in key governmental and leading voluntary sector organisations' reports on children's mental health in the 1990s (Mental Health Foundation,

1999; Kurtz, 1996; NHS Health Advisory Service, 1995). This categorisation also includes other conditions: for example, developmental disorders such as delayed speech (as well as autism) and conduct disorders such as aggression and anti-social behaviour. Other key authors in this field of study, for example Rutter and Smith (1995) in their seminal book on 'psycho-social' disorders of young people, have tended to discuss both recognised diagnosable conditions, such as eating disorders, and problems of anti-social behaviour including criminal activity. Crime, however, is not considered in this chapter (see Chapter 11).

In addition, many commentators in this area have stressed the importance of adopting a positive definition of 'mental health', rather than solely focusing on problems or disorders. Most recently, *Bright Futures*, the Mental Health Foundation (1999) report on children's mental health produced the definition in Figure 17.1, placing the emphasis on what is necessary for a child to flourish and enjoy life. More generally, it is useful to think of the concept of mental 'well-being', as well as the absence of disorders. This concept allows a consideration of broader issues, such as the levels of happiness and positive self-image of children and young people.

Figure 17.1 **A definition of children's mental health**

We believe that children who are mentally healthy will have the ability to:

- develop psychologically, emotionally, creatively, intellectually and physically;
- initiate, develop and sustain mutually satisfying personal relationships;
- use and enjoy solitude;
- become aware of others and empathise with them;
- play and learn;
- develop a sense of right and wrong;

and;

- resolve (face) problems and setbacks and learn from them.

Source: Mental Health Foundation (1999)

Prevalence and measurement of mental health problems

The task of estimating the prevalence of mental health problems is beset by definitional issues, as well as difficulties in identifying adequate measures capable of assessing the extent of mental health problems amongst children and young people. Many commentators seem to concur that at any one time up to one in five children and young people may experience some form of psychological problem (Mental Health Foundation, 1999; Kurtz, 1996 based on Target and Fonagy, 1996). Table 17.1 provides some estimates of rates of specific mental health disorders. There is widespread evidence that boys are more likely to suffer psychiatric disorders in childhood than girls, as they are more likely to exhibit behavioural problems in earlier years, whereas girls are more likely than boys to suffer from mental health problems in adolescence, as they experience a particularly high rate of emotional problems in later youth (Scott, 1996). Rates of depression, whilst similar in boys and girls in childhood, rise much faster in young women and are twice as high among adult women compared with men (Smith and Rutter, 1995). Parasuicide and eating disorders are also much more common in young women, whilst suicide and crime are more common amongst young men. These patterns may be partly explained by the fact that girls and young women are more likely to internalise their behaviour, and therefore more likely to worry, be anxious and depressed, whilst boys and young men are more likely to externalise behaviour, and therefore exhibit anti-social behaviour (McCulloch *et al.*, 1999).

There appear to be two main methods used in the research literature to measure the extent of mental health problems amongst children and young people. The first method relies on the examination of medical and psychiatric records to establish the numbers of children and young people diagnosed as suffering from particular mental health problems. The second method is the use of specifically developed mental health questionnaires, which can be used to establish the level of well-being, and give an indication of possible psychiatric morbidity, within any given population. The most widely used questionnaire is the self-completed General Health Questionnaire 12 (GHQ12) which consists of twelve questions which ask about respondents' general level of happiness, depressive feelings, anxiety and sleep disturbance in the previous four weeks, with a higher score indicating worse health. The GHQ12 is used in the annual Health Survey of England. As the GHQ12 is a self-completion questionnaire it is only suitable for use with young people and adults, not younger children. A range of questionnaires have also been designed to detect emotional and behavioural problems amongst younger children, including the Strengths and Difficulties Questionnaire (SDQ), also used in the Health Survey of England, and the Child Behaviour Checklist and the Rutter questionnaire. Such questionnaires concentrate on conditions such as hyperactivity, conduct problems, peer problems, and pro/anti-social behaviour amongst children. It should be noted that these questionnaires are commonly filled out by parents, which may bias results.

One very recent study on the prevalence of mental health problems amongst children requires special mention. In 1999, concurrent with this ESRC study, the Social Survey Division of the Office for National Statistics, carried out the first national survey of the prevalence of mental health problems amongst children and adolescents in Great Britain (Meltzer and Gatward, 2000). This focused on three categories of mental disorder: conduct disorders, emotional disorders and hyperkinetic disorders. It is important to note that the focus was on 'disorders' which had a clinically recognisable set of symptoms or behaviour, rather than a wider definition of mental health or well-being. The questionnaires (to parents, children and teachers) were based on the ICD-10 (International Classification of Diseases, tenth revision) and DSM-IV (Diagnostic and Statistical Manual, fourth revision) diagnostic measures and included the SDQ and GHQ questionnaires as well as a range of other adapted clinical measures. From a survey population of 10,438, 10 per cent of children aged between 5 and 15 were defined to have had a mental disorder (5 per cent conduct disorders, 4 per cent emotional disorders, 1 per cent rated as hyperactive).

Table 17.1   **Estimates of prevalence of mental health problems**

Emotional disorders

for example: phobias, anxiety states and depression; these may be made manifest in physical symptoms such as chronic headache or abdominal pain.

Abdominal pain without organic cause:	10% in 5- to 10-year-olds
Simple phobias:	2.3–9.2% of children
Emotional disorders with onset in childhood:	4.5–9.9% of 10-year-olds
	25–33% among clinic attenders
Major depression:	0.5–2.5% among children
	2–8% among adolescents

Conduct disorders

for example: stealing, defiance, fire-setting, aggression and anti-social behaviour

Severe tantrums:	5% of 3-year-olds in an urban community
Conduct disorders	6.2–10.8% among 10-year-olds
	33–50% among clinic attenders

Hyperkinetic disorders

for example: disturbance of activity and attention, and hyperkinetic conduct disorder

Hyperkinetic disorder	1.7% of primary school boys

1 in 200 of the whole population suffer severe hyperkinetic disorders. Up to 17% at least suffer some hyperkinetic disorders.

Developmental disorders

for example: delay in acquiring certain skills such as speech, social ability or bladder control. These may affect primarily one area of development or pervade a number of areas as in children with autism and those with pervasive developmental disorders.

Nocturnal enuresis:	8% of 7-year-old children
	1% of 14-year-old children

Eating disorders

for example: pre-school eating problems, anorexia nervosa and bulimia nervosa

Feeding difficulties	12–14 % among pre-school children
Anorexia nervosa:	0.5–1% of 12- to 19-year-olds 8 to 11 times more common in girls
Bulimia nervosa:	1% of adolescent girls and young women
Attempted suicide:	2–4% of adolescents
Suicide:	7.6% per 100,000 15- to 19-year-olds

Habit disorders

for example: tics, sleeping problems and soiling

Sleep difficulties:	13% of London 3-year-olds have persistent difficulty settling at night
Tic disorders:	1–13% of boys and 1–11% of girls
Encropesis (faecal soiling):	2.3% of boys and 0.7% of girls aged 7–8 years
	1.3% of boys and 0.3% of girls aged 11–12 years

Post traumatic syndromes

for example: post-traumatic stress disorder

Somatic disorders

for example: chronic fatigue syndrome

Psychotic disorders

for example: schizophrenia, manic depressive disorder or drug-induced psychosis

Sources: NHS Health Advisory Service (1995), Table 1 (p21) and Kurtz (1996), Annex 1 (p60) after Wallace *et al.* (1995).

Figure 17.2   **Child, family and environmental risk factors**

Child Risk Factors
Genetic influences
Low IQ and learning disability
Specific development delay
Communication difficulty
Difficult temperament
Physical illness, especially if chronic and/or neurological
Academic failure
Low self-esteem

Family Risk Factors
Overt parental conflict
Family breakdown
Inconsistent or unclear discipline
Hostile and rejecting relationships
Failure to adapt to child's changing developmental needs
Abuse – physical, sexual and/or emotional
Parental psychiatric illness
Parental criminality, alcoholism and personality disorder
Death and loss – including loss of friendship

Environmental Risk Factors
Socio-economic disadvantage
Homelessness
Disaster
Discrimination
Other significant life events

Source: NHS Health Advisory Service (1995) Tables 2, 3 and 4 (pp.23–24).

The causes of mental health problems

The causes of mental health problems amongst both children and adults are still poorly understood. Research has identified a range of factors which appear to be consistently associated with mental health problems in childhood: however the links between some of these factors are more firmly proven than others. Commentators (Mental Health Foundation, 1999; Kurtz, 1996; NHS Health Advisory Service, 1995) tend to discuss the existence of three types of 'risk' or 'predisposing' factors, as presented in Figure 17.2. Firstly, risk factors associated with the child are identified which include genetic influences as well as specific difficulties arising from factors like development delays or physical illness. It may be noted that there appears to be some conflation of risk factors and mental health disorders within this category. Secondly, 'family' risk factors include both family breakdown as well as rejecting or abusive relationships between parent and child. The third set of factors, 'environmental', are identified as including socio-economic disadvantage and associated situations such as homelessness. Similarly, 'resilience' factors have also been identified in the literature, situated again within the child, family and environment, which may protect a child, or lessen the likelihood of their developing mental health problems. Protective factors would include having caring parents and a good standard of living. It is generally agreed, and logical to assume, that a child's or young person's likelihood of experiencing mental health problems increases the greater the number of risk factors to which they are subject.

The three authors who use this categorisation all agree that socio-economic disadvantage is a risk factor for a range of mental health problems in childhood, commenting that it is either an 'acknowledged' risk factor (Kurtz, 1996; NHS Health Advisory Service, 1995) or 'it is known that children who are socio-economically disadvantaged, eg. those living in poverty or who are homeless, are at increased risk' (Mental Health Foundation, 1999). However, these statements are assertions, rather than factual statements, as little research evidence is provided to prove that socio-economic disadvantage is a contributing cause of children's mental health problems. The rest of this chapter seeks to explore these assertions in some detail by considering the available research evidence in this area.

Evidence for a link between poverty and children's mental health

A number of studies have attempted an investigation into the role of poverty in determining children's mental health in the 1990s. Most of these studies have utilised information collected through established health and community population-based surveys rather than undertaking special surveys on this subject with the exception of the new government national survey (Meltzer and Gatward, 2000).

Clarke, Bradshaw and Williams (1999) examined the association between the mental well-being of young people (aged between 11 and 15) and family resources using the British Household Panel Survey (BHPS). Utilising the last four waves of the BHPS (1994–1997), they were able to examine well-being for a sample of 1,300 children (where a child appeared more than once, the latest observation was included). Four indicators of well-being appear in the BHPS: SAD, the number of days in the last month that young people have felt unhappy or depressed; WORRY, the number of nights in the last week that they have lost sleep worrying; HAPPY, a scoring variable measuring how young people feel about school work, appearance, family, friends and life as a whole, and IMAGE, another scoring variable using six statements including 'I have a number of good qualities', 'I certainly feel useless at times', 'I am a likeable person', 'All in all, I am inclined to feel a failure', 'At times I feel I am no good at all', and 'On the whole my health is very good'. The authors looked at three indicators of poverty or economic circumstances: equivalent income of less than 50 per cent of average income after housing costs; whether the household was receiving means-tested benefits; and whether the household was lacking a number of household assets. Analysis, using both bivariate and multiple regression techniques, revealed very little evidence of a relationship between poverty and the mental well-being of 11- to 15-year-olds on any of the indicators.

The only variable which showed a clear relationship was IMAGE. Children living in families receiving means-tested benefits were found to have a lower self-image, a relationship which held when all other factors were taken into account (Table 17.2).

Table 17.2 **Logistic regression of the odds of having high (poor) IMAGE scores**

Best fitting model (77% correctly predicted)			
Receiving means-tested benefits		**Age of the young person**	
No	1.00	11	0.79
Yes	1.79**	12	0.95
Sex		13	0.58*
Male	1.00	14	1.41*
Female	2.67***	15	1.61**

Notes:
* Significant at <0.05
** Significant at <0.01
*** Significant at <0.001

Source: Clarke, Bradshaw and Williams (1999).

Earlier, and less sophisticated, analysis of the first wave of the BHPS (including approximately 700 children) found similarly weak correlations between indicators of poverty / family resources and children's well-being (Brynin and Scott, 1996; Scott, 1996). Scott (1996) also found a correlation between self-image and economic circumstances of households, and a weak relationship between happiness and family resources for boys, but this was only of borderline statistical significance. Brynin and Scott (1996), undertaking similar analysis, found no relationship between children's life satisfaction or self-confidence and the social class of their parents.

The Annual Health Survey of England (Prescott-Clarke and Primatesta, 1998), first introduced in 1990, has included questions about children's mental health since 1995. Young people aged 13–24 completed the General Health Questionnaire 12 (GHQ12) in 1995 and 1997. In addition, in 1997, the Strengths and Difficulties Questionnaire (SDQ) was given to parents to complete for children aged 4–15.

Two measurements of poverty or inequality were examined: social class of household (measured by father's occupation) and equivalised income. As with Clarke *et al.*, (1999), no clear relationship was found between GHQ12 score (for either gender) and social class of head of household or equivalised income. However, the Health Survey of England did report a statistically significant inverse relationship between income and SDQ scores for both boys and girls. Table 17.3 shows how SDQ scores increased from social classes I to V, with only 5 per cent of boys and 2 per cent of girls in social class I compared with 20 per cent of boys and 14 per cent of girls in social class V with high scores (17 or more on the scale). A similar effect was observed for equivalised income (Table 17.4) with 6 per cent of boys and 4 per cent of girls in the top quintile (household income over £24,381) compared with 20 per cent and 15 per cent in bottom quintile (up to £6,500) exhibiting high SDQ scores. There are two possible explanations for the diverging GHQ and SDQ data: mental health problems may be associated with poverty for younger, but not older children, given that the two measures are administered to different (although slightly overlapping) age groups, and / or some mental health problems, those measured by the SDQ, are associated with poverty, but others, as measured by GHQ12, are not. Girls were more likely to have higher GHQ scores than boys, whilst boys were more likely to have higher SDQ scores, which again probably reflects the different age groups as well as boys' greater propensity to suffer from behavioural problems, more likely to be observed in the SDQ measure, and girls' greater propensity to experience emotional problems, more likely to be measured by the GHQ.

The West of Scotland Twenty-07 Study, a longitudinal health study comprising a sample of 1,000 adults in Glasgow, with three cohorts, aged 15, 35 and 55 from 1987 / 88, has also been used to investigate the mental health of young people. West et al., (1990) examined differences by social class (measured by head of household) for youth on the full range of measures of health collected in the study, including accidents, general health status (mainly physical illnesses), psychological well-being and physical measures. Psychological well-being was measured by the GHQ12, using both a binary score and Likert scale. Once again, for this age group, no evidence for differences by class for psychological well-being amongst young people aged 15 was found, using either method of scoring (Table 17.5). However, statistically significant class differentials were observed for the cohort of 35-year-olds for psychological morbidity, leading the authors to suggest that 'the relative equality of youth is essentially transient'. To check that the apparent lack of class variation in mental (and physical) health in adolescence was not an artefact of the measurement of social class, Macintyre and West (1991) examined six different occupationally-based and five non-occupationally-based measures of class, only to reconfirm the lack of variation between health and social class in youth according to virtually all the measures.

Another source of information on the mental health of young people is the international WHO Health Behaviour Survey of School-Aged Children, which is carried out every four years by participating countries (some countries have missed years, for instance England has undertaken surveys in 1983/84, 1995 and 1997/8). Most recently, Haselden et al., (1999) reported on the 1997/8 English Survey which included questions on the extent to which young people felt happy, confident, lonely or helpless. The authors reported that those in ABC1 households were slightly more likely to rate themselves positively on these measures than C2DE households, but there was no statistical significance testing and the differences were minor: for example, 92 per cent of ABC1 self-reported as very or quite happy, compared with 91 per cent of C2DE households, although 70 per cent of ABC1 children said they never or rarely felt helpless but only 62 per cent of C2DE children. There was also some very slight difference, again unlikely to be of statistical significance, between social integration: for example, 57 per cent of ABC1 schoolchildren said they had hardly ever been bullied compared with 54 per cent of C2DE children.

Table 17.3 **SDQ score, by social class of head of household, and sex (children ages 4–15, 1997)**

SDQ Total	Social class of head of household						Total
Deviance score	I	II	IIINM	IIIM	IV	V	
	%	%	%	%	%	%	%
Males							
36,524	90	87	79	76	71	64	78
14–16	4	7	11	11	11	16	10
17–40	5	6	9	13	18	20	12
Females							
36,524	92	90	84	82	76	79	84
14–16	6	6	11	9	11	7	8
17–40	2	4	5	8	13	14	8
Bases (weighted):							
Males	119	501	200	529	356	95	1,878
Females	136	520	217	536	304	75	1,874
Bases (unweighted):							
Males	187	780	321	794	515	141	2,843
Females	211	809	344	815	450	114	2,862

Source: Prescott-Clarke and Primatesta (1998:355).

The evidence from the main community surveys which include variables on mental well-being suggests that ordinary young people, particularly adolescents, are more or less as likely to feel happy or have high levels of 'well-being' irrespective of the family resources available or the social class of the household. If young people of lower socio-economic status are more likely to be less happy, this difference is a slight one, and certainly not as significant as the income differentials in Britain. However, the findings of the Annual Health Survey Strengths and Difficulties questionnaire indicated that anti-social behaviour and conduct disorders were linked to social class and poverty measures. This evidence was further supported by the recent national survey of the mental health of children (Meltzer and Gatward, 2000).

Meltzer and Gatwood (2000) found a clear difference in the prevalence of mental disorders along class lines, with a particularly stark one for conduct disorders. Children in social class V families were about three times more likely to be defined as having a mental disorder compared with those in social class I (14 per cent compared with 5 per cent). Looking specifically at conduct disorders, children in social class V

Table 17.4 **SDQ score, by equivalised household income quintile and sex (children ages 4–15, 1997)**

SDQ Total	Equivalised annual household income quintile					Total
Deviance score	Up to £6,500	Over £6,500 to £10,655	Over £10,655 to £15,899	Over £15,899 to £24,381	Over £24,381	
	%	%	%	%	%	%
Males						
36,524	68	72	80	88	90	78
14–16	12	13	11	6	4	10
17–40	20	15	10	6	6	12
Females						
36,524	74	81	87	91	90	84
14–16	10	11	7	6	6	8
17–40	15	8	6	3	4	8
Bases (weighted):						
Males	472	330	326	321	240	1,878
Females	431	344	326	322	271	1,874
Bases (unweighted):						
Males	661	480	515	518	391	2,843
Females	607	507	512	522	439	2,862

Source: Prescott-Clarke and Primatesta (1998:356).

families were five times as likely to be defined as suffering from these disorders (10 per cent compared with 2 per cent respectively). Differences in prevalence rates of mental disorders were also found for household income, with 16 per cent of children in families with a gross weekly household income of under £100 having some form of mental disorder compared with 6 per cent of children in families earning £500 per week or more. In addition, the statistical odds of having a mental disorder appeared to be highly related to whether or not the parents were working. Using logistic regression, the odds of a child having a mental disorder in a family where both parents were unemployed (and by implication likely to be reliant on social security benefits) was nearly twice that of the odds of a child in a family where both adults in the family were employed.

Table 17.5 **Psychological well-being (GHQ) by social class and sex: young people aged 15**

GHQ	Gender	Non-manual	III manual	IV-V	Total	Overall/ Trend
Mean score	M	8.4	7.8	8.3	8.2	ns/ns
(Likert)	F	9.6	9.3	9.5	9.5	ns/ns
% scoring 3+	M	13.1	6.2	11.7	10.4	ns/ns
(caseness)	F	19.9	16.0	20.4	18.5	ns/ns

ns = not significant

Source: West et al. (1990), Table 4 (p669).

Two further points are relevant to this discussion. Some other specific mental disorders also show indications of class differentiation. For example, there is some evidence to suggest that children in higher social classes are more at risk of developing eating disorders, particularly anorexia nervosa (Fombonne, 1995a). One study found that the number of anorexia cases was higher in private than in State schools (Esler and Szmukler, 1985). Schizophrenia has also been linked with social class, although in this case it is difficult to establish cause and effect as early symptoms may lead to educational and work failures (Dennehy et al., 1996). In addition, a disproportionately high proportion of young Black people are diagnosed as suffering with schizophrenia (Smaje, 1995).

It is also important to highlight the particular cases of some children and young people who experience extreme versions of poverty and hardship. The clearest example is that of homeless children and young people (see Chapter 8).

Young people's own socio-economic status and mental health

Brynin and Scott (1996) have suggested that it is 'experienced rather than inherited class' which is crucial in understanding the mental well-being of young people. This hypothesis has led to a number of researchers investigating whether closer correlations may exist between young people's own emerging socio-economic class and mental health, than with their originating parental social class.

Glendinning et al., (1992) were perhaps the first researchers to investigate class-based health inequalities using both measures of social class related to parental socio-economic status, and the current social position of young people. The latter was measured by activity status (education, training, work, unemployed, non-employed); social class (based on type of employment), and educational attainment. Glendinning et al. were attempting to explain how the lack of variation by parental social class in adolescence transforms into distinct health inequalities in early adulthood, as shown by West (1990) and Macintyre and West (1991). The research was based on the Young People's Leisure and Lifestyle Project, a longitudinal national study of Scottish young people in 1987, 1989 and 1991, here looking at the 1989 group (four cohorts aged 15–16, 17–18, 19–20, 21–22; although the last three were used for young person's class), looking at general health status, disability/long-standing illness and psychological well-being (GHQ12). They found no significant relationship between health (including mental health) and social class of parents. However, both young men and women on training schemes, those unemployed and women at home were more likely to report psychological stress, although no relationship with educational attainment or social class of the young person was found. They concluded that: 'An analysis based solely on measures of social class of origin or upbringing fails to recognise the diversity of attitudes, behaviours, activities, employment, education and training that exist amongst young people'. (Glendinning *et al.*, 1992:685)

West and Sweeting (1996) used the West of Scotland Twenty-07 Study to investigate the mental health of young people according to both their parental social class and their own emerging social position. The full range of measures of mental health used in the survey were examined: the GHQ12 , a list of symptoms, Hospital Anxiety and Depression Scale (contains sub-scale of anxiety and depression), and questions on suicidal thoughts and behaviour. West and Sweeting re-confirmed West *et al.'s* (1990) earlier finding that there was very little variation between the mental health of young people aged 15 by parental social class. However, whilst parental social class remained inconclusive at age 18, distinct variations in mental health were found when young people's own socio-economic status was examined. On almost all mental health measures, unemployed young people were in poorer health; for example, 56 per cent of young unemployed men and 66 per cent of young unemployed women had GHQ12 scores of potential clinical significance compared with 33 per cent of all 18-year-old men and 42 per cent of all young women. In addition, 9 per cent of men and 7 per cent of women in the unemployed sample reported attempting suicide (compared with 1 per cent and 2 per cent respectively of those at work or on YTS). Young women at home also had very poor mental health. After controlling for prior health at age 15 (to ensure that any selection effect was taken into account), social class and sex, West and Sweeting were able to conclude that the relationship was essentially causative with odds of high GHQ scores and suicidal thoughts increased twofold or more among unemployed young people compared with those at work or on YTS and the odds of attempted suicide increased by a factor of six. At age 21, the effect of unemployment on health was even greater with odds of GHQ caseness three times more than those in work or on YTS. In addition, the study found that health worsened with increased exposure to unemployment: 79 per cent of those with three or more spells of unemployment at age 18 had higher GHQ scores and 44 per cent suicidal thoughts. Whilst numbers were small, West and Sweeting also found indications that those who expected to be unemployed in the future (at age 15 and 21) had higher GHQ scores.

A substantial body of literature exists demonstrating both the physical and mental health effects of unemployment on adults, over and above any selection effect (where those in poorer health are more likely to be unemployed). Similar findings linking unemployment to poor mental health specifically amongst young people have also been found by Banks and Jackson (1982), Donovan *et al.*, (1996), Furlong and Spearman (1989), and Banks and Ullah (1996). For example, Banks and Jackson (1982) carried out a 20 month follow-up study of two cohorts of school leavers in Leeds, and found higher levels of minor psychiatric morbidity among unemployed young people, even after controlling for age, educational level and ethnicity. It should, however, be noted that many studies of school leavers have had small samples of unemployed youth, which may limit the robustness of the research.

Finally, Brynin and Scott (1996), looking at a completely different type of measure of young people's socio-economic status, found that children with the least disposable income (both through work and pocket-money) were less happy and had a poorer self-image. However, recent analysis of the BHPS has shown that there is no relationship between parental social class or economic resources and children's personal financial resources (as discussed in Chapter 16). Currie *et al.*, (1997) looking at indicators of so-cio-economic status for adolescents as part of the Scottish WHO Health Behaviour in School-Aged Children Survey also reviewed the use of a measure of children's own socio-economic status by their personal income (earned and pocket-money) and found that this measure was weakly correlated with parental occupational class. If young adults receive similar amounts of pocket-money, and have access to similar levels of earned income, it is possible that they are to some extent protected from the income differentials of their parents. This is, however, little more than an assertion as it would be difficult to explain why the greater amount of other utilities and activities affordable by higher income families would not also be a factor in explaining young people's own socio-economic status and social inclusion or exclusion.

The indirect effect of poverty

Some studies suggest that the socio-economic status of families may have an indirect effect on their children's mental health, mediated through other factors, primarily family structure, parents' own mental health, area and parents' employment status.

Family structure

The Health Survey of England (Prescott-Clarke and Primatesta, 1998) found that children in lone-parent families were statistically more likely to have higher (ie. worse) scores on the Strengths and Difficulties questionnaire, and that young men in lone-parent households also had statistically significant, higher, GHQ scores, although these were higher, but not statistically significant, for girls.

Analysis of the BHPS (1994 wave) by Scott (1996) found that children in lone-parent families were no less likely to be unhappy than those in two-parent families. However, Brynin and Scott (1996) whilst finding no relationship between life satisfaction and family structure, found that young (but not older) children with one parent, and more so those with a step-parent, were statistically less likely to be self-confident. Clarke, Bradshaw and Williams (1999) also found some evidence, on some variables, that children of lone parents had lower well-being scores.

The most recent English WHO Health Behaviour Survey of School-Aged Children (Haselden *et al.*, 1999) found some slight differences between levels of happiness amongst children with both natural parents compared with those with step-parents and one parent (for example, 93 per cent of the former felt very or quite happy compared with

88 per cent of the other groups), but the differences on all measures were slight, usually only a few percentage points.

Most recently, Meltzer and Gatward (2000) found that children of lone parents were about twice as likely to be defined as having a mental disorder than other children (16 per cent compared with 8 per cent). Logistic regression analysis showed increased odds of about 50 per cent for children from lone parents having a mental disorder compared with couples.

On the related subject of family relations, Sweeting and West (1996), using the West of Scotland Twenty-05 study, found young people aged 15 (in 1987) who reported more conflict with parents were also more likely to have health problems (both physical and psychological health) and lower self-esteem at age 18 (in 1990). This relationship was strongest for young women.

Parental stress

The Annual Health Survey of England also reported a significant relationship, particularly strong for girls, between SDQ scores and both parents' scores on the GHQ. Young women's GHQ score was also found to be associated with their mothers' GHQ score, however there was no relationship for boys nor was fathers' GHQ score significant for either gender.

Brynin and Scott (1996) found a close relationship with life satisfaction (happy scales) of children with their mothers' GHQ scores, although not with the fathers' GHQ score, indicating that mothers who are experiencing stress are more likely to have children who are less happy; this relationship was stronger for girls than boys and for younger than older children. However, no correlation was found between mothers' stress levels and children's self-confidence (although there was only borderline significance for fathers). The authors commented:

> Whilst psychological well-being is largely a private matter there do seem to be some public policy implications insofar as there is a demonstrable link between social disadvantage and poor health and high stress levels of adults. Moreover, while there is no direct link between social disadvantage and children's psychological well-being (on the basis of this sample and the variable we have used), children are likely to be slightly less happy the more stress their mothers feel. (Brynin and Scott, 1996:57)

Area

The Meltzer and Gatwood (2000) study used ACORN, a classification which combines geographical and demographic characteristics, to look at possible differences in child mental health in families in the following six categories: thriving, expanding, rising, settling, aspiring and striving. Logistic regression showed that children in 'striving' families (which included people living on council estates and in low-income areas etc.) had nearly double the odds of having a mental disorder compared with children in 'thriving' households (which included wealthy achievers and affluent rural families).

Employment status of parents

Whilst the employment status of parents might be very closely related to poverty, a few studies seem to have found links between employment status of parents and children's well-being, where social class and income variables show no clear link. Clarke, Bradshaw and Williams (1999) found that some children whose father was unemployed appeared to have lower well-being scores. By contrast, Scott (1996) reported that boys were much less happy if their mother was working full-time.

An American model (Figure 17.3) has depicted how familial economic difficulties may indirectly lead to adjustment problems for young people via parental depression, marital conflict and pressure on parenting. Fombonne (1995b) points out that this model may have particular implications for single parents who are more likely to experience poverty. It seems likely that young people experiencing a range of negative family situations including poverty, parental unemployment, psychiatric disorder in parent, neglect, have an increased risk of mental health problems (Goodyer, 1994). Clarke, Bradshaw and Williams (1999) suggest that certain variables (eg. lone parenthood) may be acting as a proxy for poverty and vice versa in large surveys such as the BHPS. In effect, there may be some links between well-being and poverty which are being mediated through other factors.

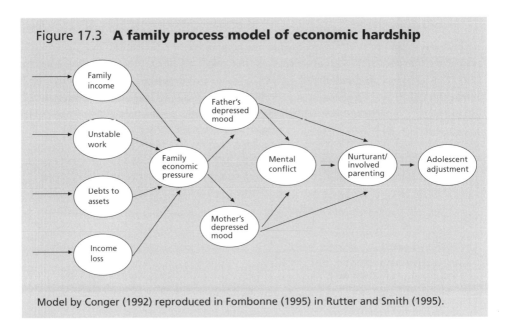

Figure 17.3 A family process model of economic hardship

Model by Conger (1992) reproduced in Fombonne (1995) in Rutter and Smith (1995).

Trends over time in children's mental health

There is a consensus that mental health problems amongst children and young people have become more prevalent in Western societies in the post-war period (Rutter and Smith, 1995; Mental Health Foundation, 1999; NHS Advisory Service, 1995). There is, however, less of a consensus, and less evidence, on the possible causes of this rise. Notwithstanding this, it appears that poverty and socio-economic factors are not one of the key reasons which would explain the rise.

A rise in disorders

It is not possible to review all the supporting evidence for the presumed rise in disorders in this chapter: that task has been completed elsewhere (Rutter and Smith, 1995). However, it is possible to give a few examples. There appears to be some evidence for increased rates of self-harm and attempted suicide in the 1970s and 1980s, although these may not have been sustained into the 1990s (Rutter and Smith, 1995). Hawton *et al.*, (1996) looking at deliberate self-poisoning and self-injury in children and adolescents under 16 years of age in Oxford found an upward trend over the period 1976–1993.

Fombonne (1995b) presents a number of studies which indicate that depressive disorders may have increased since the war. It has been documented that the number of young people diagnosed with mental health problems and/or admitted to hospital increased over the ten years leading up to the early 1990s (SCEC, 1994), but this may be accounted for by more young people presenting such problems to professional services and/or changing approaches to treatment. Lewis and Wilkinson (1993) compared a 1977 and a 1985 study, and found 'cases' of psychological morbidity increased from 22 per cent to 31 per cent; however this did not disproportionately affect young people (16–24).

Reasons for a rise in disorders

As the Mental Health Foundation (1999:11) have explained: 'It is not easy to demonstrate causal links between trends in society and impacts on children and young people.'

Rutter and Smith (1995) reviewed the international evidence on why disorders had become more frequent over the last 50 years, and, although they could not conclusively demonstrate the causes, were able to comment on the most likely and unlikely reasons for a rise in disorders. Poverty and unemployment were both felt not to be factors instrumental in explaining the rise in disorders. Rutter and Smith (1995) point out that several disorders, like crime, have been associated with social disadvantage, but that living conditions have improved during the period that psychosocial disorders have risen. They also point out that the incidence of some disorders may have declined or levelled off during the 1980s and 1990s, for example, suicide rates, at a time when some countries, including Britain, have experienced growing rates of poverty. They conclude that: 'although social disadvantage is associated with many psychosocial disorders at any one point in time, worsening living conditions do not account for the rising levels of disorders'. (Rutter and Smith, 1995)

In their review, Rutter and Smith accept that unemployment creates risks for individuals, but again point out that high levels of unemployment do not account for an overall rise in disorders as unemployment was low in the 1950s and 1960s when the greatest increase in disorders were seen. They conclude that any effect of social disadvantage is indirect, in increasing other risks such as family breakdown.

The factors that Rutter and Smith (1995) conclude are most likely to be associated with the rise in disorders include increased family discord and lack of parental support, a possible increase in stressors in general (including family break-up, more freedom, breakdown in 'love' relationships), and increasing expectations on young people at a time when it has become increasingly difficult to meet these. They also think that the growth of youth cultures and markets may have acted to create 'an isolated youth culture' with increased peer influence. Extended transitions are also suggested but it is noted that there is no evidence that those who have longer transition have greater problems. Finally, the more general shift towards individualism in society is also identified as a possible cause: 'the shift towards individualistic values, the increasing emphasis on self-realisation and fulfilment, and the consequent rise in expectations, should be studied as possible causes of disorders'. (Rutter and Smith, 1995:807)

Other authors have also stressed the changing nature of society and the increased number of risks and stressors associated with the 'unpredictable nature of life in high modernity', alongside extended youth transitions, as possible factors accounting for the growth in mental health problems amongst young people (Furlong and Carmel, 1997).

> We suggest that processes of individualisation, coupled with the stress which develops out of uncertain transitional outcomes, have implications for the health of all young people. In particular, it is argued that the protraction and desequencing of youth transitions have had a negative impact on young people's mental health. In this respect, Beck and Giddens are correct to suggest that reflexive individualisation, together with the need to establish adult identities and sustain coherent narratives in a rapidly changing social world, can lead to new risks. (Furlong and Carmel, 1997:65)

Rutter and Smith (1995) conclude that 'finding causal explanations of the increases in psychosocial disorders remains a project for the future'. Further analysis is needed on the few time-series studies which are available (like the BHPS) to see what changes in well-being occur after changes in economic and family formation (Clarke, Bradshaw and Williams, 1999). Better indicators also need to be developed which can measure the range of mental health disorders over time, including cross-national social indicators by bodies such as OECD and Eurostat (Rutter and Smith, 1995).

Conclusions

The chapter began with a hypothesis that poverty was likely to be associated with mental health and psychological problems in childhood and young adulthood. The evidence reviewed does not consistently support, nor consistently refute, this assertion. Evidence is quite strong for a link between childhood poverty and some mental *disorders*, especially conduct disorders. However, the evidence is much weaker, and often unobserved, for a relationship between childhood poverty and levels of more broadly-defined mental well-being, such as levels of happiness. Some evidence does exist which points to a relationship between older youth's own emerging socio-economic status and poor mental health, most prominently in relation to the links between unemployment and poor psychological well-being. Finally, some research studies have also noted a possible indirect effect of poverty as mediated through other factors such as household structure and parental stress. A review of the post-war increase in mental disorders amongst young people does not suggest that there is any relationship with increasing levels of poverty in Britain. In conclusion, it can be suggested that poverty is likely to be related to some aspects of the mental health of children and young people. Future research needs to concentrate on the development of more sophisticated measurements of mental health, utilising them in longitudinal studies, to increase the likelihood of these relationships being more fully understood.

Other countries

Helen Barnes

18 How other countries monitor the well-being of their children

Helen Barnes

Introduction

This chapter discusses the institutional framework and the main mechanisms which governments use to monitor the well-being of children, reviews the types of indicators collected for various domains, and addresses some of the conceptual and methodological issues involved in the selection of particular indicators as outcome measures. Writing in 1992, Jensen and Saporiti noted that there was a dearth of statistical material on children and their living conditions in many industrialised countries. Despite the large number of surveys[1] which document children's well-being, it was often not possible to carry out analysis using the child as the unit of observation, and information from disparate sources was often not brought together in a fashion readily accessible to analysts and policy makers. Preliminary efforts to collect data on how EU countries monitor child well-being were made as part of the work of the European Observatory on National Family Policies (Ditch *et al.*, 1998). This project has updated that work and extended the investigation to a wider range of 20 countries (the EU Member States, Canada, USA, Norway, Australia, New Zealand and Japan), using national informants who provided replies to standard questions as well as supplying copies of relevant reports and literature.

Institutional framework

The UK is not as unusual as is sometimes assumed in having no formal means of co-ordinating the work of the various ministries responsible for children. In most countries there is no single government department which is responsible for children and their well-being, and their interests are represented across a range of ministries. Around half the countries in the study are in this position, while the others have a Ministry which has lead responsibility for children, usually the Ministry for the Family or the Ministry for Social Affairs (see Figure 18.1). The absence of a department with lead responsibility for children can lead to a lack of coherence in the formulation of policy and a lack of co-ordination in its implementation. In terms of monitoring children's well-being it may also lead to their invisibility in official statistics and reports.

Of course, not all countries have child policies which are determined solely at a national level. In Germany, nationally-determined policies are implemented at state level, but with a fairly restricted degree of autonomy; while in Austria, Spain, Belgium, Canada, Australia and the USA, there is a fairly high level of autonomy at the state level. Child policy is largely the responsibility of the regions in Belgium and Spain, while in the Netherlands and the Scandinavian countries the municipalities have a high degree of delegated responsibility. The Scandinavian countries take the

Figure 18.1 Institutional framework for child policy

Country	Overall responsibility for children	Child Ombudsman?
Australia	No overall co-ordination	No
Austria	Ministry for Environment, Youth and Family Affairs	Yes, national and state level
Belgium	Regional	Yes
Canada	No overall co-ordination, Federal Ministries for Family	No
Denmark	Inter-Ministerial Committee	National Children's Council
Finland	No overall co-ordination	No
France	No overall co-ordination	No
Germany	Ministry for Family, Women, the Elderly and Youth	No national, some at state level
Greece	Ministry of Health and Welfare	No
Ireland	Department of Health and Children, Inter-Departmental Working Group	No
Italy	Department of Social Affairs	Two regional, no national
Japan	No overall co-ordination	No
Luxembourg	Inter-Ministerial Working Group	Yes
Netherlands	No overall co-ordination	No
New Zealand	No overall co-ordination	Yes
Norway	No overall co-ordination	Yes
Portugal	High Commission for the Promotion of Equality and the Family	No
Spain	Inter-Ministerial Committee	No
Sweden	No overall co-ordination	Yes
UK	No overall co-ordination	Two national, no UK
USA	No overall co-ordination, Ministries at State level	No

view that making child policy the responsibility of a specific ministry would tend to downgrade its importance for other ministries, while the Netherlands has actively increased the amount of decentralisation in this area in an attempt to make child policy more responsive to local needs and priorities. In other countries, such as Spain, high levels of regional autonomy are seen as creating a necessity for good co-ordination mechanisms.

There is increasing interest in the idea of *children's ombudsmen,* and they have a clear advantage in being able to advocate children's interests independently of the party political pressures which inevitably dictate the agenda of any government ministry. Nine of the twenty countries in the study have some form of Child Ombudsman (although these are by no means identical across countries) and most produce annual reports on their work. Sweden is unusual in having the Ombudsman's report published alongside official statistics in a single annual report. In addition to whether they operate at a national or regional level, child ombudsmen differ in their degree of independence from government, the level of resources which are at their disposal, and the extent to which they intervene in individual cases as well as having a broader role in lobbying and in scrutinising new legislation. For instance, the national Child Ombudsman in Austria consists of a single part-time employee, who is part of the Ministry for Children and the Family, rather than being fully independent, although there are independent ombudsmen operating in the nine *Länder* who meet regularly. In Denmark, the Children's Council is an independent body with seven full-time members of staff carrying out the functions of an Ombudsman. The Child Ombudsman has a role in scrutinising legislation for its potential impact on children in Sweden and the Flemish Community in Belgium, where child impact statements are required as part of the parliamentary process. The possibility of an extended role for the Ombudsman is currently under discussion in New Zealand.

Why and how do governments monitor child well-being?

All developed countries have some mechanisms which monitor the well-being of children and young people, including vital statistics, administrative statistics on such issues as education and health, and primary research, whether or not funded by government itself. There have been two major engines behind the renewed interest in monitoring child outcomes during the last ten years or so. These are on the one hand, the 1989 UN Convention on the Rights of the Child, now ratified by all countries in this study, whose reporting requirements have encouraged a number of governments to improve their national reporting systems (although many reports for the UN provide little data on outcomes as such, being more concerned with the legal rights of children and the various policy inputs in the national context) and on the other, a growing concern amongst academics and welfare professionals about the effects of recession and public expenditure cuts on child well-being. There has also been an extensive academic debate, especially in the USA, about the value of indicators in providing evidence about the effects of growing up in varying circumstances on children. As Miringoff and Miringoff (1997) argue, a lack of systematic reporting frameworks on child welfare can lead to policy initiatives being adopted in response to unrepresentative but widely reported cases, or perhaps even worse, to a sense of fatalism about social problems:

> 'We hear far more about "the crisis in our cities" or the "crisis amongst youth" or "an epidemic of teenage suicide", suggesting uncontrollable situations not open to solution, than we hear anything comparable to "the economy expanded by 2.3 per cent in the last quarter", which suggests a pragmatic vigilance and the possibility of rational action if trouble should occur.' (Miringoff and Miringoff, 1997:476)

De Winter (1997) argues that the focus of concern with the well-being of children has shifted over time. He presents three phases: in the first, which he describes as the era of the 'predictable child' the emphasis was on early detection of problems and on intervention by professionals to reduce the impact of health or behavioural problems across the general population. The second phase, which he describes as that of the 'social renewal child' sees an emphasis away from all children, and towards children perceived as being in a risk group. Specific, tailored interventions are then designed and implemented, for a variety of motives, including the building of human capital, solidaristic concerns for the disadvantaged, and the interest of professionals in working with certain target groups. The third phase, which de Winter argues to be currently in its ascendancy, is that of the 'moral rearmament child'. The perceived need for intervention is argued to arise less from a desire to tackle deprivation *per se* than from the dangers which young people are seen to pose to society in the form of crime, vagrancy and so on. The cause of the problems is often located in the moral failure of parents, and at worst, policy interventions can take on the appearance of a 'war against the young'. De Winter argues that these orientations towards child welfare can have at least two major effects relevant to the question of developing social indicators specifically for children. First, there is a tendency to seek explanations of causality at an individual, rather than societal level. Secondly, there is often an over-emphasis on negative, 'problem' outcomes, rather than on identifying factors which accentuate or reduce the risk of negative outcomes. A number of commentators have identified the need to focus on societal factors, including measures of such issues as social capital in neighbourhoods, exposure to violence, ethnic segregation and so on. For instance, Ben-Arieh and Wintersberger (1997) and Zubrick *et al.* (1999) argue that an ecological perspective, which takes into account factors operating within the household and the neighbourhood, as well as those operating at a broader societal level such as globalisation, insecurity and increased risk, offers the best hope of understanding the 'new morbidity' of negative child outcomes in developed countries.

This so-called 'new morbidity' manifests itself in a range of threats and risks to children's well-being which were not found, or were far less prominent, in earlier periods, and which have a less clear-cut relationship with household poverty than traditional health indicators, although they are often concentrated in areas of social disadvantage. These include exposure to violence, abuse of tobacco, alcohol and other drugs, deaths from car accidents, involvement in crime, eating disorders, and child abuse (Zubrick *et al.*, 1997; chapters by McGlone and Quilgars, this volume). Deaths from accidents, suicides and murders now outnumber natural causes of death for children and young people across the industrialised world (Elster, 1997). A number of commentators (such as De Winter, 1997; Moore, 1995) have pointed out that concerns about these new types of risks have tended to result in a bias towards the collection of data on negative, rather than positive, outcomes for children and young people.

Interest in measuring child outcomes has grown partly because of a more generalised belief in the usefulness of social indicators as tools for planning and evaluating social policy developments (Ben-Arieh, 1997). Although UNICEF have been publishing regular reports on child well-being world-wide for over 15 years, it is only in the last five to ten years that there has been a real growth in the development of indicators for children as a specific subgroup of the population. Increased monitoring of child well-being can help to identify not only groups who are at risk, and who may require preventive services, but those who have avoided risk, and whose experiences can provide positive evidence of what works. Figure 18.2 sets out the ideal standard for outcome indicators; in practice, however, government monitoring activity tends to be constrained by cost and the limitations of available data, and professional boundaries may also act as a barrier to developing broad measures of well-being. There is a tension between the subtle, but time-consuming, methods favoured by social scientists and the more readily available, but less informative, data sources which are attractive to policy-makers (Prout, 1997; Philips and Love, 1997). This is, perhaps, one reason why there have been to date few measures based on children's own perceptions.

Figure 18.2 **Criteria for indicators of child well-being**

- Comprehensive coverage
- Measure depth, breadth and duration
- Age-specific, including transition to adulthood
- Clear and comprehensible
- Positive outcomes
- Cross-culturally valid
- Consistent over time
- Anticipate future trends
- Methodologically rigorous
- Geographically detailed
- Cost-efficient
- Reflective of social goals
- Adjusted for demographic trends

From Moore (1995) *Eurosocial Report 56. New Social Indicators of Child Wellbeing.*

There is widespread agreement that regular reports on the state of children are an essential tool in raising public awareness and achieving political support for improving their living conditions (Adamson, 1995; Qvortrup *et al.*, 1994). Japan appears to have the longest history of producing regular reports on children, having done so since the nineteenth-century. Although most countries have only recently begun to produce reports on children, over half the countries in this study now produce regular reports on children, as Figure 18.3 demonstrates. A further group of five countries, including the UK, has produced *ad hoc* reports on children over the past few years. A minority of countries still produce no reports beyond those which are required in fulfilment of the UN Convention on the Rights of the Child.

Figure 18.3 **Reports on children**

Regular reports on children	Recent reports on children	None other than UN requirements
Canada	Netherlands (1996)	France
Japan	Portugal (1999)	Greece
USA	Denmark (1995)	Spain
New Zealand	UK (1994)	Australia
Germany	Austria (various dates)	Ireland
Italy		
Belgium		
Luxembourg		
Norway		
Sweden		
Finland		

The content of reports on children varies, but they tend to cover similar broad topics. Recent reports in Finland, Portugal, and the Netherlands are typical in drawing together statistical data on family demography, employment and housing conditions, together with summary information from research on children and young people's leisure activities, education, health and values. In Sweden, statistical information on children is presented alongside the report of the Child Ombudsman. In Canada and the USA, there are such a large number of reports on children, at both national and state level, that it is difficult to summarise them. A recent review of 'state of the child' reports in Canada (Rutman and Armitage, 1993) found that they tended to be quite similar in content, generally including a range of information on family structure, health, education, economic status, childcare, housing and rights issues. Most present a breakdown of information by gender, age, disability and race, although data limitations and varying objectives for the reports mean that these data are not always presented systematically.

In the USA, the Annie E. Casey Foundation, a private charitable foundation, is responsible for funding a series of 'Kids Count' reports on children at state level, and it also produces an annual report covering the country as a whole. The Foundation also produces *ad hoc* reports on issues such as child abuse, teen pregnancy, and health inequalities in children. The Federal Inter-Agency Forum on Child and Family Statistics produces an annual report on child well-being, containing 25 indicators, drawn from national surveys and vital records, including 11 standard health indicators, and nine educational indicators (Federal Inter-Agency Forum on Child and Family Statistics, 1997 and annually). Indicators of particular interest (although they are not measures of outcome) include the proportion of children reporting food poverty (often not having enough to eat at home), the proportion of young children who are read to every day, and the proportion of children whose parents are not native speakers of English and who have problems communicating in English. A longer and more detailed report, covering over 80 indicators in five broad domains (population, family and neighbourhood; economic security; health conditions and health care; social development, behavioural health and teen fertility; education and achievement), is also published every year, and attempts to provide a comprehensive overview of data relating to children and young people in the US (US Department of Health and Human Services, 1996 and annually).

Six US states (California, Florida, Minnesota, Massachusetts, Oregon, Vermont) are widely regarded as being in the vanguard of developing social indicators for children (Brown *et al.*, 1997). In California, although there have been no attempts to set benchmarks or focus on particular child outcomes at state level, a considerable amount of effort has been expended in linking administrative data, including health, education, and income data, many of which are available on the Internet. The California Children's Services Archive is an attempt to bring together information on children to create a comprehensive longitudinal dataset. It currently includes state-wide data on all live births and deaths since 1970, records of assessment, incarceration and parole by the Youth Authorities, adoption records, residential and foster care, and special educational needs, and it is planned to include data on child abuse, MedCal (the state Medicaid system), AFDC/TANF, employment and education within a five-year period. This archive has been used to produce annual reports on 'Performance Indicators for Child Welfare', focusing on child abuse and the outcomes of out-of-family placements. In Florida, there has been extensive use of outcome measures for children as part of an exercise in bench-marking which began with the establishment of the Florida Commission on Government Accountability to the People (GAP), which undertook a consultative exercise to establish a list of over 250 benchmarks across a range of domains. The first 'Benchmarks Report' was published in 1996, covering seven areas: families and communities, safety, learning, health, the economy, the environment, government. All but two of these areas contain direct measures of child well-being. Key goals identified for children and young people were creating a healthy start for children, protecting children from abuse and neglect, facilitating the recovery of children with mental health problems, enabling children to enter school ready to learn, and reducing teen pregnancy, and each is linked to a set of indicators. Vermont has also established a set of indicators linked to progress on benchmarks, as part of the Framework for Co-ordination initiative, which aims to create a single co-ordinated framework for the delivery of services to families and children.

Several countries have recently launched iniatives to improve the well-being of children which are similar to the UK 'Supporting Families' initiative. In 1997, the federal, provincial and territorial governments of Canada agreed to work together to develop a National Children's Agenda, a strategy aimed at improving the well-being of children. A major conference, Investing in Children, sponsored by Human Resource Development Canada, was held in Ottawa in October 1998 to bring together researchers and present data from the National Longitudinal Survey of Children and Youth (NLSCY). In New Zealand, the Government has a programme called 'Strengthening Families' which is designed to integrate and co-ordinate services for families at risk, defined as those experiencing multiple and persistent disadvantages which compromise family functioning and increase the risk of long-term poor outcomes (Angus, 1999; Department of Social Welfare, 1997 and 1998). Established in 1997, the strategy sets benchmark targets for 22 indicators, including outcomes, policy inputs and risk factors, which are the subject of annual progress reports (see Figure 18.4). It is notable that all but three of these are negative indicators, and that there is a shortage of indicators for children aged between seven and fourteen years of age.

Six indicators (including two positive outcome measures) have been chosen as priority targets; under-five mortality, abuse and neglect renotifications (age 0–6), the proportion of three-year-olds in education, abuse and neglect renotifications (age 7–16), teenage fertility (live births to girls aged 13–17), and the proportion leaving school with a formal qualification. Two new indicators for teenagers were added during 1998, in reponse to a perceived need for data, relating to involvement with the police.

In Ireland, a National Children's Strategy, covering a ten-year period, is to be launched during 2000, and submissions have been invited from the public to establish a set of policy goals. This initiative is being carried forward by an Inter-Departmental Group comprising senior officials from nine Government Departments and chaired by the Department of Health and Children.

It may be necessary to create a particular focus to create public interest in children's rights and child well-being. In Japan, demographic data on children is always published close to May 5th, Children's Day, which is a national public holiday. In Germany and France a Children's Parliament was recently held to raise awareness of issues affecting children and young people. In New Zealand, the Commission for Children issued a report urging people to 'vote for children' in the recent elections, and highlighting the impact of particular policies.

Which aspects of children's well-being do governments currently monitor?

There is a remarkable similarity in the *types* of child outcomes which are monitored across industrialised countries, although this does not by any means imply a consensus about which indicators are most valid or reliable, comparability of data across countries (Micklewright and Stewart, 1999), or the existence of extensive data on particular issues of policy concern (Ruxton, 1996). The following section discusses some key areas, highlights surveys and indicators which provide examples of good practice, and identifies some gaps in available data.

Poverty

All countries in the study have information showing the proportion of households with children which have incomes below 50 per cent of average (or median) household income, although data taking the child as the unit of analysis is still not readily available for all countries. Most of the countries deposit the datasets on which this is based with the Luxembourg Income Survey and LIS analysis provides estimates of the prevalence of poverty with children as the unit of analysis (Bradbury and Jantti, 1999; Danziger, Smeeding and Rainwater, 1995; Bradshaw, 1999). The incidence of poverty, in turn,

Figure 18.4 New Zealand 'Strengthening Families' target measures

Indicator (** priority indicator)	Baseline (1995 or nearest date)	2000 target	2010 target
Road traffic deaths per 100,000 (age 15–19)	31	25	not established
Youth suicides per 100,000 (age 15–19)	38.9 (M) 6.3 (F)	33 (M) 5.4 (F)	29 (M) 4.7 (F)
Hospital injury discharge rate per 100,000 (age 15–19)	2,517	2,100	1,770
Abuse/neglect renotifications per 1,000 (age 7–16)**	11.68	75% baseline	50% baseline
Live births per 100,000 females (age 13–17)**	1,121	1,090	975
Percentage smoking tobacco (age 18–24)	34.2	22	19
Drug/alcohol risk behaviour	not established	not established	not established
Serious/repeat offending per 1,000 (age 10–16)	13.76	80% baseline	65% baseline
Offenders under 16 dealt with by police	44,654	not established	not established
Prosecutions of people under 16	4,798	not established	not established
Percentage leaving school with formal qualification**	81.9	84	90
Infant mortality (per 1,000 live births)	6.7	5	4
Under-five mortality (per 1,000 live births)**	8.3	7	5
Hospital injury discharge rate per 100,000 (age 0–4)	2,401	2,040	1,680
Abuse death rate per 100,000 (age 0–14)	1.23	1.0	0.8
Abuse/neglect renotifications per 1,000 (age 0–6)**	9.08	80% baseline	50% baseline
Out-of-family placements (age 0–16), number of bednights	375,000	95% baseline	75% baseline
Percentage of pregnant women smoking	33	20	18
Birth weight under 2,500 grammes (per 1,000 live births)	59	57	55
Percentage of children entering school with hearing loss	8.3	5	4
Percentage of children aged two with completed immunisations	56	95	95
Percentage of children age three in early education**	79.9	84	90

Source: New Zealand Department of Social Welfare, 1998.

affects the degree to which there have been attempts to measure the outcomes of poverty, since countries with low recorded poverty rates are less inclined to view the issue as meriting attention. For instance, the Scandinavian countries, which have until recently had very low rates of poverty, have tended to concentrate their monitoring activities on the small proportion of children and families perceived to be at risk. In the USA, where poverty rates are much higher, and there are a large number of policy interventions with a potential influence on the well-being of children, many of the outcome measurements collected are intended to evaluate the effectiveness of specific programmes. In particular, the Welfare Indicators Act 1994 requires the publication of an annual report on the numbers of families dependent on welfare programmes, the degree and duration of such dependence, the factors which are predictive of welfare dependence and the additional data required to assess issues in relation to welfare dependence (US Department of Health and Human Services, 1997 and annually). This report contains data on a wide range of issues seen as increasing the risk of welfare dependence, including information on household structure, the duration of poverty, disability, crime and early parenthood, but a decision has been taken to exclude measures of child well-being, as they are reported elsewhere. In this context, the lack of reporting mechanisms which has existed in the UK until recently is all the more striking given its high rates of child poverty.

Both the timing of poverty and its duration may be important determinants of children's well-being. Poverty in early childhood appears to have more damaging long-term effects than that which occurs later (Duncan and Brooks-Gunn, 1997), whilst the risk of negative outcomes increases with the length of time spent in, or on the margins of, poverty (Duncan et al., 1998). Much available data on child outcomes tells us only about current income, thus masking these effects. Longitudinal and panel surveys can provide information on the timing and duration of poverty, but there are also simple ways of providing proxies for this information in administrative data, for instance by estimates of the proportion of children living in families where social assistance has been claimed for over two years, or over five years, and in cross-sectional surveys, by creating estimates of family income over the past five or ten years.

In addition to measuring income poverty, many countries also measure non-monetary indicators of poverty, such as access to a private car, over-crowded housing and so on. The European Community Household Panel Survey has been used to make comparisons of poverty across countries using these types of indicators (for example, see Ditch et al., 1998). Non-monetary poverty is obviously a more culturally-specific concept than income poverty, although one would expect to see broad consensus about what constitutes necessities across industrialised countries. What is interesting in the present context is the fact that some of the indicators currently in use may be of far less salience to children than to adults, because of their different social lives and time orientation. Two rather obvious measures which have an impact on children's experience are child homelessness (Quilgars, this volume), which is noted as being an area where data is lacking in a number of countries, and food poverty (where the child reports that there is often not enough to eat at home), which is monitored in the USA, but not elsewhere. There is a need for further work to determine which non-monetary indicators of poverty are of most significance to children and young people.

Health

All the countries studied collect standardised health information about children on a routine basis. This includes birth-weight, life expectancy at birth, age-specific and cause-specific mortality rates, rates of chronic illness (although data on disability amongst children is less often collected), dental caries, weight and age-appropriate development. Although often regarded as less useful as an indicator than in the past, because of the extent to which health standards have improved (and because they do not adequately reflect positive aspirations for well-being) data on morbidity and mortality amongst children and young people continue to show an important relationship with poverty and deprivation, both at an individual level (where the social class gradient has remained consistent, or even increased, over time) and area level. This can be seen, for instance, in the dramatic improvements in infant mortality rates in Portugal (and other South European countries) since the 1960s (Ditch *et al.*, 1998), the rise in mortality rates in the countries of former Eastern Europe during the 1990s, and the differential mortality rates amongst those living in poorer and better-off areas of the UK (Chapter 2, this volume; Harker *et al.*, 1997; Acheson, 1999) and the US (Annie E. Casey Foundation, 1999) as well as continuing regional differentials in Portugal and Italy (Ditch *et al.*, 1998, National Centre for the Documentation and Analysis of Childhood and Adolescence, 1999). Ethnicity also appears to be a major factor in differential health outcomes in a number of countries, including Italy, the UK, Canada, Australia and New Zealand. As will be discussed below, mortality from specific causes shows a strong association with poverty and deprivation.

Mortality and morbidity data, as objective measures, are less susceptible than other indicators to issues of comparability caused by variations in definition across time and place. However, problems may still arise owing to variations in the coding of ethnic origin and social class on birth and death certificates, and the recording of presenting, rather than underlying, causes of death. There have also been calls for an improvement in the recording of gestational age of low birth-weight babies, in order to differentiate between premature babies and those showing evidence of retarded growth *in utero* (Lantz and Partin, 1997).

Low birth-weight, which is more common amongst low-income and minority ethnic groups, is associated not only with higher rates of neonatal and infant mortality, but with long-term health risks, such as an increased rate of coronary heart disease (Lantz and Partin, 1997, Modood *et al.*, 1997; Acheson, 1998). The Annie E. Casey Foundation in the USA has developed a healthy birth index consisting of four items, and a three-item risk index, as well as providing regular reports on eight indicators associated with poor health at birth (see Figure 18.5).

Morbidity and mortality data are widely available, comparable across time and place, and readily understood, and therefore fulfil some of the key criteria for an effective indicator (Moore, 1995), but they are limited in other respects, particularly in providing indicators of positive health and in identifying future trends. Self-reports of physical and mental health status are widely regarded as reliable indicators amongst adults, but are less often used with children in national surveys, although they are used in the international Health Behaviour of School-Aged Children Survey (Currie, 1999).

Figure 18.5 **Key indicators for health at birth**

Healthy birth index

- weight of at least 5.5 lbs
- five-minute Agpar score of 9 or 10
- gestation of 37 weeks or more
- prenatal care started in first trimester

Birth risk index

- mother under 20 years of age
- mother unmarried
- mother has fewer than 12 years of education

Risk indicators for health at birth

- mother under 20 years of age
- second or subsequent birth to teen mother
- mother unmarried
- mother has fewer than 12 years of education
- little or no prenatal care
- mother smoked during pregnancy
- weight under 5.5 lbs
- gestation under 37 weeks

Source: Davis *et al.*, 1999, *The Right Start.*

Parental reports of health are generally recommended as survey questions for children aged under four, whilst age-appropriate questions may be asked of those in older age groups, and show consistent associations with income (Starfield, 1997; Currie, 1999). Parental, teacher and self-reports of child health are a major feature of the Canadian Longitudinal Survey, and are also found in the Western Australian Child Health Survey and the Youth Risk Behaviour Survey (YRBS) in the USA.

Two health indicators which are particularly relevant in the USA, because of the problems poor populations face in accessing health care, but may also have salience elsewhere, are the concepts of sentinel conditions (which should not occur where health care is adequate) and access occurring at inappropriate levels (Starfield, 1997). The first refers to conditions such as iron-deficiency anaemia, elevated blood–lead levels and communicable diseases such as TB, whereas the second refers to hospitalisation for conditions amenable to primary health care (such as dehydration, severe ENT infections, asthma, bacterial pneumonia, gastro-enteritis and urinary tract infections), as has been found amongst homeless children in the UK (Chapter 8, this volume). Reducing the levels of emergency admissions for gastro-enteritis and respiratory infections for babies under one year old is one of the Sure Start targets in the UK.

Accidents in childhood are monitored by a number of countries, and the clear social gradient observed in the UK is consistent with that in other countries. There are a number of explanations for this phenomenon, including the location of low-cost housing, lack of access to well-designed domestic appliances, lower levels of parental education and supervision, and poor access to childcare. The Scandinavian countries appear to have done most to reduce both accident rates, and their concentration amongst those in lower social classes (Ditch et al., 1998). Motor vehicle accidents are now the largest single cause of death for children aged 5–14 across Europe, responsible for one in five deaths in this age group in 1994 (Micklewright and Stewart, 1999). Deaths related to firearms, whether accidental, homicidal or suicidal, are also an important indicator in the US (Forum on Child and Family Statistics, 1997).

Most countries collect some information on the health behaviours of young people, including diet, exercise, use of tobacco, alcohol and illegal drugs, sexual activity and use of contraception, although few do so in a regular and representative fashion at a national level. However, a number of countries take part in the international Health Behaviours of Schoolchildren Survey (Currie, 1999). The Youth Risk Behaviours Survey in the USA and the Canadian NLSCY provide the most extensive data on these issues, and they also feature in the Christchurch Health Survey and the Western Australian Health Survey.

Increasing obesity is noted as a problem in several of the countries in the study, and is related to both changes in diet and changes in activity patterns of children, who are increasingly spending time on sedentary pursuits such as video games, rather than sport, and are often driven in their parents' cars, rather than walking (Hillman et al., 1990). Few of the countries in the study publish data on obesity regularly, although this is done in the USA, Australia, France and Canada, but the information is available in principle as part of the routine health checks on schoolchildren carried out in most countries. Several countries, including Ireland, Canada, USA and Australia monitor the number of hours spent in physically-demanding exercise each week or include a measure of the number of hours spent watching television, as in the Netherlands and the USA. Eating disorders such as bulimia and anorexia nervosa are reported as increasing amongst young women in several countries, including Australia, but few countries appear to collect reliable statistics, nor would it be easy to do so on a systematic basis, since the indicators would inevitably measure patterns of service use, rather than incidence. The Canadian National Longitudinal Survey of Children and Youth asks about body image and binge eating at age 11 and 13, while the Western Australian Child Health Survey and the USA NHANES Survey also ask a series of questions about body image and dieting.

Mental health problems are a cause of concern in many countries, with self-harm amongst females and suicides amongst young men on the increase. It is clear that there is a rather widespread deficit as far as sensitive indicators able to predict suicide risk is concerned. Hospitalisation rates for self-harm are available for some countries, as are referral rates to mental health services, but these are clearly not an objective measure and represent at most only the tip of the iceberg. The most effective indicators of mental health status are self-reports of self-esteem and mental well-being, child or young person's evaluation of the quality of the parent–child relationship, child or young person's evaluation of relationships with peers, and measures which capture the young person's sense of having a future orientation and positive options open to them. A wide variety of such measures is to be found in the Canadian NLSCY and the Western Australian Child Health Survey. One interesting finding from the NLSCY is that children from poor recent immigrant families had better mental health outcomes than Canadian-born children living in poverty (Beiser *et al.*, 1998). Although the reasons for this were not clear, they may have included the fact that poverty was a transitional stage, living standards being judged relative to conditions in the country of origin, and different family structures and parenting practices.

Substance misuse

Substance misuse is a matter of increasing concern across many countries; the Southern European countries have experienced rapid rises in the use of legal and illegal drugs by young people as their economies have developed (Ditch *et al.*, 1998). The main sources of data on substance misuse are administrative statistics (such as crime figures and hospitalisations) and self-report studies, with the result that they are likely to understate, or possibly in some cases over-state, the behaviours of interest. Many of the available survey instruments monitor behaviour amongst young people in their teens, and thus fail to capture the increasing use of legal and illegal drugs by those in younger age groups. The more sensitive indicators for alcohol use include distinctions between regular weekly, monthly and daily use of alcohol, identify 'binge' drinking (where five or more alcoholic drinks are consumed in a single session), and distinguish between spirits and other alcoholic drinks. Similar distinctions are drawn in some countries between the use of marijuana, inhalants, hallucinogens, cocaine, and other drugs. Other indicators monitored by a few countries only include surveys of attitudes towards the use of legal and illegal drugs, whether the young person has driven after drinking, or been a passenger in a car where the driver had been drinking, and the prices of common illegal drugs. The most extensive data is to be found in the USA, Australia, and Canada. As in the UK (Chapter 14, this volume), US evidence suggests that drug use is associated with smoking, although the US associations between drug-taking and truancy and early sexual activity do not hold for the UK, suggesting that it has a more 'deviant' status in the US than the UK. Both alcohol and drug use are as likely to be associated with affluence as with poverty in the UK, and living in a city also appears to predispose young people to experiment with drug use (Chapters 13, 14, this volume).

Teenage fertility

Teenage fertility is an issue of particular concern in the UK (see Chapter 6, this volume), where it has been the focus of a recent report by the Social Exclusion Unit; in New Zealand, where reducing the level of teenage pregnancy was identified as a priority target in the recent 'Strengthening Families' Strategy, and in the USA. Although most other countries in the study monitor the proportion of live births to young mothers and the age-specific abortion rate, the numbers involved are not generally so high as to warrant policy concern, and in some countries occur mostly within marriage (Micklewright and Stewart, 1999). In the US, a number of indicators which are risk factors for teenage pregnancy (including the proportion of those aged 14–18 who have had sexual intercourse, the proportion sexually active in the last three months, number of sexual partners by age 20, use of contraception at last intercourse and STD rates amongst 15- to 19-year-olds) are collected as part of the Youth Risk Behaviours Survey, which also reports on the pregnancy rate amongst young women aged 15–19, whether these result in live births or abortions, and on second-order births to teenage women. The results of the risk factors are subdivided by gender and race, and there are significant differences in risk behaviour between ethnic groups in the US, as there are in New Zealand (New Zealand Department of Social Welfare, 1997). This known association makes it important for measures of teenage fertility to be adjusted to take account of the ethnic make-up of the areas compared (Moore, 1995). Without this, raw data can tell us little about the significance of different rates in different areas, much less monitor the impact of different policies and practices on trends in teenage fertility (Prosser and Stagner, 1997). Because abortion, as well as birth, implies health risks for young women, some surveys also monitor the proportion of young women who have ever been pregnant.

Crime

Concern about children as both the perpetrators and victims of crime has become pronounced in industrialised countries over recent years, and at times this has manifested itself in ways highly consistent with De Winter's (1997) characterisation of 'a war against the young', with debates about reducing the age of criminal responsibility in several countries, and the introduction of child curfews in the UK and some US states (Chapter 11, this volume). Political debate about crime and the young is often stimulated by particularly shocking cases, as has happened with child murders in Japan (Tokoro, 1999) and the UK (McGlone and Millar, 1998) in recent years, rather than by reasoned consideration of statistical trends. Several countries have recently commissioned reports on crime and children; these include Japan, Portugal and Italy. Public concern about crime and young people is also leading to pressure for better statistics in Austria. The issue of crime is also complicated by problems of definition, and by differing ages of criminal responsibility, which make valid comparisons across time and place very difficult (Chapter 11, this volume, Prosser and Stagner, 1997). Indicators such as the numbers of children and young people arrested or convicted for particular types of offences, or the numbers of children in custody, are highly sensitive to changes in policy and practice in recording and dealing with crime, as are child victimization rates. Behavioural indicators showing a risk of increasing involvement in crime include truancy rates, staying out overnight without permission, association with young people already involved in crime, attitudes towards crime, and the extent to which young people routinely carry weapons (US Department of Health and Human Services, 1997). These carry the risk of under- and over-reporting, and are in any case, apart from truancy figures, not widely available, although both Canada and the USA collect a range of data on such issues in the NLSCY and the YRBS. The most widely available and valid objective indicators for young people and crime are the arrest rate for violent crimes committed by or against children and young people, and the death rate from child abuse and neglect (Prosser and Stagner, 1997; New Zealand Department of Social Welfare, 1998). There may also be a case for including some measures known to be risk factors for involvement in crime, notwithstanding the methodological issues referred to above.

Education

All the countries surveyed collect data on the number of children enrolled in school, and performance in examinations and most have at least some data on truancy, although in many cases the latter is not reliable. In addition, population surveys often ask about the highest levels of qualification obtained, allowing a retrospective analysis. Assessment results are not always comparable across schools or areas; this is noted as a particular issue in Japan and the USA (Tokoro, 1999; Brown *et al.*, 1997). It is not usually possible to carry out analysis of the relationship between poverty and educational outcomes for individuals from administrative data, since schools will not normally have access to income data for children. As in the UK, parental education appears to be the strongest predictor of children's educational outcomes in most countries. Because of its association with household income, it can be difficult to identify the direction of causality.

The concept of 'school-readiness' is one which is gaining increasing currency, especially in the USA and Canada. In contrast to the more broadly-defined concept of 'learning readiness', which allows for differences in development for age, 'school-readiness' is essentially a normative concept of what entry-level pupils should be like in order to fulfil school requirements and absorb the curriculum. It encompasses several dimensions: physical (including physical development and physical abilities, such as gross and fine motor skills), social (including emotional development and basic social skills), learning styles (curiosity, openness to new tasks), language development (verbal ability and signs of emerging literacy) and cognition and general knowledge (including problem-solving ability, maths and social knowledge). The Canadian NLSCY includes around 50 indicators of learning readiness. Two of the most significant predictors of school success have been found to be exposure to reading at home, and early literacy / numeracy performance in school (Phillips and Love, 1997). However, other sources argue that positive social and emotional development is more predictive of later educational success than purely cognitive measures (Aber and Jones, 1997). Once children are at school, parental expectations and parental attitudes to education and involvement with school appear to be crucial. This includes helping with homework, attending school open evenings, providing voluntary help at school, taking children to public libraries to borrow books and so on (Phillips and Love, 1997). The US regularly collects data on parents' involvement with school. The degree of social stratification in schools has also been found to be an important determinant of educational outcomes in Ireland and the USA, as pupils from all backgrounds achieve higher exam scores in schools which have a socially-mixed intake.

Positive indicators

The most widely collected measures which can be taken as objective indicators of positive child development are measures of educational success and post-compulsory educational enrolment. Other measures which are available in some countries include involvement in sport, social and community activities, and voter registration amongst young adults. Indicators of pro-social behaviour, such as empathy with others and a willingness to join in shared tasks, even amongst young children, are found in the Canadian NLSCY. The US surveys of high-school seniors ask a range of questions about peer attitudes to school grades and about the young person's future aspirations which also have a positive orientation.

Mediating Factors

As is clear both from the reviews of specific outcomes for the UK in earlier chapters, and from the comparative literature, although many of the outcome indicators collected show strong associations with poverty, the relationships are complex and causal mechanisms often obscure. This poses problems both at the level of conceptualisation and at the level of measurement. It may be difficult to identify indicators which act as a reliable proxy for key outcomes, and identifying whether a measured improvement is directly attributable to a particular policy or range of policies can be close to impossible. Although there are specific factors which are predictive of particular outcomes (for instance, age at first intercourse is obviously predictive of the risk of teenage pregnancy) there is also some evidence, and this is consistent with an 'ecological' concept of the influences on child well-being, that there is a range of mediating factors which affect outcomes, both positively and negatively, across a range of domains. These include individual factors (duration of risk, cumulative exposure to risk, self-esteem, resilience and so on) household factors (household composition, levels of maternal education, maternal depression, parenting practices, etc.) and neighbourhood factors (such as the availability and quality of services, extent of poverty and level of crime). For instance, parental depression, ineffectual parenting, multiple deprivation and neighbourhood factors are all known to have an influence on youth offending (McGlone, Chapter 11 this volume). It may be as important to monitor these mediating factors as it is to track trends in outcomes, not least because they provide early warning signs of positive or negative developments.

Individual factors

Furstenburg and Hughes (1997) suggest that measures of children's social capital (including their contacts, respect for adults, and involvement in community organisations) and knowledge and competency about the social world (such as knowledge of the entry qualifications for college or university, and how to obtain medical assistance) are important mediators of the opportunity structure available to them, and should therefore be a priority for measurement.

All the evidence suggests that a concentration of risk factors greatly increases the likelihood of adverse outcomes. Canadian evidence suggests that exposure to four or more recognised risks increases the likelihood of a range of negative outcomes significantly. A concentration of both personal and neighbourhood deprivation is associated with poor educational outcomes in the UK (Chapter 9, this volume). The Christchurch Health and Development Study has a family difficulties scale combining information

on 39 indicators of socio-economic disadvantage, family function and child-rearing practices, which is highly effective in predicting which teenagers will have multiple problems
(defined as conduct problems, police contact, early-onset sexual activity, substance abuse,
low self-esteem, depression and suicidal tendencies). Only 0.2 per cent of teenagers
from families with a score of six or under had multiple problems, compared to over a
fifth of those scoring 19 or more (Fergusson, 1998). However, it is worth remembering
that nearly all teenagers engage in some risk behaviours. A cumulative risk index developed in the USA, (based on whether or not the young person was enrolled in school,
had ever had intercourse, had ever used illegal drugs, had five or more drinks in a row
in the last month, or had stayed out overnight without permission in the last year)
found that fewer than half of fifteen-year-olds had not engaged in any risk behaviours
and that half of all seventeen-year-olds had engaged in two or more such behaviours
(US Department of Heath and Human Services, 1997).

The US literature also suggests that high rates of 'transience', whether at an individual level (frequent changes in household composition, frequent moves of
accommodation and / or school) or at a neighbourhood level (high rates of relationship
breakdown, high rates of residential mobility) may have an effect in increasing the risk
of negative outcomes, with the strongest effects being observed where there are high
rates of transience at the individual level. This may be one explanation for the poorer
mental health and educational outcomes for children living in temporary accommodation (Chapter 8, this volume).

Household factors

The importance of household structure as a mediating factor on child outcomes is well-
known, if less clearly understood. Other things being equal, children from lone-parent
households tend to have poorer outcomes than those from couple families, (McLana-
han and Sandefur, 1994; Lipman et al., 1998; Fergusson, 1998) while those in stepfamilies
often have similar (if not poorer) outcomes to the children of lone parents rather than
other couples (Furstenburg and Cherlin, 1991). However, existing data sources often do
not provide accurate information on household composition. Although many children
in the UK will spend their whole childhood with both biological parents, a minority
will experience repeated changes in household composition (Clarke, 1992) which are
not well captured by existing data sources. This deficit in data collection is one shared
with many other countries. One US source (Sandefur and Mosley, 1997) recommends
the compilation of monthly household composition histories in longitudinal surveys of
children and young people. While this sounds onerous in terms of time and cost, because only a minority of UK children experience frequent change, this would appear
unlikely to be the case in practice.

Maternal depression is associated with a range of negative outcomes, including
child abuse (Chapter 5, this volume), poorer mental health (Chapter 17, this volume)
and involvement in crime (Chapter 11, this volume). There is a consistent association
between high levels of parental (especially maternal) education and positive outcomes
for children (Duncan et al., 1994), which is particularly evident in educational and health

outcomes, and appears to be more significant than income for the former (Teachman *et al.*, 1997). Most countries have some measure of parental education, such as their highest qualification. Some countries have developed complex indicators which take account of both household income and the social capital of parents, for instance in New Zealand the Elley–Irving Scale is used to measure socio-economic status, taking into account education, income, location and occupation. Such measures are less transparent to the public than single-item indicators, but they probably provide more accurate measurement of the various factors involved in the generation of poor outcomes. Parental employment may be important as a source of social inclusion, but this is less likely if the work is short-term, poorly paid or insecure. For this reason, US data asks not about current employment status, but whether a parent's work is full-time, and year-round. The Canadian National Longitudinal Study of Children and Youth asks a range of questions of children aged 10–11 and 12–13 which are designed to measure the quality of parent–child interaction (similar questions are also found in the Australian Health Survey and the Christchurch Health and Development Survey).

Neighbourhood indicators

Neighbourhood factors become increasingly important as children become older, spend more time away from their parents and become more open to peer influences (Furstenburg and Hughes, 1997). Family environment, child care and parenting practices are the most significant influences on the development of pre-school children and remain of primary importance, but outside influences become steadily more salient with age (Duncan *et al.*, 1994; Kohen *et al.*, 1998). Factors in the neighbourhood which may mediate the experience of household poverty include the quality and cost of education, child care, leisure and health services available, the physical infrastructure (housing, provision of parkland and recreational space), and the level of social cohesion in the community (including income distribution, crime levels and the extent to which children attend schools local to their home). However, although there has been much interest in this topic, research studies have produced conflicting findings, and few have attempted to go beyond presenting evidence of associations between negative outcomes and the characteristics of low-income neighbourhoods and to discover how and why children and young people are influenced by the neighbourhoods in which they live (Furstenburg and Hughes, 1997).

Although this project is primarily concerned with outcomes rather than policy inputs, the importance of education and childcare services in mitigating family poverty may merit their inclusion in measures of child well-being. Two simple but valuable indicators used in Canada and the USA measure deficits in, respectively, the availability and quality of childcare; the proportion of children aged 6–12 who go home to an empty house ('latch-key children') and the number of times childcare arrangements have had to be changed in the last year.

Indicators of physical infrastructure which it may be helpful to measure include the number of housing units in poor repair, vacant or boarded, the extent to which the local population is expanding or declining, and residential mobility, often measured as the proportions of households which have lived in the area for fewer than five years or more than ten years (Furstenburg and Hughes, 1997).

Affluent neighbours appear to have an effect in raising IQ levels across the board, whilst poorer neighbours appear to increase the risk of externalising behaviour in all income groups (Duncan *et al.*, 1994). In the US, some attempt is made to measure the concentration of poverty, by estimating the number of poor children living in areas where over 40 per cent of households are below the poverty line.

Composite indices of well-being

It can be difficult to gain an accurate impression of whether children's well-being is improving or deteriorating, even where there are regular reports and monitoring systems in place. For this reason, some authorities favour types of index measurement including composite indicators for countries or states based on change in a number of key variables. In the US, for instance, the index of Social Health of Children and Youth uses eight variables, including infant mortality, child abuse rates, numbers failing to complete high school and child poverty rates. The simpler Index of Social Health used by UNICEF to compare industrialised countries uses infant mortality, public expenditure on education, teen suicides and income distribution and compares countries not with each other but against their own past performance (Miringoff and Opdyke, 1993). The US Kids Count reports compare counties and states on the basis of their rankings on ten key indicators (see Figure 18.6).

Such index measures have a number of advantages. They are a simple and easy to grasp reporting framework, which may be more effective than a long and complex report in gaining the attention of the media and helping to focus attention on child outcomes. They also facilitate comparisons with other countries, and between and across areas within a given country; and, because they are linked to research evidence, they can also be used as diagnostic measures, to indicate threshold levels of risk or risk avoidance (as in the healthy birth index cited above). However, they also have several major disadvantages. They are often a rather simplistic and crude way of measuring child outcomes. There is also the issue of how many items to include, which domains they should represent and in relation to which age range. Interpreting the results can also be difficult – for instance, where there is a fall in one indicator, and a rise in another, how should they be weighted? Where there is evidence of known associations (for instance between low birth-weight and minority ethnic group), any index will also need weighting to allow for different population bases. For all of these reasons, while composite indices have some merit, they must be treated with caution and are no substitute for a comprehensive report.

Some problems and issues

Although there are some differences between countries in terms of what they measure, this is more a reflection of variations in the resources devoted to the issue than of any real disagreements about which indicators are most valuable. The range of indicators which it is useful to monitor includes some measures of input, particularly concerning the incidence and duration of poverty and exposure to risk, a range of outcome meas-

Figure 18.6 Kids Count Ranking Index

Summary ranking on rates for the following child well-being indicators:

- low birth-weight (under 5.5 lbs)
- infant mortality
- child mortality
- teen mortality from accidents/homicide/suicide
- teen births
- teen high school drop-out
- teens not in school or employment
- parents not in full-time, year-round work
- living in poor household
- living in household headed by lone parent

Source: Kids Count Data Book, Annie E Casey Foundation.

ures (to include health, education and personal effectiveness), and others which are indicative of mediating factors at the individual, household or community level (including household structure, parenting, extent of neighbourhood poverty).

In terms of policy-making, there is a tension between the need to select indicators which are both robust and readily available, and reaching an understanding of the subtle and complex processes involved in generating change in key outcomes. One criticism which has been made of the increasing use of child well-being indicators in the USA (Lantz and Partin, 1997; Starfield, 1997) is that they have sometimes tended to result in rather simplistic policy responses, such as assuming that policies to improve take-up of pre-natal care will lead to an automatic improvement in infant mortality rates, rather than seeing both mortality rates and take-up of pre-natal care as reflective of underlying social and economic factors. There is also a scope for indicators to be used in a punitive fashion, as, for instance, where local or state funding is tied to the achievements of targets on indicators which are not readily amenable to change.

Data on children is collected by a huge variety of agencies, in relation to different ages and with a variety of aims. In most countries in this study, there are problems in obtaining official information about children in a single accessible format, although many countries have made significant progress towards this in recent years by producing regular reports. However, there are still many gaps in the information which is available, and these should inform thinking on the best ways to monitor child well-being in the UK. Conceptually, the ages for which data is available and presented often do not fit well with established developmental models, as for instance when data for 14- to 19-year-olds is aggregated, and different indicators will also be relevant to different stages of development. One issue which arises is whether it is necessary to measure a range of outcomes across the developmental spectrum, or whether negative outcomes for one age group can safely be taken as a proxy for negative outcomes in other age-groups or in other domains. Whilst it is obviously desirable to take a wide variety of measurements, there may be instances when it is necessary to rely on a limited number of indicators. Because of the differing salience of individual, household and neighbourhood factors for different developmental stages, there would appear to be less danger in using data from a limited number of domains than from using one age group as a proxy for another.

For almost all countries, there is a shortage of data (other than routinely collected health data) on pre-school children, which is unfortunate given that this is such a formative stage of development. It is often not possible to disaggregate data for regions or municipalities, or by ethnic group, although some countries, such as the USA, Canada, Australia and New Zealand, routinely present analysis by ethnic origin. There is also a widespread shortage of data on disabled children in most countries. Any system put in place to monitor child well-being should enable analysis of the situation of children facing particular disadvantage (Ben-Arieh and Wintersberger, 1997).

Most of the indicators collected do not relate to the child's well-being in the present moment; there are few measures of how much the child enjoys school, gets on with his or her parents and so on. It is widely acknowledged in the literature that children and young people are in the best position to act as informants on their own well-being (Dolev and Habib, 1997; Prout, 1997). Yet there are still few surveys which seek information directly from children themselves, and those which do generally interview only children over ten years old. This study found almost no evidence of children being allowed to help develop and shape the concepts which are used to measure their well-being.

Conclusion

There is real value in regular reports on children, in order to track trends in their well-being, and to generate political pressure to improve their living standards. It is notable that despite the high rates of child poverty in the UK, there has to date been far less evidence of monitoring activity than in the majority of other industrialised countries. The experience of other countries suggests that it may be more appropriate to produce reports on children bi-annually, rather than annually, partly because of the rather small changes from one year to the next, and also for reasons of cost and administrative simplicity. Although some countries produce reports less frequently, at five-yearly intervals, this would not appear to be an appropriate time period for the UK at a time when child poverty rates are high and their reduction seen as a priority.

Notes to Chapter 18

1   The US alone has 25 possible sources of survey data on children, ranging from the national data census to studies on specific areas such as teen fertility.

Conclusions

Jonathan Bradshaw

19 Conclusions

Jonathan Bradshaw

Introduction

This review of the outcomes of child poverty has sought to answer three main questions:

- First, is there evidence that the outcomes for all children have got worse over the last 20 years?
- Second, is there evidence that these worse outcomes are associated with relative child poverty in the UK?
- Third, have poor children fared worse than children who are not poor over the last 20 years or so?

This concluding chapter reviews the results and then discusses the outcomes examined in the context of the Government's proposals for monitoring its anti-poverty strategy. At the end it is proposed that some additional measures of outcomes should be incorporated into the monitoring exercise.

First some comments on the exercise that has been undertaken.

When UNICEF commissioned the national reports for their original study of child poverty and deprivation in industrial nations (Cornia and Danziger 1996) they were insistent that it should have a heavy focus on outcomes – the consequences of social and economic change – rather than inputs. It is relatively simple to describe what had happened to the level and dispersion of incomes of families with children in Britain. There is a good deal of data on changes in the labour market and in family form which would have affected children. It is also fairly straightforward to summarise what policy changes might have affected families with children, including what changes to taxation, benefits and services have had an impact on children. There is also a growing body of literature which compares policy and policy change between countries. It includes some very good comparative data on poverty and change in poverty over time, though, perhaps inevitably, it takes far too long to emerge (Bradbury and Jantti, 1999; Bradshaw, 1999; Micklewright and Stewart, 1999; UNICEF, 2000). The Luxembourg Income Survey, in particular, has become a good vehicle for the comparative analysis of income poverty both cross-sectionally and over time. The European Community Panel Survey, after a very slow start, is also becoming an important source of information, with the added benefit that the indicators of poverty in the survey extend beyond income.

However data on outcomes are much more problematic. The data emerges only slowly, often only as a result of academic endeavour. There are serious shortcomings in the coverage of some of the data and, in particular, often no adequate analysis by poverty or even socio-economic group. Where there is cross-sectional data on the association between poverty and an outcome there is rarely a time series, and even more rarely a time series which allows an investigation of the outcome's association with poverty over time.

The outcomes for children

Table 19.1 attempts to summarise the reviews of evidence that were undertaken for this study. This is a summary and, in making it, inevitably the reservations have been left out. We have deliberately restricted the summary to 'Yes', 'No', 'Probably' and so forth, and each cryptic summation is based on an overall judgement of a quantity of evidence, sometimes conflicting (and therefore is a judgement about the quality of that evidence). In the first three columns of Table 19.1 we have sought to answer the three key questions:

Has this outcome increased (got worse) over time for all children?

The judgements are:

YES for: low birth-weight, some infections, homelessness, school exclusions, crime, smoking for girls, alcohol, drugs, suicide in young men.

NO for: mortality, dental health, fatal accidents, teenage pregnancy, poor housing conditions, educational achievement.

On the other outcomes we do not know or the evidence is too mixed to call.

Is there clear evidence that this outcome is associated with poverty and its proxies?

The judgements are:

YES for: mortality, most morbidity, fatal accidents, neglect and physical abuse, teenage pregnancy, poor housing conditions, homelessness, educational attainment, smoking, suicide, mental illness.

NO for: crime, sexual abuse, alcohol, drugs, child labour.

On the other outcomes we do not know or the evidence is too mixed to call.

Is there evidence of divergence in the outcomes of the poor and the non-poor over the last 20 years or so?

Here the evidence gets particularly difficult to interpret. But the judgements are:

YES for: child mortality, low birth-weight, accidents, teenage pregnancy, bad housing conditions, educational attainment and suicide.

NO for: infant mortality, chronic illness, alcohol, drugs and child labour.

On the other outcomes we do not know or the evidence is too mixed to call.

Now, the most interesting outcomes are those where there is clear cross-sectional evidence that they are associated with poverty, but nevertheless, over the last few years they have improved. Of course they may have improved at a faster rate if we had not had the increase in child poverty that we have had. But these are outcomes where the impact of rising poverty has been mitigated or at least has not yet shown an impact. They include:

- infant mortality,
- dental health,
- fatal accidents,
- teenage pregnancy,
- bad housing conditions,
- educational attainment.

For each of these outcomes there is evidence of how they have managed to buck the trend. Thus:

- infant mortality has been reduced by improvements in infant care,
- dental health by fluoride,
- fatal accidents by accident prevention policies and reduced freedom to roam,
- teenage pregnancy by sex education, contraception and births by abortion,
- bad housing by housing improvements,
- educational attainment by investment in standards.

Similarly, the outcomes which are related to poverty and yet which have not improved and/or differences have got wider by socio-economic group are:

- child deaths,
- low birth-weight,
- accidents,
- homelessness,
- educational attainment,
- school exclusions,
- suicide.

For some of these outcomes it is possible to attribute cause. Thus:

- part of the increase in low birth-weight is associated with increased births among minority ethnic groups and an increased ability to keep premature babies alive;
- accidental deaths are the main cause of child deaths and poorer children are more likely to die on the roads and from accidents at home;
- homelessness is a crisis almost entirely restricted to the poor by definition, and access to social housing has been restricted by a whole raft of housing policies which have effected affordability and availability;
- although standards in schools may be improving overall, differentials in standards are increasing; the impact of poverty on educational attainment is profound – perhaps too profound to be overcome by investment in schools;
- school exclusions are difficult to interpret and may be partly driven by the standards agenda.

Suicide is, perhaps, the most problematic indicator of the outcomes of poverty.

The general lesson from this is that policy matters. But that policy has to address the underlying poverty as well as the outcomes. This is probably especially true of health and educational outcomes: health and educational interventions can only achieve a certain amount without action directly on poverty. How, for example, can a health intervention prevent low birth-weight when a third of pregnant women are dependent on Income Support, more or less frozen in real terms for over 20 years?

Of course how an outcome has been classified depends so much on the evidence (and our interpretation of it). So the final three columns of Table 19.1 are concerned with the evidence rather than the outcome. Judgements are made about the adequacy of the cross-sectional evidence of the link between the outcome and poverty. Then a judgement about the adequacy of the time-series evidence about changes in that association. Finally, the best source of data is specified. In brief, the conclusion is that the data is better cross-sectionally than it is longitudinally. On the 'best sources' a bias towards administrative statistics and national, regular surveys must be acknowledged. This is not to deny the value of independent, local or one–off studies. However, to get to the bottom of the outcomes of child poverty data is needed that are nationally representative, regularly collected (though not necessarily annually) and focus on poverty and outcomes.

There is no doubt that our national portfolio of data is improving. In particular the English Health Survey is an important addition. There are other sources that are relatively over-exploited and others that are relatively neglected. So, for example, the National Child Development Survey (1958 Cohort), for all the value it has given over time, is now suffering from its 1958 roots, and serious attrition. In contrast, the youth questionnaire in the British Household Panel Survey is under-exploited, as is the English Health Survey. In thinking about the future no one would argue against the case for a new birth cohort of children and one is being planned for 2001. But what is lacking is a large survey of children with a split age cohort design that locates children in their families, schools and local environments. Such a dataset is an essential tool for answering most of the questions about the relationship between poverty and outcomes.

Opportunity for All

In September 1999 the Government published *Opportunity for All* (Cm 4445, 1999) which included a set of thirteen indicators which they proposed to use *inter alia* to measure success in tackling child poverty and social exclusion (there are similar documents for Scotland and Wales). While this is a welcome step forward in national efforts to monitor the impact of social and economic change on the lives of children there are a number of criticisms to be made of the indicators chosen.

In their report the Government argue that their approach to tackling poverty and social exclusion is to 'Tackle the causes of poverty and social exclusion, not just the symptoms; create a fairer society in which everyone has the opportunities to maximise their potential; and invest in individuals and communities to equip them to take control of their lives'. The indicators, it is claimed 'reflect these strategic priorities'. 'The indicators fall into three main categories; those that focus on incomes; those that focus on wider aspects of welfare such as education, housing, health and the quality of local environments; and those that capture factors that affect people during their lives and increase the risk that they experience deprivation at a later point.'.

The indicators build on indicators and targets already in place. Some are related to the success measures proposed in the Welfare Reform Green Paper (Cm 3805, 1998).

They are also (it is said) influenced by responses to consultation, to specific targets already set in Public Service Agreements (PSAs) and to Output and Performance Analysis (OPAs) – which set out each Government Departments's aims and objectives (in terms of service provision and outcomes).

Indeed, the indicators chosen have a very strong Departmental/Whitehall feel about them. It is as if each Department has been permitted to nominate a few – some for the Department of Social Security (DSS), some for the Department of Health (DoH), some for the Department of the Environment, Transport and the Regions (DETR), some for the Social Exclusion Unit and so on.

The first two indicators are (appropriately) the Treasury's in that they relate to Sure Start which was initially conceived within HM Treasury (though it is now in the Department for Education and Employment (DfEE).

1   *An increase in the proportion of seven-year-old Sure Start children achieving level 1 or above in the Key Stage 1 English and maths tests.*

2   *Health outcomes in Sure Start areas:*
   *   *a reduction in the proportion of low birth-weight babies in Sure Start areas;*
   and
   *   *a reduction in the rate of hospital admissions as a result of serious injury in Sure Start areas.*

The first two of these indicators have the merit of being concerned with outcomes – a cognitive outcome and a physical health outcome, and there is no doubting the association between these outcomes and poverty. The third indicator is an input – the 'serious injury' part is an outcome and childhood accidents are the major cause of deaths in childhood and there is plenty of evidence that deaths from accidents are associated with poverty (though it is less conclusively linked to childhood injuries). However hospital admissions are an input which could vary with local policy (and be manipulated by local practice) as could the definition of 'serious'. In fact the indicator is defined in the document as emergency admissions during the first year of life with gastro-enteritis, respiratory infection or severe injury. It would have been more satisfactory to have chosen infant and childhood mortality and/or deaths from accidents rather than these treatments for morbidity variables. However no doubt the reason deaths were not chosen is that there would have been too few of them in Sure Start areas which, area-wise, are based on the concept of 'pram-pushable distances'.

This raises a more fundamental objection to the indicators – that they are only concerned with Sure Start areas. Sure Start has begun in an experimental phase and it is proposed that it will eventually be extended to 250 of the most deprived neighbourhoods in Britain. While it is no doubt a good idea to monitor the effects of Sure Start in these areas and these indicators are either Sure Start OPAs or PSAs, it is surely not right to present them as part of the indicators designed to evaluate a national anti-poverty strategy – especially as we shall see there are few other health outcome indicators in the list.

Table 19.1 **Summary of the outcomes and their association with povert**

Outcome	Has it increased?	Are poor outcomes associated with poverty?	Have differences become wider?
Mortality	No	Yes. Strong association with social class	No for *infant mortality.* Yes for *child mortality.* Yes for *post-neonatal* period for lone mothers.
Morbidity	*Low birth-weight:* Yes	Yes	Yes
	Congenital anomalies: Varies	Some do	Don't know
	Chronic illness: If Yes small except asthma	Yes by income	No
	Infectious diseases: Varies	Most are	Don't know
	Dental: No	Yes	Don't know
	Obesity: Probably	Probably	Don't know
	Physical activity: Don't know	Yes for 2–10s	Don't know
Accidents	Not *fatal accidents.* Don't know for *accident morbidity.*	Yes for *fatal accidents.* Possibly not for *accident morbidity.*	Probably
Child abuse	Don't know	Yes except *sexual abuse*	Don't know
Teenage pregnancy	Not in the last 20 years	Yes	Probably – certainly spatially
Environment/housing conditions	No except lone parents and ethnic groups	Yes	Yes
Homelessness	Yes up to 1991	Yes	Probably
Educational attainment	No	Yes	Yes
School exclusions	Yes	Don't know	Don't know
Crime	Yes	No	Don't know
Smoking	Yes slightly for girls	Probably but mainly after childhood	Don't know
Alcohol	Yes for frequency	No	Probably not
Drugs	Yes at least up to early 1990s	No	Probably not
Suicide	Yes for men aged 15–24	Yes	Probably
Child labour	Don't know	No	Probably not
Mental illness	Don't know	Yes	Don't know
Mental well-being	Don't know	No for 11–15s except perhaps self-esteem; but probably Yes for younger and older children and young people.	Don't know

Are the sources adequate for cross sectional analysis?	Are the sources adequate for time series analysis?	What are the best sources?
Yes but very reliant on fathers' social class	Yes but reliant on fathers' social class	Birth and death registration, ONS Longitudinal Study.
Yes	Yes but reliant on social class	ONS Birth and Mortality Statistics
No	No	Congenital Anomaly Statistics
Not really	No	Family Fund
Not really	No	GHS but Health Survey of England will be better
No	No	NSHG Cohort
No	No	Children's Dental Health Survey
Yes	Not yet	No good national sources. Health Survey of England will be better
Yes	No	Death registration, Health Survey of England
No	No	None good
No	Yes on trends	Birth and Abortion Statistics. ONS Longitudinal Survey
No EHCS too infrequent	ditto	English House Conditions Survey
Yes	No	Homelessness statistics
Yes	Improving but could be better at an individual level	Qualifications and Curriculum Authority baseline data in the future
Yes but	No	DfEE
No	No	British Crime Survey
Yes	No	GHS and smoking surveys
Yes	Getting better	GHS and surveys of drinking
No	No	British Crime Survey, ONS Surveys
No	No	?None
Yes	No	BHPS
Yes	No	ONS: Mental Health of Children and Adolescents
Yes	Getting better	BHPS and Health Survey of England

The next three indicators are, as it were, DfEE's:

3   *An increase in the proportion of those aged 11 achieving level 4 or above in the Key Stage 2 tests for literacy and numeracy.*

4   *A reduction in the proportion of truancies and exclusion from school.*

5   *An increase in the proportion of 19-year-olds with at least a level 2 qualification or equivalent.*

These are two cognitive and one behavioural outcome measure. They are all from DfEE's National Learning Targets for England. The most obvious anxiety concerns the reliability of the data on school exclusions and truancies. School exclusions affected only 0.16 per cent of pupils in 1997/8 and only 0.7 per cent of half days were missed per year through unauthorised pupil absence. These very small numbers are likely to be highly sensitive to changes in recording – upwards or downwards. There is also rather weak evidence of the association between school exclusions and poverty.

6   *A reduction in the proportion of children living in workless households, for households of a given size, over the economic cycle.*

There is no doubt that the increase in worklessness in Britain has been associated with the increase in child poverty and that our comparatively high levels of worklessness are a reason for child poverty being higher here than elsewhere. However worklessness is an input, a cause of poverty rather than an outcome of poverty. It is also not inevitably associated with poverty – in other countries the children of workless lone parents and couples do not live in poverty because their social protection systems protect them from poverty. Further, there are very substantial proportions of poor children whose parents are not workless. Adelman and Bradshaw (1998), in their analysis of the 1995/6 Family Resources Survey found that 13 per cent of poor children (living in families with equivalent incomes below half national average after housing costs) had one earner and a few even had two earners. These proportions may now have fallen as a result of the introduction of the National Minimum Wage, Working Families Tax Credit, Child Care Tax Credit and real increases in Child Benefit but the point remains – employment does not guarantee movement out of poverty and employment is never going to be the only way to abolish child poverty.

There are also reasons to question this indicator in its own right. Estimates are to be derived from the Labour Force Survey and/or the Family Resources Survey. A better and more up-to-date indicator of the same thing could be administrative data on the numbers and/or proportions of all children living in families receiving Income Support or income-tested Job Seekers Allowance. The numerator is available with little or no delay from the Department of Social Security and the denominator is obtainable simply from the Child Benefit register. All families receiving Income Support are workless, or virtually workless given the earnings disregards, and none of them have capital or other resources. Furthermore, thanks to the work of the Oxford Social Deprivation Research Unit this indicator is now part of the DETR's Index of Deprivation and available at district, ward and enumeration district level.

7   *Low income indicators:*

    a)   a reduction in the proportion of children in households with relatively low incomes;

b)   *a reduction in the proportion of children in households with low incomes in an absolute sense; and*

c)   *a reduction in the proportion of children with persistently low incomes.*

These are the Department of Social Security indicators. The first two to be derived from the Family Resources Survey and the third from the British Household Panel Survey. They are all input indicators but they are obvious candidates in any index of poverty and social exclusion – though they are not available at as local a level as benefit-claiming data is.

8   *A reduction in the proportion of children living in poor housing.*

9   *A reduction in the proportion of households with children experiencing fuel poverty.*

These are both DETR PSA targets. They are both inputs rather than outcome measures but there is no doubt that poor housing and cold conditions have an impact on all sorts of elements of children's well-being. However there are questions to be asked about whether these are the best indicators of physical well-being available. Estimates of the proportion of children living in poor housing are available from the English House Conditions Survey but the data is only available every five years. Further, in 1996 only 13 per cent of children were living in houses that were unfit or in substantial disrepair or requiring essential modernisation, and that proportion had hardly changed between 1991 and 1996. So as well as having to wait five years to observe the trend, the trend may not be a particularly sensitive indication of well-being. The same problems arise with the fuel poverty indicator. The English House Conditions Survey is also the source of data on the proportion of families with children who need to spend more than 10 per cent of their incomes to achieve a satisfactory heating regime (21 degrees C in the living rooms and 18 degrees C in the other occupied rooms). In 1996 11 per cent of lone parents and 6 per cent of couples with children experienced fuel poverty. It would be possible to obtain a more regular estimate of the proportion of households with children spending more than a certain percentage of their income on fuel from the Family Expenditure Survey, though this would not include the cold conditions element of the indicator.

An additional and perhaps better indicator that could be used is the incidence of homelessness among children and young people and/or the number of households with children in temporary accommodation. This was included as one of the 'Milestones' in the Scottish version of *Opportunities for All* (http://www.scotland.gov.uk/library2/doc07/sjtd-02.htm).

10   *A reduction in the rate at which children are admitted to hospital as a result of an unintentional injury resulting in a hospital stay of longer than three days.*

This is associated with an *Our Healthier Nation* target to reduce the rate of serious injuries from accidents and it is the national equivalent to indicator 2(b) covering the Sure Start areas. Some of the same criticisms apply. Thus hospital admissions and the length of them are an input and might vary over time and in different geographical areas according to policy and treatment regimes. It might have been better to have chosen the child mortality rate due to accidents as a more precise indicator of serious accidents, not least because it appears to be more closely associated with poverty than injuries. Or, to refine it even further, it might have been better to have chosen child deaths from traffic accidents or accidents in the home which are the two most clearly associated with poverty.

There are a number of other indicators related to physical health which might have been considered including infant mortality, child deaths, low birth-weight births, the prevalence of some congenital anomalies, self (or parental-reported) chronic illness, some infectious diseases, the prevalence of dental caries, obesity – all associated with poverty and all available from national sources on a regular basis. The absence of more health indicators in this list is surprising – given the *Acheson Report* and the *Health of the Nation* targets. The Scottish Milestones included reductions in the proportions of women smoking during pregnancy, the percentage of low birth-weight babies, dental decay among five-year-olds and increasing the proportion of women breast-feeding.

11   A reduction in the proportion of 16- to 18-year-olds not in education and training.
This indicator is selected on the grounds that it is associated with a measure proposed in the Green Paper on Welfare Reform – a reduction in the numbers of school leavers with no recognised qualifications and 'is the most powerful predictor of unemployment at age 21'. It is an input measure – and one which includes those who are in employment.

12   An improvement in the educational attainment of children looked after by local authorities.
Three-quarters of care leavers are estimated to leave school with no qualifications and the Department of Health PSA contains a target to increase that by at least 50 per cent by 2001 and by 75 per cent by 2003. This is a cognitive outcome for a very vulnerable group of young people for whom the State has a particular obligation and where there is evidence that it has failed miserably in the past. However the DfEE and the Department of Health have not yet decided how they are going to collect this information.

13   Teenage pregnancy: a reduction in the rate of conceptions for those aged under 18 and an increase in the proportion of those who are teenage parents in education, employment and training.
This is an objective of the Social Exclusion Unit report on Teenage Pregnancy. The teenage pregnancy rate includes those that eventually end in abortion, and abortion, and access to abortion, are policy inputs which can be manipulated. It is arguable that it would have been better to have selected the teenage birth rate, or the proportion of teenage pregnancies which end in births. However it is a behavioural outcome and an obvious candidate for any index.

The *Opportunity for All* report goes on to list a further 19 indicators covering people of working age and older people and are not the focus of this book. However four of the indicators for people of working age could just as well have been selected for children and young people.

20   A reduction in the number of people sleeping rough.
21   A reduction in cocaine and heroin use by young people.

22 *A reduction in adult smoking rates in all social classes.*
23 *A reduction in the death rates from suicide and undetermined injury.*

- Rough sleeping is a problem of (poor) young people but there are major difficulties in counting rough sleepers.
- The addiction indicator specifies young people, but there is little evidence that there is an association between cocaine and heroin use and poverty, and the proportion of young people using these opiates is roughly only 1 per cent.
- There are good sources of data on child smoking (and alcohol consumption) but little evidence that it is associated with poverty – at least among children.
- Suicide is a serious problem for young people (men) and appears to be associated with unemployment.

In terms of our distinction between inputs and outcomes and physical, cognitive, behavioural and mental/emotional, how do the *Opportunity for All* indicators reflect indicators of well-being? Table 19.2 summarises the position. It is difficult to classify some of them: indicators 2b and 10 are both inputs and outcomes and indicators 6 and 7 have been classified as behavioural inputs although they do nor really fit into any of the categories. However the picture that emerges from this is that there is a reasonable spread of indicators between the categories with the exception of emotional (suicide has been classified as an emotional outcome though it could be classified as behavioural). But nearly a third of the indicators are measures of inputs rather than outcomes.

Table 19.2   Classification of *Opportunity for All* Indicators

	Inputs	Outcomes
Physical	2b, 8, 9, 10	2a, 2b, 10
Cognitive	11	1, 3, 5, 12
Behavioural	6, 7	4, 13, 20, 21, 22
Emotional		23

Conclusion

What other outcome measures might have been included in the *Opportunity for All* indicators?

In identifying outcomes of child poverty that might be added to the list of *Opportunity for All* indicators we have restricted ourselves (in the first instance) to the outcomes examined in this review, which are known to have an association with child poverty and for which there is data available at national level:

- Post-neonatal mortality rates
- Child death rates
- The class or income differential between both these rates
- Accidental deaths on the roads and in the home
- Low birth-weight

- Selected congenital anomalies
- Self- or parental-reported chronic illness
- Some infectious diseases
- Dental caries
- Obesity
- Child neglect and physical child abuse
- Children in temporary accommodation
- Satisfaction with neighbourhood
- Repossessions involving children
- SDQ scores of children aged 4–15 in the Annual Health Survey of England
- Self-esteem scores for children aged 10–15 in the BHPS
- GHQ scores of young people aged 16–21 (or more) in the Annual Health Survey of England.

In addition to this there are some indicators that could be included in an index designed to monitor child poverty and which were not included in this review because they are not outcomes:

- Percentage of children in families receiving Income Support/Income related JSA (available from Department of Social Security administrative statistics).
- Percentage of children living in wards defined as (say) the 10 per cent most deprived in Britain (available from the Oxford Index 99 group).
- Percentage of wards with more than 50 per cent (say) children in families receiving Income Support/income-related JSA (available from the Oxford Index 99 group).
- Percentage of children in households lacking three or more socially perceived necessities (available along with a host of other poverty/social exclusion variables from the Survey of Poverty and Social Exclusion in Britain (Gordon *et al.*, 2000) and which could be made available regularly by incorporating questions into the GHS or FRS).
- Any of the indicators of social exclusion now included in the European Community Household Panel Survey.[1]

While there is room to argue about any of these indicators, it is to be hoped that they illustrate that there is room to build on the list in *Opportunities for All*. Britain needs to monitor the well-being of its children far better in the future than it has done in the past.

Note to Chapter 19

1 The following indicators are available in the ECHP: the percentage of children in households dissatisfied with their financial situation, with difficulties in making ends meet, unable to save regularly, who cannot afford three or more basic necessities, whose financial situation has deteriorated since the previous year, with minimum equivalised income required to make ends meet more than 105 per cent of actual income, percentage of couples with children with three or more housing problems; with financial burdens or debts.

References

Aber, J. and Jones, S. (1997) 'Indicators of positive development in early childhood: improving concepts and measures', in Duncan, G. and Brooks-Gunn, J. (1997) *Growing up Poor.* New York: Russell Sage Foundation.

Acheson, D. (chair) (1998) *Independent Inquiry into Inequalities in Health.* London: The Stationery Office.

Adamson, P. (1995) *The Progress of Nations.* New York: UNICEF.

Adelman, L. and Bradshaw, J. (1998) *Children in Poverty in Britain: An analysis of the Family Resources Survey 1994/95.* Social Policy Research Unit, University of York.

Aldridge, J., Parker, H. and Measham, F. (1999) *Drug Trying and Drug Use.* London: Home Office.

Allen, I. and Dowling, S.B. (1998) *Teenage Mothers Decisions and Outcomes,* Report 856. London: Policy Studies Institute.

Amery, J., Tomkins, A. and Victor, C. (1995) 'The prevalence of behavioural problems amongst homeless primary school children in an outer London borough: a feasibility study', *Public Health,* Nov, 109(96):421–4.

Anderson, I. (1994) *Access to Housing for Low Income People.* Centre for Housing Policy, University of York.

Anderson, I., Kemp, P. and Quilgars, D. (1993) *Single homeless people.* London: HMSO.

Anderson, I. and Morgan, J. (1997) *Social Housing for Single People? A study of local policy and practice.* Housing Policy and Practice Unit, University of Stirling.

Angus, J. (1999) *The Strengthening Families Strategy – a paper,* mimeo. New Zealand Department of Social Welfare.

Annie E. Casey Foundation (1999, and annually) *Kids Count Data Book.* Baltimore: Annie E. Casey Foundation (available free on-line at www.aecf.org).

Atkinson, A. (1998) *EMU, Macroeconomics and Children,* Innocenti Occasional Papers 68. Florence: UNICEF International Child Development Centre.

Audit Commission (1999) *Missing Out, National Report by the Audit Commission.* London: Audit Commission.

Audit Commission (1996) *Misspent Youth.* London: Audit Commission.

Baker, A.W. and Duncan, S.P. (1985) 'Child sexual abuse: A study of prevalence in Great Britain', *Child Abuse and Neglect,* 9:457–67.

Balarajan, R., Soni Raleigh, V. and Botting, B. (1989) 'Sudden infant death syndrome and post-neonatal mortality in immigrants in England and Wales', *British Medical Journal,* 298 (6675):716–20.

Baldwin, J (1998) *Young People in 1997.* Exeter: Exeter University.

Baldwin, J (1997) *Young People in 1996.* Exeter: Exeter University.

Baldwin, J (1996) *Young People in 1995.* Exeter: Exeter University.

Baldwin, N. and Spencer, N. (1993) 'Deprivation and child abuse: Implications for strategic planning in children's services', *Children and Society*, 7(4):357–75.

Baldwin, S. (1985) *The Cost of Caring*. London: Routledge.

Banks, M. and Ullah, P. (1996) *Youth Unemployment: social and psychological perspectives*. Research Paper no.61, Department of Employment. London: HMSO.

Banks, M.H. and Jackson, P.R. (1982) 'Unemployment and risk of minor psychiatric disorder in young people: cross sectional and longitudinal evidence', *Psychological Medicine*, 12:789–798.

Barry, A. E., Carr-Hill, R. and Glanville, J. (1991) *Homelessness and Health: What do we know? What should be done?* York Centre for Health Economics, University of York.

Bax, M. and Lawton, D. (1998) *Prevalence of Disabling Conditions in Childhood*. York: Family Fund Trust.

Beiser, M., Hou, F., Hyman, I. and Tousignant, M. (1998) *Growing up Canadian – a study of new immigrant children*, Working Paper W-98-24E. Applied Research Branch, Human Resources Canada.

Ben-Arieh, A. and Wintersberger, H. (1997) *Monitoring and Measuring the State of Children – Beyond Survival*. Vienna: European Centre for Social Welfare Policy and Research.

Best, R. (1995) 'The Housing Dimension', in Benzeval, M., Judge, K. and Whitehead, M. *Tackling Inequalities in Health: an agenda for action*. London: King's Fund.

Biehal, *et al.* (1992) *Prepared for Living?* London: National Children's Bureau.

Bines, W. (1994) *The Health of Single Homeless People*. Centre for Housing Policy, University of York.

Blane, D., Bartley, M., Davy-Smith, G., Filakti, H., Bethune, A. and Harding, S. (1994) 'Social patterning of medical mortality in youth and early adulthood', *Social Science and Medicine*, 39:361–366.

BMA (1999) *Growing Up In Britain: Ensuring a healthy future for our children*. London: BMJ Publishing Group.

Bondi, L. (1991) 'Attainment at primary schools: an analysis of variations between schools', *British Educational Research Journal*, 17:203–217.

Bone, M. and Meltzer, H. (1989) *The Prevalence of Disability Among Children*. London: HMSO.

Botting, B. (1997) 'Mortality in childhood' in Drever, F. and Whitehead, M. (eds), *Health Inequalities: Decennial supplement*, Series DS No.15. London: The Stationery Office.

Botting, B. (ed.) (1995) *The Health of our Children, The Registrar General's decennial supplement for England and Wales*. London: HMSO.

Botting, B. and Cooper, J. (1993) 'Analysing fertility and infant mortality by mother's social class as defined by occupation – Part II', *Population Trends*, 74:27–33.

Botting, B. and Crawley, R. (1995) 'Trends and patterns in childhood mortality and morbidity', in Botting, B. (ed), *The Health of Our Children: Decennial Supplement*. London: OPCS.

Botting, B., Rosato, M. and Wood, R. (1998) Teenage Mothers and the Health of their Children, *Population Trends 93*, ONS. London: The Stationery Office.

Botting, B. *et al.* (1996) *Health of Children*. London: HMSO.

Bradbury, B. and Jantti, M. (1999) *Child Poverty Across Industrialised Nations*, Innocenti Occasional Paper, Economic and Social Policy Series 71. Florence: UNICEF International Child Development Centre.

Bradshaw, J. (2000) 'Prospects for poverty in Britain in the first 25 years of the next century', *Sociology*, 34(1):1–18.

Bradshaw, J. (1999) Child poverty in comparative perspective, *Journal of European Social Security*, 1(4):383–404.

Bradshaw, J. (1997) 'Children in poverty', Paper presented at the launch of Breadline Britain in the 1990s, at the House of Commons 22 July 1997, University of York, Social Policy Research Unit.

Bradshaw, J. (1990) *Child poverty and deprivation in the UK*. London: National Children's Bureau.

Bradshaw, J. and Barnes, H. (1999) *How do nations monitor the well-being of their children*, Paper to the LIS Child Poverty Conference, Luxembourg, 30 September 1999–2 October 1999.

Bradshaw, J. and Barnes, H. (1998) 'Relating inputs to outcomes: Child poverty and family transfers in comparative perspective', in Ringen, S. and De Jong P. (eds.) *Fighting poverty: Caring for children, parents, the elderly and health*, Volume Five International Studies in Social Security. Aldershot: FISS/ Ashgate.

Bradshaw, J. and Holmes, J. (1989) *Living on the Edge: A study of the living standards of families on benefit in Tyne and Wear*. Child Poverty Action Group. Tyneside.

Bradshaw, J., Ditch, J., Holmes, H., and Whiteford, P. (1993) *Support for Children: A comparison of arrangements in fifteen countries*, Department of Social Security Research Report 21, London: HMSO.

Bradshaw, J., Kennedy, S., Kilkey, M., Hutton, S., Corden, A., Eardley, T., Holmnes, H. and Neale, J. (1996a) *Policy and the Employment of Lone Parents in 20 Countries*, European Observatory on National Family Policies, The EU Report.

Bradshaw, J. and Morgan, J. (1987) *Budgeting on Benefit*. London: Family Policy Studies Centre.

Bradshaw, J. and Williams, J. (2000) *Earnings and pocket money: Analysis of the British Household Panel Survey*, University of York.

Bradshaw, N., Bradshaw, J. and Burrows, R. (1998) 'Area variations in the prevalence of lone parent families in England and Wales: A research note', *Regional Studies*, 30(8):811–815.

Brennan, M. and Lanchashire, R. 'Association of Childhood Mortality with Housing Status and Unemployment', *Journal of Epidemiology and Community Health*, 1978.

Briggs, F. and Hawkins, R.M.F (1996) 'Low socio-economic status children are disadvantaged in the provision of school-based child protection programmes', *British Journal of Social Work*, 26:667–78.

Brown, B., Kirby, G., and Botsko, C. (1997) *Social Indicators of Child and Family Well-Being: a profile of six state systems*, IRP Special Report 72. University of Wisconsin-Madison.

Brynin, M. and Scott, J. (1996) *Young People, Health and the Family*. London: Health Education Authority.

Burghes, L. with Brown, M. (1995) *Single lone mothers: problems, prospects and policies*. London: Family Policy Studies Centre.

Burr, M. (1995) 'Pollution: does it cause asthma?' *Archives of Disease in Childhood*, 72:377–379.

Burridge, R. and Ormandy, D. (eds.) (1993) *Unhealthy housing: research, remedies and reform*. London: Spon.

Burrows, R. (1997) *Contemporary patterns of residential mobility in relation to social housing in England*, York: Centre for Housing Policy, University of York.

Burrows, R. and Rhodes, D. (1998) *Unpopular places? Area disadvantage and the geography of misery in England*. Bristol: The Policy Press/Joseph Rowntree Foundation.

Campbell, B. (1993) 'A teenage girl's passport to womanhood', *The Independent*, 12 May 1993.

Campbell, R. (1998) 'Children's perspectives on work', in B. Pettit (ed.) *Children and work in the UK*. London: Child Poverty Action Group.

Carlen, P. (1996) *Jigsaw: A Political Criminology of Youth Homelessness*. Buckingham: Open University Press.

Carstairs, V. and Morris, R. (1991) *Deprivation and Health in Scotland*. Aberdeen: Aberdeen University Press.

Carter, M. (1997) *The Last Resort: Living in Bed and Breakfast in the 1990s*. London: Shelter.

Carter, M. (1995) *Out of Sight ... London's continuing Bed and Breakfast Crisis*. London Homelessness Forum.

Central Statistical Office (1994) *Social Focus on Children*. London: HMSO.

Child Trends, Inc. (1997) *The Project on State-Level Child Outcomes – building common definitions and moving towards common constructs*, mimeo. Child Trends, Inc.

Clarke, L. (1999) 'Young Mothers and Their Families: Trends, Associated Factors and Consequences', in *Promoting the Health of Teenage Lone Mothers, Setting a Research Agenda*, A report of a Health Education Authority Expert Working Group chaired by K. Wellings, Health Education Authority, London.

Clarke, L. (1992) 'Children's Family Circumstances', *European Journal of Population*, 8, 309–340.

Clarke, L., Bradshaw, J. and Williams, J. (forthcoming) *Family diversity, poverty and the mental well-being of young people*, London: Health Education Authority.

Coleman, J. (1997) 'Mental Health' in J. Coleman (ed.) *Key Data on Adolescence*. Brighton: Trust for the Study of Adolescence.

Coles, B., England, J. and Rugg, J. (1998) *Working with Young People on Estates: The role of housing professionals in multi-agency work*. Coventry: Chartered Institute of Housing.

Committee of Inquiry into the Education of Children from Ethnic Minority Groups (1985) *Education for All (The Swann Report)*, London: HMSO.

Conger, R.D., Conger, K.J., Elder Jr., G.H. Lorenz, F.O., Simons, R.L. and Whitbeck, L.B. (1992) 'A family process model of economic hardship and adjustment of early adolescent boys', *Child Development*, 63, 526–541.

Connell, R. (1995) *Masculinities*. Cambridge: Polity Press.

Connelly, C.D and Straus, M.A. (1992) 'Mother's age and risk for physical abuse', *Child Abuse and Neglect*, 16, 709–18.

Cooper, H., Arber, S. and Smaje, C. (1998) 'Social Class or Deprivation?: structural factors and children's longstanding limiting illness in the 1990s', *Sociology of Health and Illness*, 20 (3):289–311.

Cooper, J. and Botting, B. (1992) 'Analysing fertility and infant mortality by mother's social class as defined by occupation', *Population Trends*, 70, Winter, 15–21.

Corby, B. (1993) *Child Abuse: towards a knowledge base*. Buckingham: Open University Press.

Corlyon, J. and McGuire (1999) *Pregnancy and Parenthood: the views and experiences of young people in public care*. London: National Children's Bureau.

Cornia, G. and Danziger, S. (eds.) (1996) *Child poverty and deprivation in the industrialised countries 1994–1995*. Oxford: Clarendon Press.

Cotterill, A. (1988) ' The geographic distribution of child abuse in an inner city borough', *Child Abuse and Neglect*, 12, 461–67.

Craig, T.K.J., Hodson, S., Woodward, S. and Richardson, S. (1996) *Off to a bad start: a longtitudinal study of homeless young people in London*. London: The Mental Health Foundation.

Creighton, S.J. (1995) 'Patterns and Outcomes', in Wilson, K. and James, A. (eds.), *Child Protection Handbook*. London: Bailliere Tindall.

Creighton, S.J. (1992) *Child Abuse Trends in England and Wales, 1988–1990*. London: NSPCC.

Currie, C.E., Elton, R.A., Todd, J. and Platt, S. (1997) 'Indicators of socio-economic status for adolescents: the WHO Health Behaviour in School-aged Children Survey', *Health Education Research*, 12, 3, 385–397.

Dale, A., Williams, M. and Dodgeon, B. (1996) *Housing deprivation and social change*. London: HMSO.

Dattani, N. (1999) 'Mortality in children aged under 4', *Health Statistics Quarterly*, 2, Summer, 41–49.

Davis, A., Raffetto, J., and Camper, D. (1999) *The Right Start: conditions of babies and their families in America's largest cities*. Baltimore: Annie E. Casey Foundation.

De Winter, M. (1997) *Children as Citizens: participation and commitment*. Oxford: Radcliffe Medical Press.

Dennehy, A., Smith, L. and Harker, P. (1996) *Not to be Ignored: Young People, Poverty and Health*. London: Child Poverty Action Group.

Department for Education and Employment (1999) *Permanent Exclusions From Schools in England 1997–98 and Exclusion Appeals Lodged By Parents in England in 1997–98*, Department for Education and Employment, SFR 11 / 1999, Government Statistical Service, London.

Department of the Environment (1991) *Homelessness Code of Guidance for Local Authorities (Housing Authorities) 1991*. London: HMSO.

Department of the Environment, Transport and the Regions (2000) *Allocation of Housing Accommodation and Homelessness: Code of Guidance on Parts VI and VII of the Housing Act 1996*.

Department of the Environment, Transport and Regions (1998) *English House Condition Survey 1996*. London: The Stationery Office.

Department of Health (1999) *Working Together to Safeguard Children: a guide to inter-agency working to safeguard and promote the welfare of children*. Consultation draft. London: DoH.

Department of Health (1998) *Our Healthier Nation*. Green Paper. Cm 3852. London: The Stationery Office.

Department of Health (1997) *On the State of the Public Health: The Annual Report of the Chief Medical Officer of the Department of Health for the year 1997*. London: HMSO.

Department of Health (1995a) *Child Protection Messages from Research*. London: HMSO.

Department of Health (1995) *Variations in Health: what can the Department of Health and the NHS do?* London: Department of Health.

Department of Health (1991). *Working together under the Children Act 1989: a guide to arrangements for inter-agency co-operation for the protection of children from abuse*. London: HMSO.

Department of Health Committee on the Medical Effects of Air Pollutants (1998), *Quantification of the effects of air pollution on health in the United Kingdom*. London: The Stationery Office.

Department of Social Security (2000) *Households Below Average Income. 1994–1998/9*. London: The Stationery Office.

Department of Social Security (1999) *Opportunity for All: tackling poverty and social exclusion*, Cm 4445. London: The Stationery Office.

Department of Social Security (1998) *New ambitions for our country: A new contract for welfare*. Cm 3805. London: The Stationery Office.

Department of Social Security (1998) *A new contract for welfare: Principles into practice*. Cm 4101. London: The Stationery Office.

Diekstra, R. F. W. (1989) 'Suicidal Behavior in Adolescents and Young Adults: The International Picture', *Crisis* 10(1):16–35.

Ditch, J., Barnes, H., and Bradshaw, J. (eds.) (1998) *Developments in National Family Policies in 1996*. Brussels: Commission of the European Communities.

Ditch, J., Barnes, H., Bradshaw, J. and Kilkey, M. (1998) *A Synthesis of National Family Policies*, European Observatory on National Family Policies, EC/University of York, 1998.

Dolev, T. and Habib, J. (1997) *A Conceptual Framework for Developing Indicators for the State of Children in Society*, in Ben-Arieh and Wintersberger, op cit.

Donovan, A., Oddy, M., Pardoe, R. and Ades, A. (1986) 'Employment status and psychological well-being: a longitudinal study of 16-year-old school leavers', *Journal of Child Psychology and Psychiatry*, 27, 65–76.

Dowding, W. and Barry, C. (1990) 'Cerebral palsy: social class differences in prevalence according to birthweight and severity of disability', *Journal of Epidemiology and Community Health*, Vol 44:191–195.

Drake, B. and Pandey, S. (1996) 'Understanding the relationship between neighbourhood poverty and specific types of child maltreatment', *Child Abuse and Neglect*, 20, 11, 1003–1018.

Drever, F. and Whitehead, M. (ed.) (1997) *Health Inequalities, Series DS No.15*. London: Government Statistical Service: The Stationery Office.

Drew, T. and King, M. (1995) *The Mental Health Handbook*. London: Piakus.

Duncan, G. and Brooks-Gunn, J., Yeung, W. and Smith, J. (1998) 'How much does childhood poverty affect the life chances of children?', *American Sociological Review*, 63:406–423.

Duncan, G. and Brooks-Gunn, J. (1997) 'Income Effects Across the Life Span: Integration and Interpretation', in *Growing Up Poor*. New York: Russell Sage Foundation.

Duncan, G., Brooks-Gunn, J. and Klebanov, P. (1994) 'Economic Deprivation and Early Childhood Development', *Child Development* 65:296–318.

Eardley, T., Bradshaw, J., Ditch, J., Gough, I. and Whiteford, P. (1996) *Social Assistance in OECD Countries: Synthesis Report*, Department of Social Security Research Report 46, London: HMSO, 1996.

Edwards, J., Walters, S. and Griffiths, R.K. (1994) 'Hospital admissions for asthma in pre-school children: relationship to major roads in Birmingham', *Archives of Environmental Health*, 49:223–7.

Elbourne, D. Pritchard, C. and Dauncey, M. (1986) 'Perinatal outcomes and related factors: social class differences within and between geographical areas', *Journal of Epidemiology and Community Health*, 40(4):301–8.

Elster, A. (1997) 'Adolescent health indicators' in Hauser, *et al.*, 1997.

Esler, I. and Szmukler, G.I. (1985) 'Social class as a confounding variable in the eating attitude test', *Journal of Psychiatric Research*, 19:171–6.

Eurostat (1997) 'Income Distribution and Poverty in the EU' in *Statistics in Focus: Population and Social Conditions*.

Evans, A. (1996) *We don't choose to be homeless – the findings of the Inquiry into Preventing Youth Homelessness*. London: CHAR.

Farrington, D. (1996) *Understanding and Preventing Youth Crime*, Findings, Social Policy Research 93, York: Joseph Rowntree Foundation.

Farrington, D. and West, D. (1990) 'The Cambridge Study in Delinquent Behaviour: a long-term follow-up of 411 London males' in G. Kaiser, and H. Kerner (eds), *Criminality: personality, behaviour, life history*, Berlin: Springer-Verlag.

Fear, N.T., Roman, E. and Reeves, G. (1999) 'Father's occupation and childhood mortality: analysis of routinely collected data', *Health Statistics Quarterly*, 2, Summer, 7–15.

Fergusson, D. (1998) 'The Christchurch Health and Development Study: An Overview and Some Key Findings', *Social Policy Journal of New Zealand*, Issue 10, June 1998.

Field, S. (1990) *Trends in Crime and their Interpretation: a study of recorded crime in post-war England and Wales*, Home Office Research Study 119, London: HMSO.

Fleming, D.M. and Charlton, H. (1998) 'Morbidity and healthcare utilisation of children in households with one adult: comparative observational study', *British Medical Journal*, Vol 316:1572–1576.

Fombonne, E. (1995a) 'Depressive Disorders: Time trends and possible explanatory mechanisms', in Rutter, M. and Smith, D.J., *Psychosocial disorders of youth*, New York: John Wiley and Sons.

Fombonne, E. (1995b) 'Eating Disorders: Time trends and possible explanatory mechanisms' in Rutter, M. and Smith, D.J., *Psychosocial disorders of youth*. New York: John Wiley and Sons.

The Food Commission. *Food Magazine* 1995:31 (October/December), cited in BMA *Growing Up in Britain: ensuring a healthy future for our children* (1999). London: BMJ.

Forrest, R. and Gordon, D. (1993) *People and Places*. Bristol: School for Advanced Urban Studies, University of Bristol.

Forum on Child and Family Statistics, US Department of Health and Human Services (1997) *Trends in the Well-Being of America's Children and Youth*.

Foster, K., Lader, D. and Cheeseborough, S. (1997) *Infant Feeding Survey*. London: The Stationery Office.

FPSC (1999) *Teenage Pregnancy and the Family*. Family Briefing Paper 9. London: FPSC.

Frost, N. (1993) 'Official intervention and child protection: the relationship between state and the family in contemporary Britain' in Violence Against Children Study Group *Taking Child Abuse Seriously: contemporary issues in child protection theory and practice*. London: Routledge.

Furley, A. (1989) *A Bad Start in Life: children, health and housing*. London: Shelter.

Furlong, A. and Cartmel, F. (1997) *Young People and Social Change*. Buckingham: Open University.

Furlong, A. and Spearman, M (1989) 'Psychological well-being and the transition from school', *British Journal of Education and Work*, 3:49–55.

Furstenburg, F. and Cherlin, A. (1991) *Divided Families – what happens to children when parents part*. Cambridge, Mass.: Harvard University Press.

Furstenburg, F. and Hughes, M. (1997) 'The Influence of Neighbourhoods on Children's Development: A Theoretical Perspective and a Research Agenda', in Hauser, op cit.

Garlick, R., Ineichen, B. and Hudson, F. (1993) 'The UPA score and teenage pregnancy', *Public Health*, 107:135–139.

Gelles, R.J. (1989) 'Child abuse and violence in single-parent families: Parent absence and economic deprivation', *American Journal of Orthopsychiatry*, 59(4):492–501.

Ghate, D. and Spencer, L. (1995) *The Prevalence of Child Sexual Abuse in Britain*. London: HMSO.

Giddens, A. (1984) *The Constitution of Society: outline of the theory of structuration*. Cambridge: Polity Press.

Gillborn, D. and Gipps, C. (1996) *Recent Research on the Achievements of Ethnic Minority Pupils*. London: HMSO.

Gillham, B., Tanner, G., Cheyne, B., Freeman, I., Rooney, M. and Lambie, A. (1998) 'Unemployment rates, single parent density, and indices of child poverty: their relationship to different categories of child abuse and neglect', *Child Abuse and Neglect*, 22(2):79–90.

Gillies, D.R., Lealman, G.T., Lumb, K.M. and Congdon, P. (1984) 'Analysis of ethnic influence on still births and infant mortality in Bradford, 1975–81', *Journal of Epidemiology and Community Health*, 38(3):214–7.

Ginns, S.E. and Gatrell, A.C. (1996) 'Respiratory health effects of industrial air pollution: a study in East Lancashire, UK', *Journal of Epidemiology and Community Health*, 50(6):631–635.

Glendinning, A., Love, J.G., Hendry, L.B. and Shucksmith, J. (1992) 'Adolescence and health inequalities: extensions to Macintyre and West', *Social Science and Medicine*, 35(5):679–687.

Goddard, E. (1997) *Young Teenagers and Alcohol in 1996*, Volume 1: England, ONS. London: The Stationery Office.

Goddard, E. and Higgins, V. (1999) *Smoking, Drinking and Drug Use among Young Teenagers in 1998*, Volume 1: England, ONS. London: The Stationery Office.

Goodyer, I.M. (1994) 'Development psychopathology: the impact of recent life events in anxious and depressed school-age children', *Journal of the Royal Society of Medicine*, 87:327–9.

Gordon, D. and Gibbons, J. (1998) 'Placing children on child protection registers: Risk indicators and local authority differences', *British Journal of Social Work*, 28:423–36.

Graham, J. and Bowling, B. (1995) *Young People and Crime*, Home Office Research Study 145. London: Home Office.

Gray, J., Jesson, D., Tranmer, M. (1993) *Boosting Post-16 Participation in Full-Time Education: a study of some key factors*, Youth Cohort Study 20, Employment Department.

Green, G., MacIntyre, S., West, P. and Ecob, R. (1991) 'Like parent like child? Associations between drinking and smoking behaviour of parents and their children', *British Journal of Addiction*, 86:745–758.

Gregg, P. and Machin, S. (1997) 'Blighted lives', in *Centre Piece*, London School of Economics: Centre for Economic Performance, 15–17.

Gunnell, D. J., Peters, P. J., Kammerling, R. M. and Brooks, J. (1995) 'Relation between parasuicide, suicide, psychiatric admissions, and socio-economic deprivation' *British Medical Journal*, 311:226–230.

Haselden, L., Angle, H. and Hickman, M. (1999) *Young People and Health: health behaviour in school-aged children*. London: Health Education Authority.

Haskey, J. (1999) 'Cohabitational and marital histories of adults in Great Britain'. *Population Trends* 96.

Hauser, R., Brown, B. And Prosser, W. (1997) *Indicators of Children's Well-Being*. New York: Russell Sage Foundation.

Hawton, K. cited in Paykel, E.S. (1998) *Handbook of Affective Disorders*. London: Churchill Livingstone.

Hawton, K. (1986) *Suicide and Attempted Suicide Among Children and Adolescents*. London: Sage.

Hawton, K., Fagg, J. and Simkin, S. (1996) 'Deliberate self-poisoning and self-injury in children and adolescents under 16 years of age in Oxford, 1976–1993', *British Journal of Psychiatry*, 169:202–8.

HEA (1999) *Reducing the rate of teenage conceptions: an international review of the evidence – USA, Canada, Australia and New Zealand*. Summary Bulletin. London: Health Education Authority.

HEA (1992) *Tomorrows Young Adults*. London: Health Education Authority.

HEA/BMRB (1996) *Drug Realities: National Drugs Campaign Survey*. London: Health Education Authority.

Health Visitors Association and the General Medical Services Committee (1988) *Homeless Families and their Health*. London: HVA and GMSC.

Hearn, J. (1998) 'Troubled masculinities in social policy discourses' in Popay, J. Hearn, J. and Edwards, J. (eds.) *Men, Gender Divisions and Welfare*. London: Routledge.

Hester, M. and Pearson, C. (1998) 'Domestic violence in work with abused children', *Findings 778*, July. York: Joseph Rowntree Foundation.

Hibbet, A. and Beatson, M. (1995) 'Young people at work', in *Employment Gazette*, April 103(4):169–177.

Hill, K. (1995) *The Long Sleep. Young People and Suicide*. London: Virago.

Hillman, M., Adams, J. and Whitelegg, J. (1990) *One False Move: a study of children's independent mobility*. London: Policy Studies Institute.

HM Inspectorate of Schools (1990) *A Survey of the Education of Children Living in Temporary Accommodation*. London: Department of Education and Science.

Hobbs, S. and McKechnic, J. (1998) 'Children and work in the UK: the evidence', in Pettit, B. (ed.) *Children and Work in the UK*. London: Child Poverty Action Group.

Hobcraft, J. (1998) *Intergenerational and Life-Course Transmission of Social Exclusion: influences of childhood poverty, family disruption, and contact with the police*, Case Paper 15, Centre for Analysis of Social Exclusion, LSE, London.

Hobcraft, J. and Kiernan, K. (1999) *Childhood Poverty, Early Motherhood and Adult Social Exclusion*, Case Paper 28, Centre for Analysis of Social Exclusion, LSE, London.

Hodgkin, R. and Newell, P. (1996) *Effective Government Structures for Children: report of a Gulbenkian Foundation Inquiry*. London: Calouste Gulbenkian Foundation.

Home Office (1998) *Crime Statistics, England and Wales 1997*. Cm 4162. London: Stationery Office.

Home Office (1997) *Aspects of Crime: young offenders 1995*. London: Home Office.

Home Office (1994) *Household Fires in England and Wales: information from the 1994 British Crime Survey*. London: Home Office.

Howarth, C., Kenway, P., Palmer, G. and Miorelli, R. (1999a) *Monitoring Poverty and Social Exclusion 1999*, New Policy Institute/Joseph Rowntree Foundation

Howarth, C., Kenway, P., Palmer, G. and Street, C. (1999b) *Monitoring Poverty and Social Exclusion: Labour's inheritance*, New Policy Institute/Joseph Rowntree Foundation.

Hutchinson (1993) 'School effectiveness studies using administrative data', *Educational Research*, 35:27–47.

Hutson, S. and Liddiard, M. (1994) *Youth Homelessness: the construction of a social issue*, Basingstoke: MacMillan.

Ineichen, B. (1993) *Homes and Health: how housing and health interact*. London: Spon.

Inside Housing (18 September 1998) London: Institute of Housing 6(1).

James, W.P., Nelson, M., Ralph A. and Leather, S. (1997) 'Socio-economic determinants of health. The contribution of nutrition to inequalities in health', *British Medical Journal*, 314(7093):1545–9.

Jarvis, L. (1997b) *Smoking Among Secondary School Children in 1996: England*, ONS. London: The Stationery Office.

Jarvis, L. (1997a) *Teenage Smoking Attitudes in 1996: an enquiry carried out by the Social Survey Division of ONS on behalf of the HEA*. London: The Stationery Office.

Jarvis, S., Towner, E. and Walsh, S. (1995) 'Accidents' in Botting, B. (ed.) *The Health of Our Children, Decennial Supplement. The Registrar General's Decennial Supplement for England and Wales.* London: HMSO.

Jenkins, J. and Keating, D. (1998) *Risk and resilience in six- and ten-year-old children.* Working Paper W-98-23E, Applied Research Branch, Human Resources Canada.

Jensen, A-M. and Solporiti, A. (1992) *Do Children Count? A Statistical Compendium.* Eurosocial Report 36/17, Vienna.

Jesson, D., Gray J. and Sime, N. (1991) *Participation, Progress and Post-Compulsory Education: England and Wales youth cohort study ,*Youth Cohort Series No 15, Sheffield University Division of Education.

Jesson, D., Gray, J. and Tranmer, M. (1992) *GCSE performance in Nottinghamshire 1991: pupil and school factors.* Nottingham: Nottinghamshire County Council.

Jones, G. (1995) *Leaving Home.* Buckingham: Open University Press.

Judge, K. and Benzeval, M. (1993) 'Health inequalities: new concerns about the children of single mothers', *British Medical Journal*, 306:677–80.

Kelly, L. (1994) 'The interconnectedness of domestic violence and child abuse: challenges for research, policy and practice', in Mullender, A. and Morley, R. (eds.), *Children Living with Domestic Violence: putting men's abuse of women on the child care agenda*, London: Whiting and Birch.

Kelly, L., Regan, L. and Burton, S. (1991) *An Exploratory Study of the Prevalence of Child Abuse in a Sample of 16- to 21-year-olds.* Child and Women Abuse Studies Unit, University of North London.

Kerfoot, M. (1996) 'Suicide and Deliberate Self-Harm in Children and Adolescents', *Children and Society*, 10:236–241.

Kiernan, K.E. (1995) *Transition to Parenthood: young mothers, young fathers – associated factors and later life experiences*, WSP Discussion Paper 113, Welfare State Programme Suntory-Toyota International Centre for Economics and Related Disciplines, LSE, London.

Kiernan, K.E. (1980) 'Teenage motherhood: associated factors and consequences – the experiences of a British birth cohort', *Journal of Biosocial Science*, 12(4):393–405.

Kilkey, M. and Bradshaw, J. (1999) 'Lone mothers, economic well-being and policies', in Sainsbury, D. (ed), *Gender and Welfare Regimes,* Oxford University Press, 1999.

Kohen, D., Hertzman, C. and Brookes-Gunn, J. (1998) 'Neighbourhood Influences on Children's School Readiness' Working Paper W-98-15E. Applied Research Branch, Human Resources Canada.

Kolvin, I., Miller, F., Scott, D., Gatzanis, S. and Fleeting, M. (1990) *Continuities of Deprivation?* The Newcastle Thousand-Family Survey, Avebury, Aldershot.

Kumar, V. (1995) *Poverty and Inequality in the UK: the effects on children*, National Children's Bureau.

Kurtz, Z. (1996) *Treating Children Well*, London: Mental Health Foundation.

La Fontaine, J. (1990) *Child Sexual Abuse*, Cambridge: Polity Press.

Lantz P. and Partin, M. (1997) 'Population Indicators of Prenatal and Infant Health', in Hauser *et al.,* 1997.

Lavalette, M. (1998) 'Child labour: historical, legislative and policy context', in B. Pettit (ed.) *Children and Work in the UK.* London: Child Poverty Action Group.

Le Grand, J. (1978) 'The Distribution of Public Expenditure: The Case of Health Care', *Economica* 45:85–88.

Leather, P. and Morrison, T. (1997) *The State of UK Housing: a factfile on dwelling conditions.* Bristol: The Policy Press.

Lee, P. and Murie, A. (1997) *Poverty, housing tenure and social exclusion.* Bristol: The Policy Press and Joseph Rowntree Foundation.

Leitner, M., Shapland, J. and Wiles, P. (1993) *Drug Usage and Prevention.* London: Home Office.

Leon, D.A., Vagero, D. and Otterblad Olausson, P. (1992) 'Social class differences in infant mortality in Sweden: comparison with England and Wales', *British Medical Journal*, 305:687–91.

Leonard, M. (1998) 'Children's contributions to household income: A case study from Northern Ireland' in B. Pettit (ed) *Children and work in the UK.* London: Child Poverty Action Group.

Levitas, R. (1998) *The Inclusive Society?.* London: Macmillan.

Lewis G. and Wilkinson, G. (1993) 'Another British disease? A recent increase in the prevalence of psychiatric morbidity', *Journal of Epidemiology and Community Health*, 47(5):358–361.

LGA Domestic Violence and Child Abuse Task Group (1998) *Domestic violence and child abuse – policy and practice issues for local authorities and other agencies.* London: Local Government Association.

Lipman, E., Boyle, M., Dooley, M. and Offord, D. (1998) 'Children and Lone Mother Families: An Investigation of Factors Influencing Child Well-Being', Working Paper W 98 11E. Applied Research Branch, Human Resources Canada.

Lissauer, T., Richman, S., Tempia, M., Jenkins, S., Taylor, B. and Spencer, N.J. (1993) 'Influence of homelessness on acute admissions to hospital', *Archives of Disease in Childhood*, 93(4)423–429.

Little, M. and Gibbons J. (1993) 'Predicting the rate of children on child protection registers', *Research, Policy and Planning*, 10:15–18.

Lobstein (1998) 'Poor Children and Cheap Calories', *Community Paediatric Newsletter.*

London Research Centre (1997) *Atmospheric emissions inventories for four urban areas.* London: DETR.

London Research Centre (1996) *Estimates of young single homelessness – a report to NCH Action for Children.* London: LRC.

London Research Centre (1991) *Length of Stay in Temporary Accommodation: a study of homeless households in London.* London: LRC.

MacIntyre, S., MacIver, S., and Sooman, A. (1993) 'Area, Class and Health: Should we be focusing on places or people?', *Journal of Social Policy*, 22(2):213–234.

MacIntyre, S. and West, P. (1991) 'Lack of class variation in health in adolescence: an artefact of an occupational measure of social class?', *Social Science and Medicine*, 32(4):395–402.

Madge, N. and Harvey, J. G. (1999) 'Suicide among the young – the size of the problem', *Journal of Adolescence,* 22:144–155.

Madge, N. (1996) *Highlight: Suicidal Behaviour in Children and Young People.* Barnados: National Children's Bureau.

Mahony, C. (1997) 'Home is where the hurt is', *Nursing Times*, 6(93):32.

Marsh, A., Dobbs, J., and White, A. (1986) *Adolescent Drinking,* OPCS. London: HMSO.

Marsh, A., Gordon, D., Pantazis, C. and Heslop, P. (1999) *Home Sweet Home? The impact of poor housing on health.* Bristol: Policy Press.

Marsh, A. and McKay, S. (1994) *Poor Smokers,* PSI Research Report 771. London: Policy Studies Institute.

Marsh, G. and Channing, D. (1987) 'Comparison in Use of Health Services Between a Deprived and an Endowed Community', *Archives of Diseases in Childhood*, 62:392–396.

Marsland, D. (1988) *The Seeds of Bankruptcy.* London: Claridge Press.

Martin, C.J., Platt, S.D. and Hunt, S.M. (1987) 'Housing conditions and ill-health', *British Medical Journal*, 294:1125–1127.

Marttunen, M. D., Hillevi, M. and Lonnqvist, J.K. (1992) 'Adolescent Suicide: Endpoint of Long-Term Difficulties', *Journal of the American Academy of Children*, 31:649–654.

Maynard, A. (1994) 'Some Aspects of Economic and Social Policy' in Jenkins, R., Griffiths, S., Wylie, I., Hawton, K., Morgan, G. and Tylee, A. (eds.) *The Prevention of Suicide*. London: Department of Health.

McCallum, I. (1993) 'Testing seven year olds – performance and context', *Projecting School Rolls and Assessing Performance*, London: London Research Centre.

McCluskey, J. (1993) *Reassessing Priorities: The Children Act 1989 – a new agenda for young homeless people*. London: CHAR.

McCormick, M.C. (1985) 'The contribution of low birthweight to infant mortality and childhood morbidity', *New England Journal of Medicine*, 312:82–90.

McCormick, A., Fleming, D. and Charlton, D. (1995) *Morbidity Statistics from General Practice: fourth national study. 1991/1992*. London: HMSO.

McCulloch, A., Wiggins, D., Joshi, H. and Sachdev, D. (1999) *Internalizing and Externalizing Children's Behaviour Problems in Britain and the USA: Relationships to Family Resources*

McNiece, R. and Jolliffe, F. (1998) 'An investigation into regional differences in educational performance in the National Child Development Study', *Educational Research*, 40(1):17–30.

Meltzer, H. and Gatward, R. with Goodman, R. and Ford, T. (2000) *Mental Health of Children and Adolescents in Great Britain*. London: The Stationery Office.

Mental Health Foundation (1999) *Bright Futures: promoting children and young people's mental health*, London: Mental Health Foundation.

Micklewright, J. and Stewart, K. (1999) *Is Child Welfare Converging in the European Union?* Innocenti Occasional Papers. Economic and Social Policy Series no 69. Florence: UNICEF International Child Development Centre.

Middle, C., Johnson, A., Alderdice, F., Petty, T. and Macfarlane, A. (1997) 'Birthweight and Health Development at the Age of 7 Years', *Child: Care, Health and Development*, 22(1):55–71.

Middleton, S., Shropshire, J. and Croden, N. (1998) 'Earning your keep? Children's work and contributions to family budget', in Pettit, B. (ed.) *Children and work in the UK*. London: Child Poverty Action Group.

Miller, L.B., Fisher, T. and Sinclair, I. (1993) 'Decisions to register children as at risk of abuse', *Social Work and Social Sciences Review*, 4(2):101–18.

Miringoff, M. and Miringoff, M.L. (1997) 'Context and Connection in Social Indicators: Enhancing What we Measure and Monitor', in Hauser *et al.*, op. cit.

Miringoff, M. and Opdyke, S. (1993) *The Index of Social Health: monitoring the well-being of children in industrial societies*. New York: UNICEF.

Mirrlees-Black, C., Budd, T., Partridge, S. and Mayhew, P. (1998) *The 1998 British Crime Survey*, Home Office Bulletin, Issue 21/98, London: Home Office.

Modood, T., Berthoud, R., Lakey, J., Nazroo, J., Smith, P., Virdee, S. and Beishon, S. (1997) *Ethnic Minorities in Britain – diversity and disadvantage*. London: Policy Studies Institute.

Moore, K. (1995) *New social indicators of child wellbeing*, Eurosocial report 56. Vienna Centre for Research in Social Policy.

Moore, K. (1997) 'Criteria for Indicators of Child Well-Being', in Hauser *et al.*, op cit.

Morrison, A., Stone, D.H., Redpath, A., Campbell, H. and Norrie, J. (1999) 'Trend analysis of socio-economic differentials in deaths from injury in childhood in Scotland, 1981–1995', *British Medical Journal*, 318:7183.

Morley, R. and Mullender, A. (1994) 'Domestic violence and children: what do we know from research?' in Mullender, A. and Morley, R. (eds.), *Children Living with Domestic Violence: putting men's abuse of women on the child care agenda*, London: Whiting and Birch.

Morrison-Smith, J. and Cooper, S. (1981) 'Asthma and atopic disease in immigrants from Asia and the West Indies', *Post Graduate Medical Journal*, 57:774–776. (cited by Raleigh, V. and Balarajan in Botting (ed.) 1995)

Morrow, V. (1994) 'Responsible Children? Aspects of Children's Work and Employment Outside School in Contemporary UK', in Mayall, B. (ed.), *Children's Childhoods: Observed and Experienced*. London: The Falmer Press.

Mortimore, P., Sammons, P., Stoll, L., Lewis, D. and Russell, E. (1988) *School Matters: The Junior Years*, Wells: Open Books Publishing.

Moynihan, P. J. and Holt, R.D. (1996) 'The National Diet and Nutrition Survey of 1.5 to 5.4 year old children: summary of the findings of the dental survey', *British Dental Journal*, 181:328–332.

National Centre for the Documentation and Analysis of Childhood and Adolescence (1999). Data supplied to the project by V. Belotte (Italy) and K. Wall (Portugal).

National Commission of Inquiry into the Prevention of Child Abuse (1996) *Childhood Matters, Volume 1: The Report*, London: The Stationery Office.

Neale, J. (1997) 'Homelessness and Theory Reconsidered', *Housing Studies*, 4(1):47–61.

Neal, J.S. (1996) *Supported Hostels for Homeless People: a review*. Centre for Housing Policy, York University.

New Zealand Department of Social Welfare (1998) *The Strengthening Families Strategy Progress Report*.

New Zealand Department of Social Welfare (1997) *The Strengthening Families Strategy*.

NCH Action for Children (1991) *Poverty and Nutrition Survey*. London: NCH.

NHS Health Advisory Service (1995) *Child and Adolescent mental health services: together we stand: the commissioning, role and management of child and adolescent mental health services*, London: HMSO.

NUT and University of Leeds (1993) *Testing and Assessing Six and Seven Year Olds: the evaluation of the 1992 Key Stage 1 National Curriculum assessment*, NUT.

Nutbeam, D. (1989) *Health for all Young People in Wales: results from the Welsh Youth health surveys 1986 and 1989*. Cardiff: Health Promotion Authority for Wales.

O'Brien, M. (ed.) (1994) *Childrens Dental Health in the United Kingdom*, OPCS. London: HMSO.

O'Donnell, C. and White, L. (1998) *Invisible Hands: child employment in North Tyneside*. London: Low Pay Unit.

O'Toole, R., Turbett, P. and Nalepka, C. (1983) 'Theories, professional knowledge and diagnosis of child abuse', in *The Dark Side of Families*. Beverley Hills: Sage.

OECD (1998) 'Recent labour market developments and prospects,' *Employment Outlook*, June 1998.

Office for National Statistics (1999) *Population Trends*, Spring. London: The Stationery Office.

Office for National Statistics (1999) *Social Trends*. London: The Stationery Office.

Office for National Statistics (1998a) *Congenital Malformations*, Series MB3, No12. London: HMSO.

Office for National Statistics (1998b) *Health Statistics Quarterly*, Winter. London: The Stationery Office.

Office for National Statistics (1998c) *Living in Britain: Results from the 1996 General Household Survey, ONS.* London: Stationery Office.

Office for National Statistics (1998d) *Mortality Statistics: Childhood, infant and perinatal, England and Wales, 1997,* Series DH3, No30. London: Stationery Office.

Office for National Statistics (1997) *Congenital Malformations,* Series MB3, No13. London: HMSO.

Office for National Statistics (1997) *Health Inequalities: Decennial Supplement,* Series DS, No15. London.

Office for National Statistics (1996) *Congenital Malformations,* Series MB3, No12. London: HMSO.

Office for National Statistics (1996) *Mortality Statistics: Childhood, infant and perinatal,* Series DH3, No29. London: HMSO.

Office for National Statistics (1995) *Congenital Malformations,* Series MB3, No11. London: HMSO.

Office for National Statistics (1995) *Mortality Statistics: Childhood, infant and perinatal,* Series DH3, No28. London: HMSO.

Office for National Statistics (1994) *Congenital Malformations,* Series MB3, No10. London: HMSO.

Office for National Statistics (1993) *Congenital Malformations,* Series MB3, No9. London: HMSO.

Office for National Statistics (1992) *Congenital Malformations,* Series MB3, No8. London: HMSO.

Office for National Statistics (1992) *Mortality Statistics: Childhood, infant and perinatal,* Series DH3, No26. London: HMSO.

Office for National Statistics (1989) *Mortality Statistics: Childhood, infant and perinatal,* Series DH3, No23. London: HMSO.

Office for National Statistics (1986) *Mortality Statistics: Childhood, infant and perinatal,* Series DH3, No20. London: HMSO.

Office for National Statistics *Birth statistics,* Series FM1. London: The Stationery Office.

OFSTED (1996) *Exclusion from Secondary Schools 1995–96.* London: HMSO.

OPCS (1996) General Household Survey: *Living in Britain: Results from the 1994 General Household Survey.* London: HMSO.

OPCS (1995) *Morbidity Statistics from General Practice: Fourth National Study, 1991–1992.* London: HMSO.

OPCS (1993) *1991 Census: housing and availability of cars.* London: HMSO.

OPCS (1988) *Occupational Mortality: Childhood Supplement 1979–80, 1982–83,* Series DS, No8. London: HMSO.

OPCS (1986) *Living in Britain: Results from the 1985 General Household Survey.* London: HMSO.

Osmond, C., Barker, D.J.P. and Winter, P. (1993) 'Early growth and death from cardiovascular disease in women', *British Medical Journal,* 307:1519–1524.

Oxley, H., Dang, T., Forster, M., and Pellizzari, M. (1999) Income inequalities and poverty among children and households with children in selected OECD: Trends and Determinants, Paper to the LIS/DGV Conference, Child Well-being in Rich and Transition Countries, 1999.

Papadopoulos, T. (2000) *Welfare Support for the Unemployed: a comparative analysis of social policy responses to unemployment in twelve EU member* states, Aldershot: Ashgate.

Parker, H. (1998) *Low Cost but Acceptable: a minimum income standard for the United Kingdom: families with young children.* Family Budget Unit. Bristol: Policy Press

Parker, H. (1997), *Modest but Adequate,* London: Family Budget Unit.

Parsons, C. (1994) *Excluding Primary School Children.* London: Family Policy Studies Centre.

Parsons, L. (1991) 'Homeless families in Hackney', *Public Health,* 105:287–296.

Parsons, L., Duley, L. and Alberman, E. (1990) 'Socio-economic and ethnic factors in still birth and neonatal mortality in the NE Thames Regional Health Authority (NETRHA) 1983', *British Journal of Obstetrics and Gynaecology,* 97(3):237–44.

Parton, N. (1993) 'Taking child abuse seriously' in Violence Against Children Study Group *Taking Child Abuse Seriously: contemporary issues in child protection theory and practice,* London: Routledge

Parton, N. (1985) *The Politics of Child Abuse,* Basingstoke: MacMillan Education.

Parton, N., Thorpe, D. and Wattam, C. (1997) *Child Protection, Risk and the Moral Order,* London: MacMillan.

Paterson, L. (1992a) 'Social class inequalities in Scottish school leavers' access to higher education' in Maguiness, H. (ed.) *Educational Opportunity: the challenge of under-achievement and social deprivation,* Local Government Centre, Paisley College, 5–16.

Paterson, L. (1992b) 'Socio-economic status and educational attainment: a multi-dimensional and multi-level study', *Evaluation and Research in Education,* 97–121.

Paterson, L. (1992c) 'Social class in Scottish Education' in Brown, S. and Riddell, S. (ed.) *Class, Race and Gender in Schools,* Glasgow: Scottish Council for Research into Education.

Pelton, L.H. (1978) 'Child abuse and neglect: the myth of classlessness', *American Journal of Orthopsychiatry,* 48(4):608–17.

Pettit, B. (ed.) (1998) *Children and Work in the UK.* London: Child Poverty Action Group.

Phillips, D. and Love, J. (1997) 'Indicators for school readiness, schooling and child care in early to middle childhood', in Hauser *et al., op cit.*

Piachaud, D. and Sutherland, H. (2000) *How effective is the British Government's attempt to reduce child poverty?* CASE Paper 38, London: LSE/STICERD.

Pitts, J. 'Juvenile Justice', (April – October 1997) in *Community Care Research Matters,* Issue 3, Sutton, Surrey.

Pitts, J. 'Juvenile Justice', (October 1996 – April 1997) in *Community Care Research Matters,* Issue 3, Sutton, Surrey.

Platt, S. (1984) 'Unemployment and suicidal behaviour: a review of the literature', *Social Science and Medicine,* 19(2):93–115.

Platt, S. and Kreitman, N. (1984) 'Trends in parasuicide and unemployment among men in Edinburgh, 1968–1982', *British Medical Journal,* 289:1029–1032.

Platt, S.D., Martin, C.J., Hunt, S.M. and Lewis, C.W. (1989) 'Damp housing, mould growth and symptomatic health state', *British Medical Journal,* 298:1673–8.

Pleace, N. and Quilgars, D. (1999) 'Youth homelessness' in Rugg, J. (ed.) *Young People and Housing.* London: Routledge.

Pleace, N., Ford, J., Wilcox, S. and Burrows, R. (1998) *Lettings and Sales by Registered Social Landlords 1996/97: annual report of the CORE data 1996/97.* London: The Housing Corporation.

Pleace, N., Burrows, R. and Quilgars, D. (1997) 'Homelessness in contemporary Britain: conceptualisation and measurement', in Burrows, R., Pleace, N. and Quilgars, D. (eds.) (1997) *Homelessness and Social Policy.* London: Routledge.

Plotnick, R.D. (1993) 'The effect of social policies on teenage pregnancy and child-bearing', *Families in Society,* June.

Pole, C., Bolton, A. and Mizen, P. (1998) *The paid employment of children in Britain*, (draft paper): Department of Sociology, University of Leicester.

Pond, C. and Searle, A. (1991) *The Hidden Army: citizen at work in the 1990s*. London: Low Pay Unit.

Power, S., Whitty, G. and Youdell, D. (1995) *No Place to Learn: homelessness and education*. London: Shelter.

Prescott-Clarke, P. and Primatesta, P. (ed.) (1998) 'The Health of Young People 1995–97'. 2 vols. Vol. 1: *Findings, Health Survey for England*. London: HMSO.

Pritchard, C. (1992) 'Is there a Link Between Suicide in Young Men and Unemployment? A Comparison of the UK with Other European Community Countries', *British Journal of Psychiatry*, 160:750–756.

Prosser, W. and Stagner, M. (1997) 'Children in Dire Straits: How Do We Know Whether We Are Progressing?', in Hauser *et al.*, op cit.

Prout, A. (1997) 'Objective or subjective indicators or both? whose perspective counts?', in Ben-Arieh, H. and Wintersberger, H. (1997) *Monitoring and Measuring the State of Children – Beyond Survival*. Vienna: European Centre for Social Welfare Policy and Research.

Prynne, C., Paul, A., Price. G., Day. K., Hildre and Wadsworth, M. (1999) 'Food and nutrient intake of a national sample of four-year-old children in 1950: compared with the 1990s', *Public Health Nutrition*, Volume 2, Issue 4, London.

Quilgars, D. and Pleace, N. (1999) 'Services for young people in housing need' in Rugg, J. (ed.) *Young People and Housing*. London: Routledge.

Qvortrup, J., Bardy, M., Sgritta, G. and Wintersberger, H. (eds.) (1994) *Childhood Matters*. Aldershot: Avebury.

Ramsay, M. and Partridge, S. (1999) *Drug Misuse Declared in 1998: results from the British Crime Survey*, Home Office Research Study 197. London: Home Office.

Ramsay, M. and Percy, A. (1997) 'A national household survey of drug misuse in Britain: a decade of development', *Addiction*, 82:931–937.

Ramsay, M. and Spiller, J. (1997) *Drug Misuse Declared in 1996: latest results from the British Crime Survey*, Home Office Research Study 172. London: Home Office.

Reading, R. (1997) 'Social Disadvantage and Infection in Children', *Sociology of Health and Illness*, 19(4):395–414.

Reading, R., Langford, I.H., Hayanes, R. and Lovett, A. (eds.) (1999) 'Accidents to pre-school children: comparing family and neighbourhood risk factors', *Social Science and Medicine*, (48:3).

Reading, R., Openshaw, S. and Jarvis, S. (1990) 'Measuring child health inequalities using aggregations of enumeration districts', *Journal of Public Health Medicine*, 12:160–167.

Richman, S., Roderick, P., Victor, C.R. and Lissauer, T. (1991) 'Use of acute hospital services by homeless children', *Public Health*, 105(4):297–302.

Roberts 1997 'Socio-economic determinants of health: children, inequalities and health', *British Medical Journal*, 314:1122.

Roberts, H., Smith, S. and Bryce, C. (1995) *Children at risk? Safety as a social value*. Buckingham: Open University.

Roberts, I., Leah, L. and Barker, M. (1998) 'Trends in intentional injury deaths in children and teenagers (1980–1995)', *Journal of Public Medicine*, 20(4):463–466.

Roberts, I. and Pless, B. (1996) 'Social policy as a cause of childhood accidents: the children of lone mothers', *British Medical Journal*, 311:7010.

Roberts, I. and Power, C. (1996) 'Does the decline in child injury mortality vary by social class? A comparison of class-specific mortality in 1981 and 1991', *British Medical Journal*, 313:7060.

Robinson, D. and Pinch, S. (1987) 'A geographical analysis of the relationship between early childhood death and socio-economic environment in an English city', *Social Science Medicine*, 25(1):9–18.

Roll, J. (1992) *Understanding Poverty: a guide to the concepts and measures.* London: Family Policy Studies Centre.

Roth, A. and Fonagg, R. (eds.) *What Works for Whom?: a review of the effectiveness of the psychotherapies.* New York: Guildford.

Rowlingson, K. and McKay, S. (1998) *The Growth of Lone Parenthood,* Report 850. London: Policy Studies Institute.

Royal College of Physicians of London (1994) *Homelessness and Ill Health: report of a working party of the Royal College of Physicians.* London: The Royal College of Physicians.

Royal Commission on Environmental Pollution (1997) *Transport and the Environment: developments since 1994.* London: The Stationery Office.

Ruddock, V., Wood, R. and Quinn, M. (1998) 'Birth statistics: recent trends in England and Wales', *Population Trends* 94, Winter 1998. London: The Stationery Office.

Rutter, M. and Giller, H. (1983) *Juvenile Delinquency: trends and perspectives.* Harmondsworth: Penguin.

Rutter, M., Giller, H. and Hagell, A. (1998) *Antisocial Behaviour and Young People.* Cambridge: Cambridge University Press.

Rutter, M. and Smith, D. J. (1995) *Psycho-social Disorders in Young People. Time trends and their causes.* London: John Wiley.

Rutter, M. and Smith, D.J. (1995) 'Towards causal explanations of time trends in psycho-social disorders of young people' in Rutter, M. and Smith, D.J., *Psycho-social disorders of youth.* New York: John Wiley and Sons.

Ruxton, S. (1996) *Children in Europe.* London: National Children's Bureau.

Sammons, P. (1995) 'Gender, ethnic and socio-economic differences in attainment and progress: a longitudinal analysis of student achievement over nine years', *British Educational Research Journal*, 21(4):465–483.

Sammons, P., Nuttall, D. and Cuttance, P. (1993) ' Differential school effectiveness: results from a reanalysis of the Inner London Education Authority's Junior School Project Data', *British Educational Research Journal*, 19(4):381–403.

Sammons, P., West, A. and Hind, A. (1997) 'Accounting for variations in pupil attainment at the end of Key Stage 1', *British Educational Research Journal*, 23(4):490–511.

Saxena, S., Majeed, A. and Jones, M. (1999), 'Socio-economic differences in childhood consultation rates in general practice in England and Wales: prospective cohort study,' *British Medical Journal*, 318(7184):642–658.

Schagen, I. (1994) 'Multilevel analysis of the Key Stage 1 National Curriculum assessment data in 1991 and 1992', *Oxford Review of Education*, 20:163–171.

Schuman, J. (1998) 'Childhood, infant and perinatal mortality, 1996: social and biological factors in deaths of children aged under three', *Population Trends*, 92:5–14.

Scott, J. (1996) *Changing British Households: how are the children?*, paper presented to the conference on European Societies or European Society? Social Exclusion and Social Integration in Europe, Blarney, Ireland, March.

Scottish Community Education Council (1994) *Being young in Scotland*, SCEC.

Secretary of State for Health (1999) *Saving Lives: our healthier nation*. London: HMSO.

Selman, P. (1996) 'Teenage motherhood then and now: a comparison of the pattern and outcomes of teenage pregnancy in England and Wales in the 1960s and 1980s', in H. Jones and J. Millar (eds.) *The Politics of the Family.* Aldershot: Avebury.

Sharples, P., Storey, A., Aynsleygreen, A. and Eyre, J.A. (1990) 'Causes of fatal childhood accidents involving head-injury in Northern Region: 1979–1986', *British Medical Journal* 301:6762.

Sheppard, M. (1997) 'Double Jeopardy: the link between child abuse and maternal depression in child and family social work', *Child and Family Social Work*, 2:91–107.

Shuttleworth, I. (1995) 'The relationship between social deprivation, as measured by individual free school meal eligibility, and educational attainment at GCSE in Northern Ireland: a preliminary investigation', *British Educational Research Journal*, 21(4):487–504.

Smaje, C. (1995) *Health, Race and Ethnicity: making sense of the evidence.* London: Kings Fund Insititute.

Smith, D.J. and Rutter, M. (1995) 'Time trends in psychosocial disorders of youth' in Rutter, M. and Smith, D.J., *Psychosocial disorders of youth*. New York: John Wiley and Sons.

Smith, R. (1999) 'Eradicating Child Poverty', *British Medical Journal*, 319:203–204.

Smith, S.J. (1989) *Housing and Health: a review and research agenda*, Centre for Housing Research, University of Glasgow.

Smith, T. (1993) 'Influences of socio-economic factors on attaining targets for reducing teenage pregnancies', *British Medical Journal*, 14(1):1232–5.

Smith, T. and Noble, M. (1995) *Education Divides: poverty and schooling in the 1990s*. London: Child Poverty Action Group.

Smith, D.J. and Tomlinson, S. (1989) *The School Effect: a study of multi-racial comprehensicves.* London: Policy Studies Institute.

Smyth, M. and Robus, N. (1989) *The Financial Circumstances of Families with Disabled Children Living in Private Households.* OPCS Surveys of Disability in Great Britain, Report 5. London: HMSO.

Social Exclusion Unit (1999) *Teenage Pregnancy.* Cm 4342. London: The Stationery Office.

Social Exclusion Unit (1998a) *Bringing Britain Together: a national strategy for neighbourhood renewal*, Cm 4045. London: The Stationery Office.

Social Exclusion Unit (1998b) *Rough Sleeping Report*, Cm 4008. London: HMSO.

Social Exclusion Unit (1998c) *Truancy and School Exclusion.* Cm 3957. London: The Stationery Office.

Soni Raleigh, V. and Balarajan, R. (1995) 'The health of infants and children among ethnic minorities', in Botting, B. (ed.), *The Health of Our Children: Decennial Supplement*. London: OPCS.

Sooman, A. and Macintyre, S. (1995) 'Health and perceptions of the local environment in socially contrasting neighbourhoods in Glasgow', *Health and Place*, 1(1):15–26.

Sparkes, J. (1999) *Schools, Education and Social Exclusion*, Centre for Analysis of Social Exclusion Paper 29. London: London School of Economics.

Spencer, N.J., Logan, S., and Gill, L. (1991) 'Trends and social patterning in birthweight in Sheffield 1985–1994', *Archives of Diseases in Childhood*, 81 (Foetal and Neonatal Edition):138–140.

Spencer, N.J. (1996) *Poverty and Child Health*. Oxford: Radcliffe Medical Press.

Squires, T. and Busutill, A. (1995) 'Child fatalities in Scottish house fires, 1980–1990: a case study in neglect', *Child Abuse and Neglect*, 19(7):865–73.

Staples, B. and Pharoah, P. (1994) 'Child Health Statistical Review', *Archives of Diseases in Childhood*, 71(6):548–554.

Starfield, B. (1997) 'Health Indicators for Pre-adolescent School-Age Children', in Hauser *et al., op cit.*

Stark, E. and Flitcraft, A.H. (1988) 'Women and children at risk: a feminist perspective on child abuse', *International Journal of Health Services*, 18(1):97–118.

Statistics New Zealand (1998) *New Zealand Now – Children*. Wellington: Statistics New Zealand.

Stepien, D., Murray, L., Lawrence, B. and Clark, A. (1996) *Homelessness, Schooling and Attainment: an interim report on the effects of temporary accommodation on children in early years of schooling*, Portsmouth City Council/ LDJ Educational in association with University of Portsmouth.

Stevenson, O. (1996) 'Emotional abuse and neglect: a time for reappraisal', *Child and Family Social Work*, 1:13–18.

Stitt, S., Griffiths, G. and Grant, D. (1994) 'Homeless and Hungry: the evidence from Liverpool' *Nutrition and Health*, 9(4):275–87.

Strachan, D.P. (1991) 'Damp housing, mould, allergy and childhood asthma', *Proc. Royal College Physicians of Edinburgh*, 21:140–6.

Strachan, D.P. (1988) 'Damp housing and childhood asthma: validation of reporting of symptoms', *British Medical Journal*, 297:1223–1226.

Strachan, D.P., Anderson, H.R., Limb, E.S., O'Neill, A. and Wells, N. (1994) 'A national survey of asthma prevalence, severity and treatment in Great Britain', *Archives of Disease in Childhood*, 70:174–178.

Strand, S. (1999a) 'Ethnic group, sex and economic disadvantage: associations with pupils' educational progress from Baseline to the end of Key Stage 1', *British Educational Research Journal*, 25(2):179–202.

Strand, S. (1999b) 'Baseline assessment results at age four: associations with pupil background factors', *Journal of Research in Reading*, 22(1):14–26.

Strand, S. (1997) 'Pupil progress during Key Stage 1: a value added analysis of school effects', *British Educational Research Journal*, 23(4):471–487.

Straus, M.A. (1980) 'Stress and physical child abuse', *Child Abuse and Neglect*, 4:77–88.

Study of Education and Society, University of Edinburgh/Shelter (Scotland) (1998) *Homelessness and Children's Education*, Precis, No 78, Scotland: Scottish Homes.

Sweeting, H. (1995) 'Reversals of Fortune? Sex differences in health in childhood and adolescence', *Social Science Medicine*, 40(1):77–90.

Sweeting, H. and West, P. (1996) 'The relationships between family life and young people's lifestyles', *Findings*, April.

Taitz, L., Nicholson, J. and King, J. (1987) 'Unemployment and child abuse', *British Medical Journal*, 294:1074–75.

Target, M. and Fonagy, P. (1996) 'The psychological treatment of child and adolescent pyschiatric disorder' in Roth, A. and Fonagy, P. (eds.) *What works for whom?: a review of the effectiveness of the psychotherapies*. New York: Guildford.

Taylor, G. and Jones, S. (1990) *A Crying Shame: the child victims of homelessness*. London: The London Boroughs' Association.

Teachman, J., Paasch, K. and Carver, K. (1997) 'Social Capital and the Generation of Human Capital', *Social Forces*, June 1997.

Thomas, A. and Niner, P. (1989) *Living in Temporary Accommodation*. London: HMSO.

Thomas, S. (1995) 'Considering primary school effectiveness: an analysis of 1992 Key Stage 1 results', *The Curriculum Journal*, 6:279–295.

Tokoro, M. (1999) Report prepared for project.

Tomorrow's Young Adults: 9–17 year olds look at alcohol, drugs, exercise and smoking, HEA 1992. London: HEA.

Towner, E.M.L., Jarvis, S.N., Walsh, S.S.M. and Aynsley-Green, A. (1994) 'Measuring exposure to injury risk in school-children aged 11–14', *British Medical Journal*, 306:925–28.

Townsend, P. and Davidson, N. (ed.) (1982) *Inequalities in Health, The Black Report*, London.

UNICEF (2000) *A league table of child poverty in rich nations*, Innocenti Report Card No. 1, Florence: Innocenti Research Centre.

US Department of Health and Human Resources (1997, and annually) *Indicators of Welfare Dependence*. Annual Report to Congress.

Utting, D., Bright and Henricson, C. (1993) *Crime and the Family: improving child-rearing and preventing delinquency*, Occasional Paper 16. London: Family Policy Studies Centre.

Victor, C.R. (1992) 'Health status of temporarily housed populations and residents of North West Thames Region', *British Medical Journal*, 305:387–91.

Victor, C.R., Connelly, J., Roderick, P. and Cohen, C. (1989) 'Use of hospital services by homeless families in an inner-London health district', *British Medical Journal*, 229:725–727.

Vimpani, G. and Zubrick, S. (1998) 'The Collaborative Development of Indicators of Social and Family Functioning – Project Summary', mimeo. Perth: TVW Telethon Institute for Child Health Research.

Vinson, T., Baldry, E. and Hargreaves, J. (1996) 'Neighbourhoods, Networks and child abuse', *British Journal of Social Work*, 26:523–43.

Vostanis, P., Gratten, E. and Cumella, S. (1998) 'Mental health problems of homeless children and families: longtitudinal study', *British Medical Journal*, 316:899–902.

Wadsworth, M. (1979) *The Roots of Delinquency*, Martin Robertson, Oxford.

Wadsworth, J., Burnell, I., Taylor, B. and Butler, N. (1983) 'Family type and accidents in pre-school children', *Journal of Epidemiology and Community Health*, 37:2.

Wallace, S.A., Crown, J.M., Cox, A.D. and Berger, M (1995) *Epidemiologically based needs assessment: child and adolescent mental health*, Wessex Institute of Public Health.

Webster, D. (1999) 'Lone Parenthood: Two Views and Their Consequences', in I. Anderson and D. Sim (eds.), *Housing and Social Exclusion*, Chartered Institute of Housing, London.

Webster, D (1997) *The relationship between unemployment and lone parenthood: a multiple regression analysis*. Unpublished paper. Glasgow City Council.

Wellings, K., Wadsworth, J., Johnson, A. and Field, J. (1996) *Teenage Sexuality, Fertility and Life Chances*, London School of Hygiene and Tropical Medicine, London.

West, P. (1997) 'Health inequalities in the early years: is there an equalisation in youth?', *Social Science and Medicine*, 44(6):833–58.